ACCOUNTING FOR MANAGERS

ACCOUNTING FOR MANAGERS

Anand Kumar Sharma

ANMOL PUBLICATIONS PVT. LTD.
NEW DELHI - 110 002 (INDIA)

ANMOL PUBLICATIONS PVT. LTD.
H.O.: 4374/4B, Ansari Road, Darya Ganj,
New Delhi-110 002 (India)
Ph.: 23261597, 23278000

B.O.: No. 1015, Ist Main Road, BSK IIIrd Stage
IIIrd Phase, IIIrd Block,
Bangalore - 560 085 (India)
Visit us at: www.anmolpublications.com

Accounting for Managers

First Published, 2006

ISBN 81-261-2689-2

PRINTED IN INDIA

Published by J.L. Kumar for Anmol Publications Pvt. Ltd., New Delhi - 110 002 and Printed at Mehra Offset Press, Delhi.

Contents

Preface

"Accounting for Managers" as a paper is being taught at M.Com., M.B.A. and Other Management Courses at various universities and institutions. This book is designed as an introductory text to the above paper, encompassing vital information on all pertinent aspects. Thus the material presented here would be of interest as well as of great use to the students, teachers and professionals of Management Courses. This book will provide complete knowledge of financial management, preparation of financial statements, depreciation, fund flow and cash flow, management accounting, costing methods, budgeting control, variance analysis, marginal and absorption costing etc. to the students.

The major topics dealt in this book are—Financial Management; Accounting for Preparation of Financial Statements; Inventory Valuation; Depreciation; Fund Flow Analysis; Statement of Cash Flow; Concept of Management Accounting; Methods of Costing; Budgets and Budgetary Control; Standard Costing and Variance Analysis; Marginal and Absorption Costing etc.

It is hoped that all those will benefit from the contents of this book for whom it is meant. The author will feel amply rewarded, if motive is achieved.

Editor

1

Financial Management

Financial management is that managerial activity which is concerned with the planning and controlling of the firm's financial resources. The nature of Financial management refers to its functions, scope and activity. The scope and objectives of the Financial management have gone fundamental changes. As a separate activity or discipline, it is of recent origin. It was regarded as a branch of Economics. Still, it has no unique body of knowledge of its own and it draws heavily on Economics for its theoritical concepts.

The Finance in the modern business world is the life blood of the business economy. Without finance neither any business can be started nor successfully run. As a matter of fact, finance may be said to be the key of success of a concern. It may be described to be the circulatory system of the economic body. Husband and Dockery in 'Modern Corporation Finance' state, "In an organism composed of myriad of separate enterprises, each working for its own ends but simultaneously making a contribution to the system as a whole, some force is necessary to bring about direction and co-ordination. Something must direct the flow of economic activity and facilitate its smooth operation. Finance is the agent that produces this result."

Financial Management is one of the four important functional areas of the process of management. The major objective of any business firm is to make a profit for its owners by producing goods or services for sale in the market. To reach this goal the firm purchases the various factors of production and then produces the output it sells. This all requires funds.

The central features of Financial Management is its formulation of the firm's strategy in determining the most effective use of the funds currently at the disposal of the firm and in selecting the most favourable sources of additional funds that the firm will need in the near future.

In simple words, financial management refers to Management of Finance To define financial management, we should define two terms-Finance and Management. Finance refers to Money or funds available to a firm. Management means planning, organising, directing and controlling of activities of the firm. Thus Financial Management may be defiqed as planning, organising, directing, and controlling of financial activities in a business enterprise. Financial Management is the application of general managerial principles to the areas of financial decision making.

Thus Financial Management is that area of general management which is concerned with the timely procurement of adequate finance from various sources and its utmost effective utilisation for the attainment of organisational objectives. It encompasses within its purview all aspects of financial activity in an enterprise. Financial Management has been defined differently by different authors. According to some scholars, Financial Management is merely concerned with the procurement of funds at reasonable terms. This approach, however, limits the scope of financial management by ignoring its utilisation aspect. At the other extreme, some other authors have related Financial Management with cash only. Since every business activity is concerned with cash, this approach is too broad to be meaningful. According to modern finance experts, Financial Management is concerned both with the procurement and their effective utilisation. This approach gives equal weightage to both procurement and utilisation aspects of finance. Thus, it is a managerial or, problem-centred approach to Financial Management, and so satisfactorily acceptable for the purpose of our discussion.

Thus we see that finandal management is an operational function clothed in a special garment. It involves financial planning, financial forcasting and provision of finance as well as the formulation of financial policies. Hunt William and Donaldson have very rightly called it as "Resource Management" Some definition of Financial Management are as follows:

J.F.Bradley, "Financial Management is the area of business management devoted to a judicious use of capital and a careful selection of sources of capital in order to enable a business firm to move in the direction of reaching its goals."

J.L. Massie, "Financial Management is the operational activity of a business that is responsible for obtaining and effectively utilising the funds necessaty for efficient operations."

Archer & Ambrosio, "Financial Management is the application of the planning and control functions to the finance function.

J.F. Weston & E.F. Brigham, "Financial Management is an act of financial decision making, harmonising individual motives and enterprise goals."

Howard & Upton, "Financial Management may be defined as that area or set of administrative functions in an organisation which relate with arrangement of cash and credit so that the organisation may have the means to carry out its objectives as satisfactorily as possible."

H.G. Guthman & H.E. Dougall, "Business Finance can be broadly defined as the activity concerned with planning, raising, controlling and administering of funds used in the business."

It is clear from the above definitions that Financial Management is that specialised function of general management which is concerned with the timely procurment of adequate funds and their effective utilisation for the efficient functioning of the business enterprise. Financial Management, therefore includes financial planning, procurement of finance, investment of funds and financial control. The study of financial management of corporations includes all financial aspects like issue of shares and debentures, internal financial control, procurement of additional capital, elimination of financial crisis, determination of policies relating to reserves, surpluses, dividends, depreciation, investments, etc.

OBJECTIVES OF FINANCIAL MANAGEMENT

One of the basic and most important objectives of a business enterprise is to earn maximum profit by maximising the output at the minimum cost. Financial Management is also an important area of

General Management. The main objective of Financial Management is, therefore, to earn maximum profits out of the available resources. However, some scholars on the subject have objected on the use of term 'profit maximisation'. According to them the objective of Financial Management should be to earn 'reasonable profit' in place of 'profit maximisation'. Theoretically it is right,because if reasonable profits are earned by the management, this would avoid the exploitation of any section of society. But in practice, the objective of Financial Management is not to make 'reasonable profit' but to earn 'maximum profit'. In fact, the modern investors are also inclined to invest their funds in those enterprises which earn profits at higher rate.

Solomon Ezra, an expert on Financial Management, has also expressed his views by saying that "the proper goal of Financial Management is wealth maximisation." Other objectives of Financial Management are also centred on the objective of wealth maximisation. In sum, the main objective of Financial Management is to maximise profits and wealth. The rest of its objectives depend on the objective of wealth maximisation.

SCOPE OF FINANCIAL MANAGEMENT

Financial Management is an important area of General Management. The scope of finance function is, therefore, not so narrow as conceived by some of the thinkers on the subject. If we confine its scope to the raising of funds for the business, it would fail to provide answers to many problems which arise after the funds have been procured. These problems include: *(i)* Whether the investment made is likely to cover the risks involved? *(ii)* Whether the purpose of investment to be made is socially desirable? *(iii)* How does the cost of capital is affected by the mixture of financial resources? Thus, the scope of finance function covers not only the acquisition of funds from different sources but also their effective utilisation as well. Thus, the scope of Financial Management is quite wide and includes the following functions within its purview:

1. Financial Planning. This relates to the assessment of financial requirements for different projects undertaken by an enterprise and the selection of sources for the procurement of the estimated finance. Financial planning includes the determination of objectives, policies and procedures pertinent to finance, estimating the size of capitalisation, construction of capital structure, advance planning for the possible changes in future etc.

2. Organisation of Finance Function. Organisation of finance department and sub-departments, determination of functions, powers and responsibilities of treasurer and controller as well as the activities concerning the maintenance of account books also fall within the scope of Financial Management.

3. Procurement of Finance. Activities relating to the procurement of required capital in accordance with the estimated capitalisation and proposed capital structure for the efficient functioning of the business also fall within the scope of Financial Management.

4. Effective Management of Assets. Deliberations on financial aspects relating to purchase of fixed and floating assets as well as the arrangement of their timely supply fall within the purview of Financial Management. Active assistance and advise to top management with regard to different financial aspects of effective management of assets such as-policies regarding management of fixed assets, inventory policy, sales and collection policies, policies regarding cash, personnel mangement policy and policies regarding determination of sales price etc., are also included within the scope of Financial Management.

5. Financial Control. Financial control is inevitable to ensure that the available funds are being utilised effectively and efficiently to the achievement of organisational goals. Control on financial system is observed by modern financial control measure like-capital budgeting, flexible budgeting etc.

6. Management of Income. Effective management of income of an enterprise also falls within the scope of Financial Management. It involves the preparation of various statements like-balance sheet, income statement, profit and loss account etc., in accordance with the existing law and the prevailing business practices. It also involves the determination of net profit and its allocation as dividends to shareholders and retained earnings for future investments.

7. Analysis and Appraisal of Financial Performance. With a view to bring necessary changes in future policies and procedures, an appraisal of financial performance of the enterprise is made as against the previous year with the help of modern techniques of financial analysis. These techniques include ratio analysis, trend analysis, funds flow analysis, cost-volume-profit analysis, variance analysis, return on investment etc. Thus, the appraisal of financial performance of an enterprise also falls within the scope of Financial Management.

8. Miscellaneous. In addition to the above functions, receipt and disbursement of cash, payment of various taxes, arrangements of insurance of assets, maintenance of fmancial records, negotiations with banks and financing corporations, development of financial data for decision making, arrangement of financial reporting for the management etc., are the major routine functions included in the scope of Financial Management.

Thus, from the above discussion it is evident that Financial Management is an area of Financial decision making, harmonising individual motives and enterprise goals. In this sense, it covers not only financial planning, financial forecasting, finance raising but optimum use of funds as well as the financial control.

IMPORTANCE OF FINANCIAL MANAGEMENT

In the modern business society, Financial Management is drawing increasingly more and more attention of all those who are responsible for running financial administration. There is always a problem with every organisation for managing its expanding and ambitions plans with its limited financial resources. The financial management has, therefore been assigned the task of planning, organising and controlling the long and short term financial needs of the firm.

The development during the last four decades have proved the Financial Management as the foremost important managerial function. Now-a-days the policy statement of any business concern invariably includes four activities *(i)* Production *(ii)* Personnel *(iii)* Marketing and *(iv)* Finance., Finance provides the necessary stimulus for continued business operations of all types. As Irwin Friend observed—"A firms success and even survival, its ability and willingness to maintain production and to invest in fixed or working capital, are to a very extent, considerably determined by its financial policies, both past and present."

Finance may be rightly called as a binding force as it is so intermiinged with production, marketing and personnel functions that it is very difficult to appreciate its part. In reality financial operations are a costant force of liasion among and within the units of enterprise. Thus, it can be concluded that financial management is directly concerned with fund rusing operation. In addition to raising funds financial management is directly concerned with production marketing and other functions also with in an enterprise whenever decisions are made about the acquisition or distribution of assets.

The importance of Financial management cannot be over-emphasised. It is indeed the key to successful business operations. Money or Finance is a universal lubricant which keeps the enterprise dynamic. The Financial management, therefore, has gained much importance over the time. It has now assumed an important place in the business management because the success of a business firm largely depends upon the financial policies developed by the Financial Management.

Financial Managment is one of the most pivotal functional-areas of management, as the effectiveness of a business enterprise largely depends on the efficient utilisation of its financial resources. In fact sound financial management is a key to successful business operations, and thereby to the growth and success of business undertakings. The importance of financial management has enormously enhanced during the last decade due to a number of factors including persistent inflation, labour agitation for increase in wages and bonus, governmental regulation of business technological change requiring high capital intensity in business, operations, increasing competition and growing concern for social responsibility. The importance of financial management may be discussed under the following heads:

1. Importance to Business Executives. Financial Management is one of the most significant functional areas of management. The subject is of prime importance to the business executives for the efficient functioning of their enterprises. Financial management helps the business executives in making all the strategic managerial decisions.

It assists the managers in determining the financial needs of the enterprise and allocation of funds to specific capital projects. Financial management also plays an important role in the determination of dividend policy, merger and acquisition decisions, credit policy, etc. The modern tools and techniques of financial management enable business managers to effectively manage the working capital of the firm. Budgets serve as chief instruments of financial planing and control in the hands of business executives. Managers are the trustees of shareholders' funds. They provide capital to a company with the expectation of earning a competitive rate of return from their investment. In order to attract and retain the share capita it is necessary for the managers to fulful the expectation of shareholders by distributing reasonable dividends to them. This is only possible when business executives have full knowledge of the principles of financial management. The dominant objectives of every business enterprise is to maximise the profits by maximising the production at the least cost. Financial management leads the managers in achieving this objective, and helps them in discharging their obligations to different parties. Financial management is, therefore, of pivotal significance to the business executives not only in co-ordinating various functional activities and smooth functioning of an enterprise but also in effective decision making for the successful and efficient functioning of the undertaking.

2. Importance to Potential Investors. Investors of different classes are also benefitted by the subject of finandal management. Investors generally arrange to invest their savings through security dealers and financial brokers. But it is not expected that they would always take rational decisions regarding the selection of company as well as securities. Thus, the investors having knowledge of the principles of financial management can themselves take a satisfactory decision on this subject, and can safely earn regular income on their accumulated capital. Speculator investors can also avail the advantage of the knowledge of financial management. Besides this, corporations are also able to earn maximum profits with the help of efficient financial management. Consequently, the investors get maximum rate of return on their investment.

3. Importance to Shareholders. The knowledge of financial management is equally useful to shareholders. Although shareholders are the owners of a company, but the management of corporations is left on the elected board of directors. It is, therefore, necessary for the shareholders to appraise that to what extent the managers/directors are discharging their duties in the interest of shareholders. If shareholders are well acquainted with the principles of financial management, they can safeguard their interest in the company by suitably appraising its financial position. If the managers/directors of the corporation do anything against their interest, the shareholders can make them to follow a suitable financial policy. Thus, the knowledge of financial management is invitable for the shareholders in order to preserve and protect their inherent interest in the company. The shareholders can lead the company to earn more profits by persuading and forcing the managers/directors of the company to follow a suitable financial policy, and consequently they can receive higher dividends on their investments.

4. Importance to Financial Institutions. The existence of financial institutions absolutely depends on effective financial management. Thus, it is indispensable for them to be well versed with every aspect of financial management for the profitable employment of their funds. Investment banks, underwriters, trustee companies, commercial banks and other financial institutions must have full knowledge of financial management. Otherwise, they would remain unsuccessful in achieving their goals and in providing guidance to their customers willing to invest their savings.

5. Importance to Employees. The main objective of employees is to maximise their financial and non-financial benefits. On the basis of sound financial management, the managers of an enterprise can protect their interests by raising the productivity and effcienicy of the employees. Thus, employees are also benefitted by sound financial management.

6. Importance to Government. It is also essential for the government to have full knowledge of every aspect of financial management. Government attempts to effectively utilise the funds collected from the public in the form of taxes. In the absence of full knowledge of financial management, it becomes impossible for the government to attain maximum social welfare out of the public expenditure. Thus, the economic and social revolution of any country largely hinges upon sound financial management by its government.

7. Importance to Other Parties. All such parties as economists, students of commerce and management, politicians, sociologists etc., having interest in the economic problems of the country, are also benefitted by the knowledge of financial management. In the absence of full knowledge of the principles of financial management, it is difficult to undertake reliable studies on economic problems of a country.

It is clear from the above discussion that the importance of financial management has enormously increased during recent years due to a number of factors including persistent inflation, dear money policy of the government, rapid technological changes, severe competition, governmental regulation of business and growing concern for social responsibility. It is not only useful to managers, shareholders, potential investers, financial institutions, employees and the Government, but also equally important for economists, sociologists, politicians etc., having interest in the economic problems of the country. The subject of financial management is also of immense interest both to the academicians and the practising managers. It is of interest to the academicians because the subject is still in developing stage and there are still some controversial areas where unanimous solutions have not been reached as yet. The practising managers are interested in the subject because among the most crucial decisions of the firm are those which relate to the finance. Thus a complete understanding of the fmancial management providing them with conceptional and analytical insights to make these decisions skillfully, is very essential.

FINANCE FUNCTION

One needs finance or money to make money. Finance is the life blood of modern economic system. There must be a continuous flow of money or funds in and out of a business. Provision of sufficient funds at the required time is the key to success of a business concern. In fact finance may be said to be the circulatory system of the modern economic. Today, something must direct the flow of economic activity and facilitate its smooth operation. Finance is the agent that produces this result. As Irwin Friend states, "A firm's success and even survival its ability and willigness to marginal production and to invest in fixed or working capital, are to a very extent, considerably determined by its financial policies both past and present.

With the passage of tune and changing circumstances, the nature and concept of finance function has also undergone considerable changes. For analysing the different concepts of finance function, the definitions of finance function may be classified into the following three groups:

1. In the rust group, opinions of all such scholars are included who stress on the availability of funds. According to this concept, "Finance function is merely the task of providing funds needed by an enterprise on most favourable terms." In the words of F.W. Paish, "In a modern money using economy finance function may be deemed as the provision of the money at the time it is wanted." This approach is too narrow as it is exclusively concerned with the procurement of funds covering only the study of financial institutions and instruments from which money can be obtained. It ignores the other more important aspects of finance function.

2. In the second group, we include the definitions which relate the finance function with cash. According to this concept, "Finance function is concerned with cash." This approach to finance function is too wide to be meaningful as almost every business transaction involves cash. Hunt and William Donaldson have followed the same approach. This approach has too much widened the scope of finance, as it requires the financial managers to go into details of every business activity, be it concerned with purchasing production, marketing, personnel administration, research or other associated activities This approach is also not satisfactory.

3. In the third group, we include the definitions which suggest that finance function deals with procurement of funds and their effective utilization in the business. This is more acceptable approach for the purpose of our discussion. This is a balanced approach to the mangement of finance as it does not limit its scope merely to the

raising of funds but also involves decision making with regard to the procurement and effective utilization of funds. The modern experts on the subject as J.F. Bradley Soloman Ezra. Howard & Upton, Weston & Brigham, Archer & Ambrosio, Guthman & Dougal, Van Home, J.L. Massie; etc., have used the term in the same sense. According to them, finance function is not only concerned with the procurement of funds but also with effective utilization of funds for the attainment of the organisational objective as satisfactorily as possible. Since it emphasises the effective utilization of capital and a careful selection of sources of capital, this approach is also known as 'managerial approach' or 'problem centred approach' of finance function. Therefore, this is a balanced approach to finance function as it gives equal weightage to both procurement and utilization aspects of finance.

Thus under the above definition a finance manager has to take decisions after taking into consideration various alternatives, expected utilisation and available sources of funds. He is also expected to play a role in planning financial needs of a business concern. Thus finandal functions in a good business,establishment cover:

(a) Financial Planning,

(b) Forecasting the sources of income and expenditure,

(c) The method of raising funds,

(d) Proper allocation of funds,

(e) Control over the finance and

(f) Responsibility for bringing performance closer to targets.

In this way financial functions have much to cover and contribute in the growth and development of an establishment.

Scope of Financial Functions. From the definitions given bove, it becomes clear that the scope of financial functions is not so narrow, as some of us make us believe. If the scope of finance function is confined simply to the raising of funds then obviously that will be very narrow and limited because in every establishment there are many problems, which arise after the funds have been raised, namely whether the investment made is likely to cover risks or not, the purpose for which capital is to be invested is desirable and in keeping with social objectives and so on. Therefore a proper and reasonable scope of finance functions is to concern itself not only with the raising of funds but also with their effective utilisation as well. Thus acquisition and utilisation both are co-equal aspects in a financial function. If this is accepted as the scope of financial function then that will help in deciding an establishment as to what assets should a company acquire? What should be the amount of money to which the company should commit itself? What should be the methods of raising funds and to which extent? What should be the rate of growth of a company? And what should be the extent of its liabilities and so on.

What is not Covered under Finance Functions? Of course the scope of finance functions in an establishment is very wide, but one should not come to the conclusion that everything of an establishment is covered under it. In every establishment, there are bound to be *(a)* finance functions and *(b)* non-finance functions. The later are not covered under the scope of the former. These include, *e.g.*, the problems connected with the participation of labour in management, the procedure of recruitment, laying down qualifications for different categories of person needed for the establishment, matters dealing with advertisement techniques, and so on. These are administrative and technical matters and financial functions have little to do directly with them.

Profit Maximisation vs. Wealth Maximisation

We have discussed above the goals of financial management. Now the question arises of the choice *i.e.* which should be the goal of decision making profit maximisation or wealth maximisation. Certain objections have been raised against the goal of profit maximisation which strengthen the case for wealth maximisation as the goal of business enterprise. The objections are:

(1) *Profit cannot be ascertained well in advance* to express the probability of return as future is uncertain. It is not at all possible to maximise what cannot be known. Moreover, the term profit is vague and has not been explained clearly what it means. It may be total profit before tax or after tax or profitability rate. Profitability rate, again is ambiguous as it may be in relation to capital employed, share

capital, owner's funds or sales. This vagueness is not present in wealth maximisation goal as the concept of wealth is very clear. It represents value of benefits minus the cost of investment.

(2) *The executive or the decision maker may not have enough confidence in the estimates or future returns* so that he does not attempt further to maximise. It is argued that firm's goal cannot be to maximise profits but to attain a certain level or rate of profit holding certain share of the market or certain level of sales. Firms should try to 'satisfy' rather than to 'maximise'.

(3) There must be a balance between expected return and risk. The possibility of higher expected yields are associated with greater risk to recognise such a balance and wealth maximisation is brought in to the analysis. In such cases, higher capitalisation rate involves. Such combination or expected returns with risk variations and related capitalisation the cannot be considered in the concept of profit maximisation.

(4) *The goal of maximisation of profits is considered to be a narrow outlook.* Evidently when profit maximisation becomes the basis of financial decisions of the concern, it ignores the interests of the community on the one hand and that of the government, workers and other concerned persons in the enterprise on the other hand

(5) *The cirterion of profit maximisation ignores time value ractor.* It considers the total benefits or profits into account while considering a project where as the length of time in earning that profit is not considered at all. Whereas the wealth maximisation concept fully endorses the time value factor in evaluating cash flows.

Keeping the above objection in view, most of the thinkers on the subject have come to the conclusion that the aim of an enterprise should be wealth maximisation and not the profit maximisation Prof. Soloman of Stanford Univeristy has handled the issue very logically. He argues that it is useful to make a distinction between profit and 'profitability'. Maximisation of profit with a view to maximising the wealth of shareholders is clearly an unreal motive. On the other hand, profitability maximisation with a view to using resources to yield economic values higher than the joint values of inputs required is a useful goal. Thus, the proper goal of financial management is wealth maximisation.

THE OBJECTIVES OF A FIRM

A business firm exists for certain objects and goals. The primary purpose of a business firm is to produce and distribute goods and services to the society in which it exists. But a business firm can never have only one purpose or objective. To manage a business means to balance a variety of goals. Therefore, a business firm has a number of objectives. According to Peter Druker, the possible objectives of a firm may be : market standing, innovation, productivity, economical use of physical and financial resources to run the business profitabilty, (or increasing the profitability), improved performance and development worker's performance and co-operation, public responsibility and so on. These all can be classified as *(a)* Profit objectives, and *(b)* Service objectives.

(a) Profit Objectives

Profit is basic to the philosophy of the free enterprise system (*i.e.*, private sector). Adam Smith saw profits as the device which transforms the selfishness of mankind into channels of useful service "It is not from the benevolence of the brutcher, the brewer or the banker that we expect our dinner" wrote Adam Smith, "but from their regard to their self interest."

According to Peter Druker, profit serves three purposes:

1. It measures the net effectiveness and soundness of business efforts. It is the ultimate test of business performance.
2. It is the 'risk premium' that covers the cost of staying in business replacement, obsolescence, market risk and uncertainty.
3. Finally, profit ensurs the supply of future capital for innovation and expansion and thus enhance the wealth of the society.

These three functions of profit underline the need for a minimum profit needed for survival and prosperity of business enterprises.

It is from this basis that most profit objectives are derived. We shoot for a 'return on capital of 25 per cent before taxes', is accountant's shorthand way of saying. "A return of 25 per cent before taxes is the minimum we need to get the kind of capital we want, in the amounts we need and at the cost we are willing to pay." Thus we take up a new project only if it fulfils our profit objective. Some companies define their profit. objectives in terms of profit as a percentage of sales. It is now generally agreed that profit as a percentage of capital employed (ROI, *i.e.*, Return on Investment) is a better measure of performance, though technically it also suffers from a number of flaws.

A business organisation in a free enterprise competitive economy keeps both long range and short range profit objectives in view while formulating its policies and plans.

It may be emphasised that ROI as an objective is suitable only in the case of free enterprise economics where there is free competition and forces of supply and demand are allowed freely to govern prices. Railways, in India cannot have as much profit as they like since they are a monopoly public utility concern and cannot therefore raise fares and freights as high as required. Similarly in the context of other monopoly public sector units, profit loses its importance as an objective. Other measures of performance (defined or not so well defined) as contribution to national income, social return and productivity assume greater importance than profit.

Even in the private sector a monopoly drug manufacturer may not be allowed to have ROI as his prime objective since he can raise his ROI very high but only at the cost of people at large who are compelled to buy medicines from him. In all such cases the society has to define the quantum of reasonable profits that may be allowed to such enterprise. In our country therefore profit as an objective has to be seen in the context of four economy of shortage, seller's market absence of free competition and the limited role of the public sector in the national economy. Thus, profit should be one among the many and not the only objective of the business.

(b) Service Objective

The second objective of business firms has been defined as service motive. A business firm operates in the society so it has certain responsibilities towards the society. A civilised society is organised on the basis of some ethical principles and promises for its members and business managers have to conform them. A firm consists of a number of diverse interests and often the objective of a company management is to have the best working compromise among the interest concerned. The parties having interest in a firm are : the shareholders, employees, customers' society and government. The shareholders want fair retrun on their investment, customers want products of good quality at reasonable prices, society requires economical and efficient use of scarce resources of production, and the government wants that firm must pay taxes regularly and it must obey the rules and regulations. These all responsibilities can be summarized in a single term as the social responsibility of business firms. There are various areas of social responsibility. Perhaps the finest and foremost important area is to efficiently utilise and conserve corporate resources to produce economic wealth, maintaining the financial health of the firm itself and bring about economic welfare to the society. From this basic thing flow other derivative social obligations. From a social point of view, it is desirable of enterprises to voluntarily recognise their essential social obligations. As eating is not the only aim of human life, the profit earning cannot be said to be the only aim of a business firm.

Do Social Obligations Conflict with the Profit Objective?

The answer 'is not necessary'. Since the .first social obligation of management is to manage the corporate resources efficiently and since the other social obligations are derivative of this basic social obligation the profit objective does not come into conflict with the social obligations. The profit objective should be the rallying point of both business and society. It is to be so formulated and pursued that it at once becomes the cause and effect of observing the legitimate social obligation by management. As Peter Druker says, "A company can make a social contribution only if it is highly profitable. A bankrupt company is least capable to attract and retain talented personnel is unlikely to be an asset for the community and is bound to be pushed into oblivion by the society itself."

So we can say that the basic goal of business enterprise for profitable operations is not undesirable. Considering the inherent risks involved and the supporting and motivating role of the profit it plays in the survival and growth of the enterprise, a firm should aim at earning a reasonable profit. But 'profit through service' should be the motto of management. Managers are duty bound to maintain and sustain the economic performance capabilities of their enterprise as part of their social obligations. They can be successful in discharging their other social obligations only when they prove their leadership skills in effective and economic deployment of enterprise resources for profitable operations. Only then will society be inclined to confer social leadership role to managers to uphold the cherished values.

FUNCTIONS OF FINANCIAL MANAGER

The financial manager occupies a key position in the top management team. He plays an important role in the making of all strategic financial decisions. Besides the traditional functions of raising funds, he is also responsible for financial planning, allocation of funds to specific projects, determination of dividend policy, merger and aquisition decisions, credit policy, management of assets etc. For the sake of convenience, the functions of a financial executive can broadly be classifed as—*(I)* Executive finance functions, *(II)* Routine finance functions, and *(III)* Incidental finance functions. The details are as follows:

(I) Executive Finance Functions. Executive finance functions include all such financial decisions which involve administrative skill in planning and execution. Some of the basic executive functions are as follows:

1. Financial Forecasting. The financial manager is concerned with the determination of the need for capital funds for the efficient operation of the company. He has to forecast the cash inflows and outflows from the proposed investment projects and existing operations relative to the current availability of cash resources. This forecasting and analysis provides the basis for estimating the need for additional financial resources. However, this function makes the financial executive to perform a tight-rope dance, maintaining a nice balance between the objectives of liquidity and profitability. The financial manager attempts to match the inflows and outflows of cash to eliminate the idle cash balance earning nothing to the corporate enterprise. Since cash inflows originate in sales which is uncertain, it is quite difficult to precisely predict the cash inflows to meet the time-bound obligations as the payment of bills etc. Thus, the dilemma relating to this function is of liquidity vs. profitability.

2. Allocation of Funds. One of the most important functions of the financial manager is the allocation of funds to specific capital projects. The most important aspect of this function is capital budgeting. The financial manager is responsible for collecting the relevant information pertaining to investment proposals competing for capital allocation, forecasting incremental cash inflows during the future period, comparing the projects against one another and against the criteria of profitability and risk, and identifying the most profitable projects. Funds are finally allocated in terms of the optimum discounted net cash inflows and acceptability of the incremental risk level. Capital investment decisions are the most crucial decisions in determining the future size and composition of fixed assets and also effect the working capital requirements. (Decisions regarding allocation of funds also influence the risk complexion of the company, and affects the investors, and creditiors,) decisions to commit their financial resources to the undertaking.

3. Raising Financial Resources. The financial manager is responsible for the procurement of funds from various sources including suppliers' credit, lease financing, notes payable, loans from banks and other financial institutions, issue of shares and debentures, public deposits, retained earning and foreign collaborations. Each of these sources of finance has certain unique characteristics associated with it pertaining to cost, maturity, managerial control, burden to assets, by and other terms and conditions imposed by the lenders. Keeping this in view, the financial manager determines the mix of various financial resources in the financial structure of the company. financing decisions therefore, determine the financial structure of the enterprise. While making the financing decisions, the financial executive has to estimate the financial risk reesulting from its influence on the commposition of financial structure. Too much of debt-capital increases the financial risk, and too little debt may prevent opportunities to minimise the composite cost of capital maximize profitability.

4. Establishing Assets-Management Policies. Management of fixed and current assets is yet another important function of the financial managers. The investment policy in fixed and current assets is popularly known as assets-manangement policy. The investment decision regarding current assets is known as working capital management. The establishment of sound and consistent assets-management policies is an indispensable pre-requisite for the effective financial management. The financial manager spends more tune with the management of current assets rather than fixed (non-cash) assets. Current assets including cash, marketable securities, bills receivables and inventories comprise the working capital of the company. Management of cash involves cash forecasting so that an adequate amount of cash is available at all times for meeting the firms obligations. At the same time, there should be not idle cash funds resulting in loss of interest. The financial manager faces the dilemma of Liquidity vs. Profitability as it is never possible to forecast cash inflows accurately. The more he tries to protect the company against the risk associated with the non-payment of bills on time, the more he runs the risk of losing interest on idle funds.

It may be noted that the financial manager is not .directly involved in the determination of the volume of inventories, which lies in the domain of production and marketing executives. The financial manager, however, develops data relating to the cost of ordering and carrying inventories which lies at the base of determination of the economic order quantity of inventories. The financial executive is more concerned with providing the requisite funds for purchasing and carrying inventories, as well as their performance. With regard to bills receivables, the financial manager is responsble for the formulation of the company's credit policy as well as for supervising the collection of receivables. He attempts to keep the bills receivables to the lowest limit which is consistent with need for credit sales as part of marketing strategy.

5. Dividend Policy, Decisions and Allocation of Net Profits. The financial manager also plays an important role in the determination of dividend policy of the company. It involves the determination of dividend payout ratio, *i.e.*, the proportion of net profit that should be paid in cash to shareholders. Dividend policy decisions result in the determination of retained earnings available for future investment. The optical dividend policy is that which maximizes the shareholders' wealth.

6. Financial Planning and Control. Chief instruments of financial planning are budgets, cash flow statements, proforma profit and loss account and balance sheet. The financial manager exercises control on financial performance by comparing the actual performance against the above plans. He also employs ratio analysis to measure financial performance in such areas as debt-equity relationship, inventory turnover, contribution margin, liquidity etc.

ROUTINE FINANCE FUNCTIONS

Routine functions mainly comprise the work of routine nature which is necessary for the execution of financial decisions at the executive level. Some of the important routine finance functions are as follows:

1. Receipt and disbursement of cash.
2. Maintenance of financial records.
3. Preparation of financial statements.
4. Negotiations with banks and financing corporations.
5. Custody and safeguarding of securities, insurance policies and other valuable documents.
6. Development of financial data for decision-making.

EPISODIC OR INCIDENTAL FINANCE FUNCTIONS

1. Preparation of financial plan on promotion of company.
2. Financial re-adjustment at the time of financial crisis.
3. Valuation of firm at the time of merger or re-organisation.
4. All other incidental functions.

RESPONSIBILITIES OF FINANCIAL MANAGEMENT

The significance of financial management has enormously enhanced during recent years due to a number of factors including persistent inflation, govenmental regulation of business, speedier technological change, labour agitations for more wages and bonus increasing competition and growing concern for social responsibility. These factors have cast the financial manager in the role of a top level executive, as well as a staff specialist. He is increasingly under pressure to reconcile the conflicting goals of shareholders' wealth maximization and social responsibility. The responsibilities of fianancial management or financial manager widely differ from one enterprise to another. The main responsibilities of the financial manager may be outlined under the following heads:

1. Financial Planning. The Main responsibility of the financial manager in a large company is to determine the financial deeds of the enterprise for its smooth operations. For the fulfilment of this responsibility, the financial manager has to forecast, as precisely as possible, the cash inflows and outflows resulting from the new investment programmes and existing operations. While he has to ensure the availability of an adequate amount of funds at all times for meeting the company's obligation, at the same time he has to see that there should be no idle cash funds resulting in loss of interest. In the performance of his duty relating to financial planning, the fmancial executive has to formulate the company's financial plan, to determine the capital structure, and to advise the top management on strategic financial decisions.

2. Raising Financial Resources. The acquisition of funds is another chief responsibility of the financial manager. The alternative fmancial resources available to him include suppliers' credit, lease financing, issuance of shares and debentures, notes payable, loans from banks and financial institutions and foreign collaborations. Each of these sources of finance has certain unique characteristics accompanied with it relating to cost, maturity, managerial control, encumbrance of assets, and other terms and conditions imposed by the lenders. The financial manager determines the mix of various kinds of resources in the financial structure of the company. While making the financing decisions, the financial manager has to estimate the financial risk resulting from the alternative source of finance, especially from the borrowed capital. He must also ensure that the acquisition of funds from the proposed sources of finance does not adversely affect the interests of the concerned parties including the ordinary shareholders, creditors, employees and the society. He must also take into account that the concerned source of finance does not adversely affect the elasticity in capital structure.

3. Allocation of Funds. One of the most important responsibilities of the ancial manager is to co-ordinate with other top managers in the allocation of capital funds among various assets. For this purpose, he employs the techniques of capital budgeting dealing with the commitment of capital funds to investment projects whose benefits will be realised in the future. The financial manager is responsible for gathering information relating to the investment proposals competing for capital allocation, forecasting incremental cash inflows and outflows during the future period, comparing the projects against one another and against the criteria of profitability and risk, and identifying the most profitable projects. Finally, he allocates the capital funds to the most acceptable projects in terms of the optimum discounted net flows and acceptability of the incremental risk level.

4. Controlling the Use of Funds. The financial manager is also responsible for the effective utilisation of funds. For the fulfilment of this objective, he exercises control on cash, marketable, securities, inventories, etc. He prepares budgets, cash flow statement, proforma profit & loss account and balance sheet for exercising financial control by comparing the actual performance against the above plans. He also uses ratio analysis to measure financial performance in such areas as debt-equity relationship, inventory turnover, contribution margin, liquidity, etc. For effectively controlling the use of funds, financial manager determines the cash policy, credit policy, sales and collection policy, inventory and assets-management policy etc. of the firm. He also advises the top management on different financial aspects relating to the optimal utilisation of the available funds.

5. Dividend policy and Allocation of Net Profits. The financial manager is also responsible for determination of dividend policy and allocation of net profit. It involves the determination of dividend payout ratio, *i.e.*, determination of the portion of profit, that should be paid in cashto shareholders. After paying all taxes, the comapny may allocate the net profits in either of these three ways: *(i)* Paying dividends to the shareholders as a return on their investment; *(ii)* distributing the profit money to the employees in profit sharing plans; and *(iii)* retaining the profit earning for the expansion of business in future. Since the second alternative is a matter of fixed policy, the financial manager has to pay considerable attention in determining the portion of net profits to be paid in cash to the shareholders, and that to be retained for future investments. The optimal dividend policy is that which maximises the shareholders' wealth, and the financial executive is responsible for making the most favourable dividend policy decisions.

6. Social Responsibility. Although the primary responsibility of the financial manager is the maximization of shareholders' wealth, but he is equally responsible to the society. The social resposibility of the financial executive is that he should actively participate in providing regularly the quality products at cheap prices to the consumers. He performs this responsibility by following sound financial policies and effective control on the use of funds.

7. Other Responsibilities. In addition to the above, the financial manager is also responsible to the shareholders for maximising their wealth by maintaining the financial health of the company and increasing the productivity of the available capital funds. He is also responsible to the employees for satisfactory wage rates and favourable working , conditions. Moreover, he is responsible to the government for complying with a host of laws, taxes, rules and regulations.

In the light of the above dicussion, we can conclude that the responsibilites of the financial manager have enormously increased during the recent years. He is increasingly under pressure to reconcile the conflicting goals of shareholders' wealth maximization and social responsibility.

ORGANISATION STRUCTURE OF FINANCE FUNCTION

With the development of the management science, the concept of finance function has also changed considerably, and keeps changing along with the evolution of the content of financeas a dynamic management activity. Generally, the finance functions are the same in every business enterprise, but the organisation of these functions is not standardised and widely differs from one enterprise to another depending upon its size, nature of business, prevailing customs etc. Thus, in case of proprietory form of business, the owner himself performs the finance functions. In case of partnership, all partners or some of them perform the finance functions. Similarly, in a typical large company, the financial manager performs these functions with the help of other fmance .experts.

'Organisation of finance function' refers to the division and classification of various functions to be performed by the finance department. Financial Management in the most pivotal functional area of management, as the effectiveness of a business enterprise significantly depends on the efficient utilisation of its financial resources. Financial decisions do not only affect wage policy, inventory policy, labour policy etc. but also the existence of the business concern. Thus, the finance function can not be decentralised like other functional areas of management such as marketing, personnel, production etc. The administration and control of finance should, therefore, rest with the top management. Such administrative and controlling powers must vest in the Board of Directors or in the Finance Committee.

As stated above, the organisation structure of finance function generally depends on the size and nature of business, and so differs from one enterprise to another. In a typical large company, the organisation of the finance department may be big as compared to a small one.

In large companies, management is separated from ownership because of widely-held shares with the result that the shareholders exercise very little control over the operations of the company. The ordinary shareholders of the company, therefore, control its operation by electing the Board of Directors to whom the management is responsible. With the view to help the Board of Directors in the execution of policies, a managing director is appointed. The managing director manages the affairs of the company in accordance with the Board of Directors' directions. Under the managing director are appointed the production, personnel marketing and financial managers. Each of them is an expert of his field, and has many sub-departments working for him.

Since the managing director has to solve all the problems associated with production, marketing, personnel, finance, etc., he can .not be supposed to be the expert of financial matters. Since effective planning and control of funds is indispensable for the efficient functioning and successful operations of the company, a finance committee is constituted for providing proper guidance and advise to the board of directors as well to the managing director. The committee functions between the board of directors and the managing director. The finance committee is comprised of one or two directors from the board of directors, managing director and the departmental heads including the financial manager. The managing director is the chairman of the committee. The committee guides and advises the board of directors in respect of financial planning and control. It also directs the managing director and the chief finanacial manager with regard to the financial affairs of the company. Thus, the finance committee serves as an intermediary link between the board of directors and the departmental managers.

With the diversification in production and increase in departments and sub-department, the top management in large corporations is too much occupied to undertake a detailed analysis of financial problems. Thus, in large corporations, other committees such as capital appropriation committee, pension and profident fund committee etc., are also appointed in addition to the finance committee.

The chief financial manager is mainly appointed to look after the activities of the finance department. The financial manager is a top manager and reports to the managing director in a line board of directors which is generally responsible for strategic financial decisions such as decisions relating to investment of funds in projects for plant expansion, product diversification etc., firm, credit policy, issue of shares and debentures, bonus, executive compensation etc. The financial manager often has two subordinate officers, *viz.*, the controller and the treasurer.

The controller is the chief accounting officer of the company, and has reporting to him executives incharge of budgeting, financial forecasting, general accounting, cost accounting, internal audit, statistics accounts payable etc. The controller is responsible for budgeting, dividend policy, taxation, analysis of financial performance, fmancial forecasting and control, working capital management etc. The controller, thus, deals with the internal finance functions. He is responsible to the chief financial manager as well as to the finance committee.

The treasurer is responsible for the custody, receipt and disbursement of cash, procurement of financial resources including negotiation with banks and financial institutions, and the firm's credit policy. He supervises the executives responsible for procurement funds and cash management.

It is clear from the above dicussion that the organisation of finance function or a finance department is detemined by the size and nature of the business. The external factors such as state intervention in the industrial finance, corporate taxation policies etc., also affect the organisation of finance function. In small firm, all financial functions are performed by the owner himself. In medium scale enterprises, these functions are performed by the fmancial manager with the help of a small staff. In a typical large company, the finance function is performed by the financial manager with the help of the controller of finance and the treasurer who supervise the executives incharge for different financial functions. The above organisation chart of the financial department of the large company may not necessarily be an ideal one. The organisation of the financial department will be ideal only when it is capable of effective financial planning and control, and quick reporting, for the strategic financial decisions.

❑

2

Accounting for Preparation of Financial Statements

Every business organisation keeping the complete records of its mercantile transactions on double entry book-keeping principles prepares two important statements namely, Profit and Loss Account Income Statement and Balance Sheet (Position Statement) at the end of every financial year which is generally a period of one calendar year. These statements are known as financial statements or Annual Accounts which are based on the balances of ledger accounts. A financial statement may be defined as a statement which provides financial informations relating to an organisation's economic activities in a condensed and orderly form for the guidance of the interested parties.The Profit and Loss Account or Income statement contains the items of revenues and expenditure and the net result in the form of profit or loss for a given period of time. On the other hand, the Balance Sheet or Position Statement provides information relating to assets, liabilities and owner's equity on a given date. Sometimes, certain schedules explaining critical items are attached to the financial statements. For example, an insurance company in India is required to append "Classified Summary of Assets' in a prescribed form which is considered as a part of Balance Sheet. In the recent years, some progressive companies have started preparing statement of changes in financial position and publish the same alongwith their annual accounts with a view of providing informations regarding changes in the position of Fund which is not clear from the traditional Balance Sheet. Thus, by financial statements, we mean the Income Statement and Balance Sheet and any other schedule or statements attached thereto to explain the informations contained in these statements.

Purpose of Construction

The financial statements — Income statement and Balance Sheet are constructed primarily to know the operating results and state of economic affairs of any concern. In case of sole proprietory concerns and partnership organisations, the construction and publication of financial statements is not compulsory as is the case with joint stock companies which are compulsorily required under law to maintain the records of their transactions and publish the statements for the information of the investors, creditors and others. Generally, the sole traders and partnership firms also keep proper records and prepare the Profit and Loss Account and Balance Sheet because these documents serve much purpose. The construction of the financial statements is advantageous to the business houses in the following manner:

1. The Profit and Loss Account shows the profit or loss position for a given period of time. The management can manage the income only when it becomes known to them through the preparation of the Income Statement.
2. The operating expenses are brought into the Income Statement to determine the net profit. The management can know the position of administration expenses and take steps to control them if they are excessive.
3. The management can exercise better control over properties, assets and liabilities by the preparation of Balance Sheet which provides an aggregate view of assets, liabilities and owners' equity.
4. The figures of sales, gross profits and net profit, if compared for the last few years, show the direction of change, the knowledge of which is very important for the management. Such information is readily available from the Income Statement.
5. Financial statements can be produced in courts in support of owners claims for income tax, insurance claims, etc.

6. The statement of changes in financial position which is published by some companies is a very useful statement for managerial decision-making. It reveals those changes which cannot be understood from the Balance Sheet.
7. The lending institutions ask for the annual counts when an entrepreneur approaches them for financial accommodation. Thus, the annual accounts facilitate the task of borrowings by an undertaking.
8. An existing company, when raising additional capital by issuing its unissued capital, has to publish the information relating to the position of its capital, reserves, profits, dividends, etc. for the last few years. The financial statements provide such informations to the management without any inconvenience.

Parties Interested in Financial Statements

Apart from the management, there are many other parties who are interested in the financial statements of public companies. Following parties, directly or indirectly, become interested in the annual published financial statements of companies:

1. Shareholders. Shareholders are the real owners of joint-stock companies. Since the management and ownership is divorced in a company form of organisation, the shareholders have no access to the internal records of their companies and they have to depend upon the published statements for their decision-making. The shareholders are interested in the study of the profit earning capacity and solvency of the company in which they have made investments. The Profit and Loss account and Balance Sheet read alongwith the director's Report and Chairman's speech throw sufficient light on the issues, such as profitability and solvency and future prospects of an undertaking. The financial statements provide an objective basis for the potential shareholders to invest or not in a particular company.

The financial statements are of great help to a company which intends to acquire controlling interest in any other company. The company desirous of purchasing majority of shares of another company is not as much interested in the declared rate of dividend, as in the future earning capacity of the latter. A critical study of the financial statements for the last few years guide the holding companies in their decision for purchase of controlling interest in subsidiary companies.

2. Debenture-Holders. The debenture-holders are the long-term creditors who are interested in the safety of their funds and the regularity of the payment of interest by the company. Generally, debentures enjoy floating or fixed charge on the assets of the company and the company can provide safety to debenture-holders only if it is able to maintain its fixed assets. The maintenance of assets and payment of fixed charge in the form of interest depends upon the profit-earning capacity of the company. Any organisation can enjoy long and continued life if it grows steadily. An intelligent study of the financial statements can guide the debenture-holders about the existing financial condition and future prospects of a company.

3. Creditors. The creditors of a company are the persons who have supplied materials on credit or rendered some service to the company. They are interested that the debtor company remains solvent atleast in the short period, so that their claims are paid in time. Short-term solvency of a company can be judged with the help of the data contained in the Balance Sheet.

4. Trade Unions. Trade Unions effort is to raise the wages of their fellow workmen. They have to keep an eye on the profits of the company in their efforts of wage-maximisation. Where there is profit-sharing scheme, the workers are entitled to share in the profits of the company. The trade unions have to see the profit position which becomes clear from the Income Statement of the company. If the bonus is linked with productivity or profits, the Income Statement in the hands of the trade unions is a very useful document to determine the share of bonus accruing to the workers.

5. Parliamentarians. Parliamentarians and legislators are specifically interested in the financial statements of public undertakings. They study the published and other accounts of public enterprises with a view to know the operational, efficiency and solvency of such enterprises. The financial statements provide them necessary informations for raising issues on the working of public enterprises in the parliament and state legislatures.

6. Tax Authorities. Tax authorities are interested in the Income Statement of the enterprises which come within the purview of income tax. They ask the tax-paying enterprises to submit the detailed statement of their income for the financial year. It is the Income Statement which provides the basis for assessing the taxable income by tax authorities.

7. Research Scholars. Research scholars and academicians also make use of financial statements of companies to understand their growth and development. The data contained in the annual published accounts are a good source of secondary data which are extensively used in research studies.

8. Lending Institutions. Bankers and specialised financial institution are always interested in the financial statements of those companies which approach them for financial accommodation. On the basis of financial statements for the last few years, the lending institutions decided about the earning capacity and large-term solvency of the borrowing units.

9. Government and Controlling Agencies. In order to know how far an industrial enterprise is discharging its social responsibility, the state and central government departments dealing with the industry also study the financial statements of concerning companies. Controlling Agency like SEBI is obviously interested in the financial statements of companies for exercising better control over them to serve and protect the interests of investors. Similarly, stock exchanges are specifically interested in the listed companies financial statements.

Objective of Analysis

The analysis of financial statements means a critical examination of statements for better understanding and drawing fruitful conclusions. It is only an analytical study of statements which can help draw dependable conclusions. Therefore, analysis becomes a pre-requisite for interpretation of financial data in the form of annual accounts and statements. The technique of analysis depends upon the objective of analysis. Different persons have different objectives. For example, the object of short-term creditors is primarily to know.about the short-term solvency and the long-term creditors, such as debenture holders and financial institutions aim at knowing the long-term solvency of the enterprises to which they have lent money. There are investors who are interested in the declared rate of dividend; other investors, such as holding companies are interested in the earning capacity and growth and development of the enterprise. Thus, different persons will analyse the financial statements from different objects in mind.

Accuracy of Financial Statements

The analyst should first ensure that the financial statements which form the basis of his crucial decisions are accurate, adequate and fit for the purpose of analysis. Generally, the audited Profit and Loss Account and Balance Sheet are considered dependable statements. If the analyst is compelled to use the un-audited accounting statements, he should first ascertain their truth. It is very difficult to verify the correctness of the Income Statement and Position Statement without the basic information in the form ofledger accounts and other records. However, a comparative study of the important items such as depreciation, reserve for bad and doubtful debts, goodwill, un-written off capital expenditure, statutory reserves, etc. will reveal the trend and the causes for any unusual change in the trend may be enquired into by the financial analyst. Sometimes, the companies change the method of charging depreciation and valuation of inventory items. In such a case the data of different years loose their comparability. Similarly, the revaluation of assets remarkably change the net worth of the enterprise. The financial analyst should try to find out all such and other similar unusual changes which are brought out by managerial action. The joint stock companies are required to prepare their published accounts on the prescribed proforma and in accordance with the guidelines provided in the Acts. The financial analyst should see that the final accounts have been drawn up according to law and nothing has been left or concealed. Once the analyst is satisfied about the accuracy of published final accounts and statements, he can safely proceed to further analyse them for the purpose of drawing conclusions. However, he should always keep in mind the limitations of financial statements.

Limitations of Financial Statements

The main financial statements are Profit and Loss Account and Balance Sheet. They suffer from certain limitations such as,

1. Concept of Accounting period is not technically correct. The Profit and Loss Account is prepared for an accounting year which is generally a period of one year. This gives rise to the problem of cost and income allocation. In fact, real profit or loss can be calculated only at the end when the unit is closed down. The annual accounts can best be considered as interim reports.

2. The financial statements do not show qualitative changes which undoubtedly affect greatly the performance of an undertaking. The financial accounts do not account for events such as change in management, labour strikes, changes in government policies affecting enterprise, etc. The financial analyst should try to assess the impact of qualitative changes on the profitability of the concerning enterprise.

3. The profit or loss figure as shown by a Profit and Loss Account is not necessarily a correct figure which is influenced by the personal judgement of the management regarding depreciation, inventory valuation and provisions for various reserves and contingencies. The management can manipulate profit/loss figure to serve their interests. The financial analyst should see that the income has been rightly computed by following consistent accounting policies.

4. Cyclical fluctuations affect the working results of an undertaking. For example, the money incomes of an enterprise may go up without any increase in the volume of its business due to inflationary pressure. Under such a situation an increase in money income is not meaningful and the enterprise cannot be said to have grown at all. But the financial analyst may draw a different conclusion if he does not take into account the impact of inflation on money incomes which is not clear from the traditional final accounts. The consideration of physical quantities of production and sales will be useful for drawing logical conclusions under conditions of inflation.

5. Balance Sheet is a static document, which means, a document showing the economic position of an enterprise on a given date. The Balance Sheet is prepared on the last day of a financial year, *i.e.*, on 31st December, 31, March or 30th June. Generally, the Balance Sheet is prepared and published very late after the close of the accounting year. The Balance Sheet looses much of its significance and practical utility due to a long time-gap between the close of an accounting year year and the actual publication of the same. A financial analyst should always bear this limitation in mind.

6. Financial statements are historical in nature. They tell nothing about future. Since the financial analyst is concerned with analysis and interpretation for formulation of future business policies, he should restructure the statements in such a manner, that they become more intelligible and useful for projections for future.

7. Assets shown in the Balance Sheet might not be shown at their fair or current values. Goodwill is an item which is closely related to profits. If a company suffers loss continuously for the last few years, it clearly means that it no more enjoys the goodwill as shown in the books of the company. But the companies continue to show goodwill at the usual figure despite continuous losses. Similarly, companies in general do not account for the impact of inflation on their fixed assets and liabilities and show them at cost values. The financial analyst should take precaution and give due recognition to the assets valuation as done by a company.

The management is, generally, not in a position to understand readily the financial statements in their traditional form. But, when the statements are presented to management in an analytical form with brief explanations on critical items, it becomes easier to understand them to take decision without inconvenience and loss of time.

Method of Construction

Financial statements are the summaries of the mercantile transactions for a specified period of time. They are based on the balances of ledger which contains various types of accounts according to the nature of enterprise. The mercantile transactions are first recorded in the primary book, *i.e.,* journal which is divided into subjournals or subsidiary books, such as Cash Book, Purchases Book. Sales Book, Bills Book, Purchases Returns Book, Sales Return Book, Journal Proper, etc. Entries in the journal are made according to the set rules of book-keeping and accounts. The entries as recorded in the sub-journals or subsidiary books are transferred to Ledger which shows the classified summary of all the accounts. Ledger is a principal book of accounts which contains different types of accounts relating to purchases, sales, incomes, expenditure, personal accounts of Debtors and Creditors, accounts of properties and assets, etc. At the end of the financial year or at the time when the construction of final accounts is desired, a trial balance is prepared with a view to judge the arithmetical accuracy of account books and facilitate the task of preparation of Final Accounts. A trial Balance is a statement of debit and credit balances of different types of accounts which are in operation on a particular date. The Final Accounts show the ledger balances or balances as collected in the form of a Trial Balance in an orderly and systematic from in accordance with the requirements of the law under which the enterprice is set up. Thus the accounting cycle which started from journalising the mercantile transactions ends with the preparations of Final Accounts, which. represent the recorded facts. The recorded facts form the basic raw materials for the construction of Final Accounts.

Final Accounts of a concern depends not only on the recorded facts which provide objectivity but also on the personal judgements. of management and accounting conventions which introduce subjectivity in accounting. For a student of management accounting, it is important to understand the concepts, principles and conventions underlying the accounting informations which are presented in the form of Income statement and Balance sheet.

Accounting Principles

Accounting is an organisation is done by following certain principles which are the result of long experiences of those who have been associated with accounting theory and practice. Accounting principles provide general-guidelines for measurement and recording mercantile transactions. They also guide in the preparations of Final

Accounts to ensure objectivity and comparability of accounting data. Tltere are certain accounting principles which are generally accepted by all accountants and professional bodies and institutes. Generally accepted principles of book-keeping and accountancy may be studied under two categories *viz. (a)* Accounting Concepts and *(b)* Accounting Conventions.

Accounting Concepts

Accounting concepts means the ideas, assumptions or conditions upon which the accounting system is based. A brief explanation of different accounting concepts is provided hereunder:

1. Separate Entity Concept. According to this concept, the entity of business is different from that of its owners for the purpose of maintaining records of business activities. It means the private incomes, expenditures, properties and assets of proprictors arc kcpt separate and not mixed up with business transactions. Accordingly, the Income statements and Balance sheets of an undertaking will show exclusively the trading results of that undertaking. The separate entity concept may be expended to different segments of a concern for knowing the operating results of each segment separately. A company within the same group always enjoys separate legal entity and its success or failure has nothing to do with the progress and performance of other group companies.

2. Money Measurement Concept. This concept treats money as a unit of measurement of all the transactions which take place in an organisation. All those transactions which can be measured in terms of money or money's worth are brought into books of accounts and other events which cannot be interpreted directly in monetary units are excluded from the purview of accounting. This concept assumes that the value of money as a measuring rod remains stable. A management accountant, while analysing the financial statements should bear in mind the implications of the concept as there are so many events like change in managements, strikes and lock-outs, change in government fiscal and monetary policies, international economic and political events, etc., which considerably influence the operational performance of any organisation. The assumption of stable money value is also not realistic under the changing business scenario all around.

3. Cost Concept. Cost concept suggests that a transaction should be recorded with the actual cost involved though an entirely different value may be placed on it. If, for example, an asset is acquired for Rs. 50,000 or exchanged with any other asset which is valued at Rs. 50,000, then it should be shown in account books at Rs. 50,000, despite the fact that its real value to the organisation is more than this value. This concept provide objectivity in accounting by preventing the arbitrary values for recording purposes. However, there are implications of recording transactions at cost values, and a management accountant should clearly understand them as his job is to analyse and interpret financial statements for decision-making. He should realize that the cost values of assets rarely correspond with their market or current values and as such the Balance Sheet fails to reflect the current economic position of an enterprice which has not changed the post-acquisition costs of assets. Similarly, cost values are not relevant when acquisitions and mergers takes place. Estimated realizable values forms the basis to calculate the purchase considerations in cases of amalgamation and absorption of companies.

4. Going-concern Concept. It. is based on the assumption that the business concern will continue to functions in the foreseeable future or there is no chance of its being liquidated in the near future. Such an assumption help the management to design long-term accounting policies regarding income generations and cost expiration. The principle of continuity implies the utilization of resources whereas liquidation is concerned with sale of assets or disposition of resources. According to going-concern cóncept, the assets in a Balance Sheet are shown at cost less depreciation as against realisable values' in case of a "quit concern." A financial analyst should-check up whether or not the final accounts have been drawn up following the going-concern concept.

5. Dual Aspect Concept. Every business transaction has dual or two aspects and both the aspects should be taken into account if book-keeping has to be done an scientific basis. The dual aspects are the receiving aspects (debit) and giving aspect (credit) and a scientific system of book-keeping takes into account both the aspects involved are the cash receipt and the debenture-holders who have subscribed the debentures of the company, Entry for this transaction will be made on the receipt side of Cash Book and also an the credit side of the debenture Account in the ledger, Cash is an asset and debenture a liability carrying same value. Thus assets of any concern will be equal to its liabilities. Double Entry system of book-keping is a scientific system based an dual-aspect concept of accounting. Large scale business firms keep their accounts an Double Entry principle of book-keeping, which enable than to prepare Final Accounts. Small business firms and petty shop-keepers may instead maintain records of their transactions on single entry basis (incomplete or unscientific system) when a Cash Book and personal accounts of debtors and creditors are desired to be kept.

6. Accounting Period Concept. This concept presumes that the performance of any undertaking can be measured at short intervals during its long life. The period for which income measurement is done and Balance Sheet prepared is termed as an accounting period which is usually a period of twelve months, the management accountant should note the length of Accounting period while making comparison of financial statements for two or more years. If the accounting period is not the same in all the cases, he should express the performance on an uniform annualised basis. The accounting period for internal reporting, may be even shorter, say a period of one month or three month may be choosen for the preparations of interim reports. In case of Joint ventures which are the partnerships for a short period, the accounting period terminates with the completion of joint venture business.

7. Matching Principle. Correct measurement of profit for an Accounting period is possible only if the Matching principle is rightly applied in the measurement of profit. According to this principle, expenses incurred in an accounting year should be matched with the revenues recognised in that year. For the purpose of accounting, revenue from sales is considered as having been realized when the sales transaction has been finalised between the seller and buyer and necessary entry made in the account books. All expenses relating to such a sale should be brought in the income statement according to the requirements of matching principle. It would be incorrect if all sales are shown as revenue but the commission is shown only on the collected sales. Matching principle makes a clear distinction between expired costs and unexpired costs. Expired cost is the cost which is consumed to generate revenue in the same accounting year whereas unexpired costs belong to the future years and as such all expired costs are debited to Income Statement and unexpired costs are excluded any carried forward. Similarly, cost of a fixed asset expired as a result of wear and tear (depreciation) is shown as expense and asset at cost less depreciation is shown in the Balance Sheet

Application of the matching principle is not always an easy jobs. Some costs like depreciation cannot be precisely measured; it can be estimated in the light of the depreciation policy being adopted in the organisations. Financial analyst, while ascertaining the accuracy of financial statements, should see that the matching principle has been properly followed.

Accounting Conventions

Accounting conventions means the traditions or customs which are in use in the construction of Final Accounts. The conventions are so powerful that they are generally accepted and followed by all financial accountants. Following are most important accounting conventions:

1. Material Disclosure. This convention implies that all material facts should be shown in the Final Accounts. A material fact is one which is likely to effect the decision of a financial analyst. Method of valuation of inventory and investments, provision for bad debts and expected losses, unrealised profits due to revaluation of assets, loss of foreign markets due to international competition or tariff restrictions, change in accounting policies, etc., are some of the examples of material informations which are vital for decision-makers. The informations may be shown in the body of financial statements or by way of notes attached thereto.

2. Consistency. The convention of consistency suggests that the accounting practices and met ods should be consistently followed or they should not be allowed to change from one year to another in the interest of comparability of accounting informations. For example, method of changing depreciation should remain the same in different accounting years. It may, however, be noted that consistency does not mean rigidity, and the management is bound to follow a particular practice or method for an indefinite period. A desired change may be incorported but it should be properly indicated to enable the users to understand the financial statements in the right perspective.

3. Conservatism. According to this convention, an accountant is required to provide for all expected lo ses and ignore the expected gains till they are actually realised in the measurement of income for a particular accounting period. Provision for bad and doubtful debts and valuation of inventory at cost price or market price, whichever is less are the practices which are in tune with the convention of conservatism. Conservative approach in accounting may result in the under estimation of profits and creation of secret reserves in the Balance Sheet, which are against the principle of full disclosure. The idea of conservative accounting practice is to playa safe game under conditions of risks and uncertainties. However, the convention should be followed cautiously as it may mislead the users of accounts by presenting a picture which does not depict the true and fair view of operating results and economic position of the enterprise. The financial analyst should check whether the assets have been under-valued and liabilities over-stated in the Balance Sheet for a realistic analysis and interpretation of the same.

Recording Transactions

Double entry system of book-keeping and accountancy is the only system which provides a scientific basis for recording mercantile transactions to understand the operating results and economic state of affairs of any enterprice. According to this system, the dual aspect of every transaction.is recognised and entries are accordingly made in relevant accounts. For the purpose of recording, the transactions have been classified into three broad categories of accounts namely:

(1) Real Account, *(2)* Personal Accounts, *(3)* Nominal Accounts, and rules for making entries in account books specified.

1. Real Accounts. Real accounts are those accounts which are concerned with things such as goods, cash, machinery building, furniture etc.

2. Personal Accounts. There are the accounts which are related with the names of persons. A person may be a natural person like—Ram, Raheem, Anthony or an artificial person such as State Bank of India, Life Insurance Corporation, Reliance Industries Limited, which are the creatures of law, sometimes an account represents a person and hence called a representative personal account. For example, capital Account is a representative personel account which represents a body of shareholders who have contributed towards the equity capital of the company.

3. Nominal Accounts. Nominal Accounts deals with the items of revenue income, expenditure, profits and losses, Wages A/c, Rent A/c, Advertising Expenditure A/c, Commission A/c, Dividend A/c, Interest A/c, etc., are the examples of nominal accounts.

Recording of Transactions

There are two set of books which are maintained to keep record of all the transactions which take place in an organisation. First set consists of the primary books of accounts. Journal is the primary book which is further sub-divided into many sub-journals or subsidiary books. Following sub-journals or subdsidiary books are generally kept in a large scale business enterprise:

1. Cash Book
2. Petty Cash Book
3. Purchases Book
4. Purchases Return Book
5. Sales Book
6. Sales Return Book
7. Bills Receivable Book
8. Bills Payable Book
9. Journal Proper.

Entry made in any of the above account books also finds corresponding place in the Ledger which forms another set of books. Ledger contains detailed summary of transactions relating to a particular accounts. For example, all the transaction concerning Ram may be seen under Ram's Account in the ledger.

Double Entry Book-Keeping

The entries in the primary books *i.e.*, journal are made according to the set rules of journalising transactions. Every transactions involves two accounts and entries are to be made in both the accounts. For every debit, there is a corresponding credit entry. The general rule to make an entry is,

Debit what comes in credit what goes out	For Real Accounts
Debit the Receiver Credit the Giver	For Personal Accounts
Debit Expenses & Losses Credit Incomes & Gaines	For Normal Account

The Book-keeper has to identify the two accounts involved in a transactions. It is possible that a transaction may involve both the real accounts, one real account and another personal account, one nominal account and other personal account, one real and other nominal account, etc.

Illustration—1

Enter the following transactions in the books of a proprietor:

2004			*Rs.*
Jan.	1.	Introduced capital	80,000
Jan.	5.	Purchased goods for, cash	25,000
Jan.	10.	Purchased furniture	5000
Jan.	12.	Sold goods for cash	5000
Jan.	13.	Cash sales	3000

Contd.

2004		*Rs.*
Jan. 15.	Credit Sales to Ram	8000
Jan. 20.	Received cash from Ram	5000
Jan. 22.	Deposited cash in Central Bank	20,000
Jan. 25.	Purchased good an credit from Singh & Sons	15,000
Jan. 28.	Paid to Singh & Sons	10,000
Jan. 31.	Paid Rent of office building	1,000
Jan. 31.	Bank Interest received	500
Jan. 31.	Wages paid	3,500

Journal

Date	*Particulars*	*Ledger Folio*	*Debit (Rs.)*	*Credit (Rs.)*	*Kind of Account*
1	*2*	*3*	*4.*	*5*	*6*
2003					
Jan 1	Cash Account Dr		80,000		Real A/c
	To Capital A/c			80,000	Personal A/c
Jan 5	Goods(Purchases) A/c Dr		25,000		Real A/c
	To Cash A/c			25,000	Real A/c
Jan 10	Furniture A/c Dr.		5,000		Real A/c
	To Cash			5,000	Real A/c
Jan 12	Cash A/c Dr		5,000		Real A/c
	To goods (sales)			5,000	Real A/c
Jan 13	Cash A/c Dr		3,000,		Real A/c
	To goods(sales)			3,000	Real A/c
Jan 15	Ram's Account Dr		8,000		Personal A/c
	To goods(sale)			2,000	Real A/c
Jan 20	Cash A/c Dr.		5,000		Real A/c
	To Ram			5,000	Personal A/c
Jan 22	Central Bank A/e Dr.		20,000		Personal A/c
	To eash			20,000	Real A/c

Contd.

1	*2*	*3*	*4.*	*5*	*6*
Jan 25	Goods(Purchases) A/c Dr		15,000		Real A/c
	To Singh & Sons			15,000	Personal A/c
Jan 28	Singh & Sons A/c Dr		10,000		Personal A/c
	To cash			10,000	Real A/c
Jan 31	Rent Account Dr		1,000		Nominal A/c
	To cash			1,000	Real A/c
Jan 31	Cash Account Dr		500		Real A/c
	To Interest			500	Nominal A/c
Jan 31	Wages A/c Dr		3,500		Nominal A/c
	To cash			3,500	Real A/c

Ledger

Individual accounts of persons, property & assets, expenses, incomes, etc. are opened in another book called ledger. An Account depicts the summary of transactions which have taken place at different time periods and the net effect of those related transactions for a given period of time. Ledger is a principal book which helps in the preparations of annual accounts to know the net result of the business and the position of assets and liabilities. There are two sides of an accounts namely Debit side and Credit side. Debit side is on the left hand side and credit is on the right-hand side.

Illustration-2

Prepare ledger accounts on the basis of the journal entries of the previous illustrations:

CAPITAL ACCOUNT

(Dr.) (Cr.)

Date	*Particulars*	*J.F*	*Amount*	*Date*	*Particulars*	*J.F*	*Amount*
2003				1994			
Jan. 31	To balance c/d		80,000	Jan. 14	By cash		80,000
			80,000				80,000

CASH ACCOUNT

2003			2003		
Jan. 1	To Capital	80,000	Jan. 5	By Good	25,000
Jan. 12	To goods	5,000	Jan.10	By Furniture	5,000
Jan. 13	To goods	3,000	Jan. 20	By Ram	5,000
Jan. 31	to interest	500	Jan. 22	By Central Bank	20,000
			Jan. 28,	By Singh & Sons	10,000
			Jan. 31	By Wages	3,500
			Jan. 31	By Rent	1,000
			Jan. 31	By Balance c/d	24,000
		88,500			88,500

GOODS (PURCHASES) ACCOUNT

2003			2003		
Jan.5	To Cash	25,000	Jan. 31	By Balance c/d	45,000
Jan. 25	To Singh & Co	20,000			
		45,000			45,000

GOOD (SALES) ACCOUNT

2003			2003		
Jan. 31	To Balance c/d	16,000	Jan. 12	By Cash	5,000
			Jan. 13	By Cash	3,000
			Jan. 15	By Ram's A/c	8,000
		16,000			16,000

FURNITURE ACCOUNT

2003			2003		
Jan.10	To cash	5,000	Jan. 31	By Balance c/d	5,000
		5,000			5,000

RAM'S ACCOUNT

2003			2003		
Jan 15	To goods (sales)	8,000	Jan. 20	By Cash	5,000
				By Balance c/d	3,000
		8,000			8,000

CENTRAL BANK ACCOUNT

2003			2003		
Jan. 22	To Cash	20,000	Jan. 31	By balance d/d	20,000
		20,000			20,000

SINGH & SONS ACCOUNT

2003			2003		
Jan. 28	To Cash	10,000	Jan. 25	By goods (purchases)	15,000
Jan. 31	To Balance c/d	5,000			
		15,000			15,000

RENT ACCOUNT

2003			2003		
Jan. 31	To Cash	1,000	Jan. 3	By Balance	1,000
		1,000			1,000

INTEREST ACCOUNT

2003			2003		
Jan. 31	By Balance	500	Jan. 31	By Cash	500
		500			500

WAGES ACCOUNT

2003			2003		
Jan. 31	To Cash	3,500	Jan. 3	By Balance	3,500
		3,500			3,500

Trial Balance

A Trial Balance is a schedule of debit and credit balances of ledger accounts. It is prepared to check the arithmetica accuracy of accounts and facilitate the task of preparation of Final Accounts. The two sides of a Trial Balance must tally if there is no accounting error in the books. However, there are some errors which do not affect the agreement of a trial balance. The errors which are not disclosed by a Trial Balance are as under:

1. Errors of Principle. These are the errors which are caused due to the violation or wrong application of the rules of making entries in the primary books of accounts. For example, if an expenditure of capital nature is treated as revenue expenditure and entry made accordingly, then it will not make any difference and the two sides of Trial Balance would agree.

2. Errors of Omission. If a transaction has been left to the entered in the primary books, then also it will not affect the agreement of the Trial Balance.

3. Errors of Commission. If a wrong amount is entered in the journal, it would not have any effect in the Trial Balance. Similarly, if a wrong account is debited or credited, than also the Trial Balance would not disagree.

4. Compensatory Errors. A compensatory error is one which neutralises the wrong effect of any other error, and thus does not affect the agreement of a Trial Balance. For example, if X' s a count is debited by Rs. 150 instead of Rs. 50 and simultaneously another unt say Y's account is posted on credit side by Rs. 50 instead of entering with the same amount on the debit side of Y's Account. These are the accounting errors but their affect on Trial Balance will be nil.

Preparation of Trial Balance

Trial Balance is prepared with the balances of accounts as shown in the ledger. The balance of an account is said to be a debit balance if the debit side is bigger than the credit side. The balance is the credit balance if the credit side is bigger than the debit side. Debit balances of individual accounts are brought in the Debit column of the Trial Balance. Similarly, the credit balances are shown in the credit column. The agreement of the total of Debit balances and credit balances of accounts appearing in a Trial Balance is generally a proof of the arithmetical accuracy of books.

Illustration-3

Using the ledger balances from the illustration No 2 prepare the Trial Balance as on 31st January 2003.

TRIAL BALANCE AS AT 31ST JAN. 2003

	Debit Balance	*Credit Balance*
Capital A/c	—	80000
Cash A/c	24000	—
Goods (Purchases)A/c	45000	—
Goods (Sales)A/c	—	16000
Furniture A/c	5000	—
Central Bank A/c	20,000	—
Ram's A/c	3000	—
Singh & Son's A/c	—	5000
Rent A/c	1,000	—
Interest A/c	—	500
Wages A/c	3500	—
Total	1,01,500	1,01,500

Unsold stock Rs. 35000

Stationary bill unpaid Rs. 300

Preparation of Final Accounts

Final Accounts—Profit & Loss Account and Balance Sheet may be prepared any time the management desires to know the operating results and economic position of the enterprise: The Profit & Loss Account shows the profit earned or loss suffered for a given period of time but the Balance Sheet depicts the economic portion at a point of time.

Trading or Manufacturing Account may be separated to know the gross profit. Other part of the P.& L. A/c will show the net results in the form of profit or loss. The companies also prepare a separate account to show the appropriation of profits. The Profit & Loss Account may be prepared either in an account form or in horizontal form. If the Account is prepared in an account form, then all the items of costs, expenses and losses are shown on the left-hand side or debit side and all items of income and gains are represented on the right hand or credit side.

Strictly speaking, the Balance Sheet is not an account but it is a statement of assets and liabilities. It has two sides-right hand side to show asseis and left-hand side to represent liabilities. The two sides of a Balance Sheet are always equal. The assets and liabilities in a Balance are shown either according to fixity or liquidity of assets and liabilities. The companies are required to prepare their Balance Sheets in accordance with the prescribed performa under the Act.

Illustration-4

Prepare the Profit & Loss Account to measure the profit for one month and the Balance to show economic position as at 31st Jan. 2003 from the Trial Balance of illustration no.3.

Trading And Profit & Loss Account
For The Month Ending at 31st Jan. 2003

Expenditure	*Rs.*	*Income*	*Rs.*
To Opening Balance	nil	By goods (sales)	16000
To Good (Purchase)	45000	By unsold stock	35000
To Wages	3500		
To Gross Profit c/d	2500		
	51000		51000
To Rent	1000	By Gross Profit b/d	2500
To Stationary bill payable	300	By Interest	500
To Net Profit carried to Balance Sheet	1,700		
	3000		3000

BALANCE SHEET AS AT 31ST JAN, 2003

Liabilities	***Amount***	***Assets***	***Amount***
Capital A/c	80,000	Furniture	5,000
Profit & Loss (cr.)	1,700	Unsold stock	35,000
Singh & Sons A/c		Ram (debtor)	3,000
(creditors)	5,000	Central Bank	
		(cash with Bank)	20,000
Stationary bill			
(outstanding Exp.)	300	Cash in hand	24,000
	87,000		87,000

The above case to explain the accounting cycle is a simple one as it has taken into account few transactions for a month only. In actual practice, more elaborate final accounts are prepated.It will be useful to consider items of assets and liabilities which usually appear in the Balance Sheet of a large scale business enterprice organised in the form of a public limited company.

Liabilities		***Assets***	
- Share capital		Land & Buildings	—
Equity share capital	—	Plant & Machinery	—
Preference share capital	—	Furniture and Fixtures	—
- Share premium A/c	—	Patent & trade marks	—
- General reserve	—	Goodwill	—
- Dividend equalisation	—	Capital works in progress	—
Fund	—	Investments	—
- Investment fluctuation fund	—	Stock in trade	—
- Debenture redemption	—	Work in progress	—
- Reserve A/c	—	Sundry debtors	—
- Workmen compensation		Accrued Incomes	—
Fund		Bill receivable	—
- Contingency reserve A/c	—	Advance with suppliers	—
- Profit & Loss A/c	—	Cash and Bank balances	—
- Revaluation reserve		Miscellaneous expenditure	
- Loans		(to the extent not written off)	

Liabilities		*Assets*	
- Public deposits	—	Profit & Loss Account	—
- Debentures	—		
- Sundry creditors	—		
- Bill payable	—		
- Bank overdraft	—		
- Unclaimed dividend	—		
- Tax payable	—		
- Outstanding expenses	—		
- Receipts in advance	—		

Nature of Assets and Liabilities

The assets of an organization may be classified as under:

Fixed Assets. Fixed assets are the assets which are acquired not for re-sale but for keeping them permanently. The consumption of such assets is gradual and they give service for fairly.. long-period of time, Land & building, plant and machinery, furniture, etc. are the good examples of fixed assets, Intangible assets like goodwill is also a fixed asset.

Current Assets. Current assets are also termed as floating assets. These are the assets which keep on changing their shape and volume. Cash in hand and bank balances, stock-in-trade, sundry debtors, Work-in-progress, bills receivable, etc., are the examples of current assets. Current assets may be classified into. *(a)* liquid Assets, and *(b)* Non-liquid assets. A liquid asset is one which is in the form of cash or near-cash current asset. A near-cash asset is defined as an asset which is convertible into cash with convenience and without loss at a very short-notice. Cash Balances, very good debtors, marketable securities bills receivable are the examples of liquid assets. Non-liquid assets consist of all those current assets which cannot be converted into cash at a short notice. These consist of stock-in-trade, work-in-progress, debtors which remains outstanding for more than six months. Current assets are needed to meet the usual expenditure of business.

Miscellaneous Expenditure. (To the extent not written off). Technically speaking, an expenditure not represented by any tangible or intangible asset cannot be an asset. When expenditure on any item is heavy, it is capitalized instead of showing the total as a business expense in the Profit & Loss Alc of the year in which it is incurred. For example, heavy expenditure on massive advertising campaign. in any year is capitalised and the portion of expenditure not written off is shown on the asset side of the Balance Sheet under the head 'Miscellaneous Expenditure.' Similarly, pre-operative and preliminary expenses are capitalised and written off gradually over.a period of 3-5 years.

Profit and Loss Account (Debit Balance). Technically speaking, Debit Balance of Profit & Loss Account cannot be an asset but it is treated so for technical reasons. A company is required to show its capital at paid up value which means the loss in any year cannot be deducted from the capital. Thus the alternative is either to deduct the loss from general reserve or show it as an asset. Generally, the Profit & Loss (debit) is shown on the asset side for the time being. It is written off against the profit of the subsequent years.

Nature of Liabilities

A company's owings to its equity shareholders and other creditors may be termed as liabilities which are classified into three broad categories as under:

1. Owners Equity. It represents paid up share capital and reserves and surplus. According to separate entity concept, these are the liabilities of a company to its owners-shareholders. However, these are not such liabilities which call for payment during the life time of the company. These become payable to shareholders only in the event of winding up of the company. Reserves and surplus can, however, be used for writing down capital loss, if any, and payment of bonus to shareholders by its capitalization.

2. Long-time Liabilities. Outsiders' claims to be paid after more than one year's time constitute long-term liabilities. Debentures, loans from specialised financial Institutions and public deposits are the long-term liabilities which are repayable after 2-5 years in future.

3. Current Liabilities. These are short term financial obligations which arise due to dealing with the outsiders in the usual course of business. Sundry creditors, bills payable, outstanding expenses, tax payable, etc., are all short-term or current liabilities as they arise in the normal course of business and are to be paid within a year's time.

Contingent Liabilities

Contingent liabilities are not the actual liabilities but they become actual liabilities on the happening of a certain unfavourable event in the future. Debts not acknowledged as debt for which the case is lying in the court, is a glaring example of a contingent liability. Since, the contingent liabilities are not actual liabilities, they are shown in the Balance Sheet by way of footnotes only.

Sometimes, liabilities are also recognized as Internal and External liabilities. Owners Equity including all free reserves and credit balance of profit and loss A/c is Internal liability as it has not to ,be paid to any outsider but to the shareholders of the company. On the other hand, External liabilities represent the claims of outsiders. All long-term and current liabilities as explained above constitute external liabilities.

PRESENTATION OF FINANCIAL STATEMENTS

Income Statement

An Income statement may be presented either in horizontal form ('T' form) or in vertical form (single-column form). Part I of Schedule VI of the Indian Companies Act has laid down the proforma for presentation of Final Accounts by companies incorporated under the Act. The idea is that the companies highlight maximum informations and a uniformity is maintained for better understanding and comparison of accounting data. Presently, the Indian companies prepare and publish their final accounts in verticular form and the necessary details are shown in the schedules attached thereto. An idea can be formed from the Balance Sheet and the Income Statement of an Indian Company CURC (India) Limited for the year 1989.

STATEMENT CONTAINING SALIENT FEATURES OF BALANCE SHEET AND PROFIT & LOSS ACCOUNT ETC. AS PER SECTION 219 (1) (B) (IV)

USHA RECTIFIER CORPORATION (INDIA) LIMITED

ABRIDGED BALANCE SHEET AS AT 31ST DECEMBER 1989

Particulars	*Figures as at the end of*	
	Current Financial Year (Rs.000)	*Previous Financial (Year Rs.000)*
1	*2*	*3*
I. Sources of Funds		
1. Shareholders Funds		
(a) Capital		
(i) Equity	135993	55971
(ii) Preference	—	—
(iii) Share Application Money	—	32365
(b) Reserves & Surplus		
(i) Capital Reserve	2530	2500
(ii) Revenue Reserve	90152	26590
(iii) Revaluation Reserve	46527	43832
(iv) Share Premium A/c	43625	—
(v) Surplus in Profit and Loss Account	74249	30313
2. Loan Funds		
(a) Debentures	890143	120475
(b) Public deposits	3417	4881
(c) Secured Loans (other than debentures)	41706	165931

1	*2*	*3*
(d) Unsecured Loans	4814	76
(e) Debenture Application Money	152768	11650
	1439158	494584
II. Application of Funds		
1. Fixed Assets		
(a) Net Block-(Original cost less depreciation)	242744	233601
(b) Capital work in progress	530654	29567
2. Investments		
(a) Government Securities	170905	—
(b) Investment in subsidiary companies		
(a) Quoted	—	—
(b) Unquoted	123810	8821
(c) Others		
(a) Quoted	—	—
(b) Unquoted	101	1
3. (i) Current Assets, Loan and Advances		
(a) Inventories	160710	185372
(b) Sundry Debtors	353865	114072
(c) Cash and Bank Balance	33938	18312
(d) Other current assets	—	—
(e) Loans and Advances		
(i) To subsidiary companies	8663	1385
(ii) To others	64382	52563
	621558	371704
Less:		
(ii) Current Liabilities and Provisions		
(a) Liabilities	189060	137874

1	*2*	*3*
(b) Provisions	65041	15255
	254101	153129
Net Current Assets (i-ii)	*367457*	*218575*
4. Miscellaneous expenditure to the extent not written off or adjusted	3487	4019
5. Profit and Loss Account	—	—
	1439158	494584

USHA RECTIFIER CORPORATION (INDIA) LIMITED ABRIDGED PROFIT AND LOSS ACCOUNT FOR THE PERIOD ENDED 31 DECEMBER 1989

Particulars			*Figures as at the end of*	
			Current Financial Year (Rs.000)	*Previous Financial (Year Rs.000)*
1			*2*	*3*
I. Income				
Sales			1313390	441505
Other income			6264	16883
Total			1319654	458388
II. Expenditure				
Cost of goods consumed / sold				
(i) Opening Stock	93011	40904		
(ii) Purchase	1101561	379931		
Less: closing stock	93616	93012		
			1100956	327823
Manufacturing expenses			34291	30571
Selling expenses			5989	6796
Salaries, Wages and other employee benefits			11933	12367
Managerial remuneration			714	136

1	2	3
Interest	27874	15466
Depreciation	11297	7348
Auditor's remuneration	124	85
Total	1193178	400592
III. Profit/Loss before Tax (I-Ii)	126476	57796
IV. Provision for taxation	1500	1500
V. Profit after Tax	124976	56296
VI. Proposed Dividend:		
-Equity Shares	61103	17944
VII. Transfer to Reserves and Surplus	63873	54380

Note: In the financial year ended on 31st Dec., 1988 a sum of Rs. 16028 thousands has been written back to that year's profits from Investment Allowance Reserve.

Analysis of Financial Statements

Analysis of financial statement is a technical job which can be perfonned properly only by a knowledgeable and experienced financial analyst. In order to he successful in his analysis and interpretation, a financial analyst must possess thorough knowledge of accounting theory and practice and he must understand various tools and techniques of accounting and their application in the analysis and interpretation of data. The knowledge of the requirements of the law relating to the organisation is must for a financial analyst. In addition to this, he must also understand the industry. environment in which the unit is operating. His personal qualities such as penetrating vision and insight, tectfulness alertness, leadership qualities, etc., help him greatly in the successful discharge of his functions as financial analyst.

Techniques of Analysis

There are various techniques which are used to understand the financial statements in a comprehensive manner. Following are the methods which are generally employed to analyse the financial statements:

1. Comparative statements
2. Common size statements
3. Trend analysis
4. Technique of accounting ratio.

Comparative Statements

Joint stock companies are required to provide in their annual published accounts the corresponding figures for the year immediately preceeding the current financial year so as to provide a comparative picture of their business affairs. The decision-makers prefer to study the picture of not only for one or two years but for few more year in the fast. The Income Statement and Balance Sheet in their usual form are not much useful from management point of view. Therefore, the analysts re-arrange the information in different group as the group study alongwith the individual items is more meaningful for the purpose of interpretation and decision-making. If two or more companies have to be compared (inter-firm comparison), the analyst should take care that the group are homogeneous. He should also bear in mind the size of the enterprise in terms of capital investment and turnover. A comparative financial statement may be presented in anyone of the following forms:

A. Absolute figures for the years of comparison

B. Absolute figures alongwith variations (in absolute figures)

C. Absolute figures' alongwith variation in terms of pecentage or ratio.

D. Individual items as percentage of a base year.

It may be noted that the absolute figures, especially when they represent large amount are not easy to remember; therefore, it is advisable that the figures are expressed as a percentage or ratio.

Illustration-5

On 31st December 2003 the Profit and Loss Account and Balance Sheet of Jay India Ltd. stood as under:

PROFIT & LOSS ACCOUNT FOR THE YEAR ENDED AT 31ST DECEMBER, 2003

2002	*Expenditure*	*2003*	*2002*	*Incomes*	*2003*
20,000	To opening Stock	20,000	280,000	By Sales	4,00,000
1,20,000	To Purchases	1,50,000	20,000	By Closing Stock	50,000
10,000	To Carriage Inward	15,000			
50,000	Direct wages	90,000			
20,000	Gas, water and Power	50,000			
80,000	To Gross Profit	1,25,000			
3,00,000		4,50,000	3,00,000		4,50,000
8,000	To Salaries	9,000	80,000	By Gross Profit	1,25,000
2,500	To Rent and Taxes	3,000			
1,000	To Printing and stationery	1,500			
800	To Advertising	1,000			
2,000	To Interest on loans	1,000			
65,700	To Net Profit	1,09,500			
80,000		1,25,000	80,000		1,25,000

You are required to compare the performance of the company by re-arranging the data suitably and give your comments on the operational performance of the enterprise.

COMPARATIVE INCOME STATEMENT

Particulars	*2002*	*2003 decrease (±)*	*Increase decrease (±)*	*Increase*
1	*2*	*3*	*4*	*5*
1. Sales	2,80,000	4,00,000	+ 1,20,000	+43%
2. Purchases	1,20,000	1,50,000	+ 30,000	+25%
Carnage inward	10,000	15,000	+ 5,000	+50%
Direct wages	50,000	90,000	+ 40,000	+80%
Gas, water and power	20,000	50,000	+ 30,000	+ 150%

1	*2*	*3*	*4*	*5*
3. Direct cost of Production,	2,00,000	3,05,000	1,05,000	52%
Opening stock	20,000	20,000	—	—
	2,20,000	3,25,000	1,05,000	+52%
Less closing stock	20,000	50,000	30,000	+ 150%
4. Cost of sales	2,00,000	2,75,000	75,000	+37%
5. Gross margin	80,000	1,25,000	+ 45,000	+56%
6. Operating expenses:				
Sales...	8,000	9,000	+ 1,000	+12½%
Rent and taxes	2,500	30,000	+500	+20%
Printing & stationery	1,000	1,500	+500	+50%
Advertising	800	1,000	+200	+25%
Total operating Expenses	12,300	14,500	+ 2,200	+ 18%
Net operating Income	67,700	1,10,500	+ 42,800	+63%
Less interest charges	2,000	1,000	1,000	-50%
Profit after Interest but Before taxes	65,700	1,09,500	+ 43,800	+67%

Comments

An analysis of the Income statement in the above form clearly shows the variations in the individual item of 2003 on compared to their corresponding figures in 2002. An increase of 43 % in sales has led to an increase of 56% in gross Margin which represent an ecouraging position. The operating cost has gone up only by 18% which shows an efficient control over a overhead charges. A study of the composition of direct cost reveals that the increase in direct wages and gas water and power has been 80% and 150% respectively. Such an increase seems disproportionately high as compared to increase in the volum of sales. The increase in these items need to be further investigated in order to ascertion real causes for such an abnormal increase in these direct expenses of production. However, the over-all performance of the enterprise in 1985 as compared to 1984 is quite satisfactory.

Comparative Balance Sheet

Comparative Balance Sheet can be prepared in the same manner as the income statement as shown in the above illustration. The management accountant while presenting a comparative Balance Sheet under suitable heads, should be very clear about that structure of different assets and liabilities. The assets may be grouped under four major heads *viz.* *(a)* Liquid assets, *(b)* Non-liquid assets, *(c)* Fixed assets, and *(d)* pre-operative expenses not written off. Similarly, the liabilities may be grouped into trade liablities and long-term liabilities. The break-up of Balance Sheet in this manner will provide a better picture of the state of affair of an enterprise:

Illustration-6

On 31st December 2004, the Balance Sheet of Perfect Engineers (India) Ltd. stood as under:

BALANCE SHEET AS ON 31ST DECEMBER 2004

2003 (Rs.)	*Capital and Liabilities*	*2004 (Rs.)*	*2003 (Rs.)*	*Property and Assests*	*2003 (Rs.)*
4,00000	Share Capital	5,00,000	2,50,000	Land and Building	2,95,000
60,000	General Reserve	80,000	4,50,000	Plant and Machinery	4,05,000
8,000	Investment Fluctuation Fund	10,000	50,000	Furniture and FIxtures	75,000
6,000	Worlcmen compensation fund	15,000	1,00,000	Investtnents	1,50,000
			1,25,000	Stock in trade	2,00,000
2,00,000	15% Debentures	3,00,000	58,000	Sundry debtors	1,50,000
2,00,000	Loans from IDBI	1,50,000	30,000	Bills Receivable	56,000
2,00,000	Fixed Deposit	3,00,000	20,000	Marketable securities	40,000
80,000	Sundry creditors	1,00,000	25,000	Cash Balances	50,000
4,000	Rent outstanding	6,000	50,000	Pre-operation Exp.	40,000
11,58,000		14,61,000	11,58,000		14,61,000

You are required to re-cast the above Balance Sheet so as to reflect the financial position move clearly.

Solution

COMPARATIVE BALANCE SHEET AS ON 31-12-2004

	2003	*2004*	*Increase/ decrease*	*Increase/ (%)*
1	*2*	*3*	*4*	*5*
1. Fixed Assets:				
Land and Building	2,50,000	2,95,000	+ 45,000	+ 18%
Land and Machinery	4,50,000	4,05,000	45,000	10%
Furnitures	50,000	75,000	+ 25,000	+50%
Total Fixed Assets	7,50,000	5,75,000	+ 25,000	+33%
2. Investment	1,00,000	1,50,000	50,000	+50%
3. Current Assets:				
(a) Liquid Assets:				
— Cash balances	25,000	50,000	+ 25,000	100%
— Debtors	58,000	1,50,000	+ 92,000	159%
— Bills Receivable	30,000	56,000	+ 26,000	+ 87%
— Marketable Securities	20,000	40,000	+ 20,000	+ 100%
	1,33,000	2,96,000	+ 1,63,000	+ 123%
(b) Non-liquid Assets:				
— Stock-in-Trade	1,25,000	2,00,000	+ 75,000	+60%
Total Current Assets	2,58,000	4,96,000	+ 2,38,000	+92%
4. Pre-operative expenses	50,000	40,000	- 10,000	-20%
Total Assets	11,58,000	14,61,000	3,03,000	+26%
1. Capital and Intemal liabilities				
— Share capital	4,00,000	5,00,000	+ 1,00,000	+25%
— General Reserve	60,000	80,000	+ 20,000	+33%
— Investment Fluctuation Fund	8,000	1,000	+ 2,000	+25%
— Workmen Compensation Fund	6,000	15,000	+ 9,000	+ 15%
Total Capital	4,74,000	6,05,000	+ 1,31,000	+28%
2. Long term liabilities				
— Debentures	2,00,000	3,00,000	1,00,000	+50%
— Loans from IDBI	2,00,000	1,50,000	- 50,000	-25%
— Fixed Deposit	2,00,000	3,00,000	+ 1,00,000	+50%
Total long term liabilities	6,00,000	7,50,000	+ 1,50,000	+25%

1	2	3	4	5
3. Current liabilities:				
— Sundry creditors	80,000	1,00,000	+ 20,000	+25%
— Rent Outstanding	4,000	6,000	+ 2,000	+50%
Total current liabilities	84,000	1,06,000	+ 22,000	+26%
Total Liabilities	11,58,000	14,61,000	3,03,000	+26%

Comments

A comparative study of assets structure reveals that there has been negligible increase of 3.3% in the total fixed assets in 2004 in comparison with 2003. The investments have gone up by 50% and there has been considerable increase in liquid and non-liquid assets as they have gone up by 123 % and 60% respectively. Whether such an increase in current assets (92%) truely shows the liquid position is an issue which should be decided in the light of the current liabilities of the company. The decrease in the preparation expenses clearly shows that the company has written of such expenses to the tune of 20% during the current year.

As regards the liabilities, the shareholders funds as represented by capital and other reserves have gone up by 28%. These has been marked increase of 150% in the workmen compensation Fund due to transfer of Rs. 9000 in the current year, long-term liabilities and current liabilities have increaced by 25% respectively. The management should further investigate the causes for marked variations in current assets and workmen's compensation fund with a view to review their credit policy and the policy for building up of the workmen compensation fund.

Common Size Statements

The Profit and Loss Account and Balance Sheetcan also be presented in the form of Common-size statements. A statement in which individual items are expressed as a per centage of same common base is termed as an common-size statement. In a common-size Profit and Loss Account, the sale figure is generally taken as base (sale - 100) to calculate the proposition of other items figuring in the Profit and Loss a/c and a common size Balance Sheet expresses individual assets and liabilities as percentage of total assets/liabilities.

Common-size comparative statements provide a better historical perspective of an undertaking. Any significant departure from the normal trend need further investigation to as certain the reasons for unusual movement in the figures so that due care is taken in the formulation of future plan.

The Profit and Loss Account as Balance Sheet as given previously are presented below in the from of common-size statements.

COMMON-SIZE PROFIT AND LOSS ACCOUNT

	2003		2004	
	Amount	*% to sales*	*Amount*	*% to sales*
Sales	2,80,000	100	4,00,000	100
1. Cost of production	2,00,000	71.4	3,05,000	100
2. Cost of Sales	2,00.000	71.4	2,75,000	68.7
3. Gross Margin	80,000	28.3	1,25,000	31.2
4. Operating Expenses	12,300	4.4	14,500	3.6
5. Net Operating Profit	67,700	24.2	1,10,500	27.6
6. Profit after interest	67,500	23.4	1,09,500	24.9

COMMON SIZE BALANCE SHEET

Items	*2003 Amount*	*% of total assets*	*2004 Amount*	*% to total Assets*
1	*2*	*3*	*4*	*5*
A. Land and Buildings	2,50,000	21.6	2,95,000	20.2
Plant and Machinery	4,50,000	38.8	4,05,000	27.7
Furniture and Fixtures	50,000	4.4	75,000	5.2
Fixed Assets	7,50,000	64.8	7,75,000	53.1
B. Investments	1,00,000	8.6	1,50,000	10.2
C. Cash Balances	25,000	2.2	50,000	3.4
Debtors	58,000.	5.0	1,50,000	10.4
Bills Receivable	30,000	2.6	56,000	3.8
Marketable Securities	20,000	1.7	40,000	2.7
Liquid Assets	1,33,000	11.5	2,96,000	20.3

1	*2*	*3*	*4*	*5*
Stock-in-trade (Non-liquid asset)	1,25,000	10.8	2,00,000	13.7
Total current assets	2,58,000	22.3	14,61,000	34.0
D. Pre-operating Exp.	50,000	4.3	40,000	2.7
Total Assets	11,58,000	100	14,61,000	100
Capital and liabilities:				
Share capital	4,00,000	34.5	5,00,000	34.2
General Reserve	60,000	5.2	80.000	5.5
Investment Fluctuation Fund	8,000	0.7	10,600	0.7
Workmen Compensation Fund	6,000	0.5	15,000	1.0
Total Shareholders fund	4,74,000	40.9	6,05,000	41.4
Long Term liabilities:				
Debentures	2,00,000	17.3	3,00,000	20.5
Loans	2,00,000	17.3	1,50,000	10.3
Fixed Assets	2,00,000	17.2	3,00,000	20.5
Total long term liabilities	6,00,000	51.8	7,50,000	51.3
Current liabilities:				
Sundry creditors	80,000	6.9	1,00,000	6.8
Rent Outstanding	4,000	0.4	6,000	0.4
Total current liabilities	8,4000	7.3	1,06,000	7.2
Total Liabilities	11,58,000	100	14,61,000	100

Observations

The common-size Balance sheet shows the assets and liabilities structure in relation to total assets/liabilities. As is vident from the above, the fixed assets in 1995 formed 53.1 % of the total asset in the same year. The current assets accounted for 34% which consisted of liquid and non-liquid assets of 203% and 13.7% respectively. Preoperative expenses were only 2.7% of the total assets. It may be understood that the asset structure of any enterprises defends upon its very nature. In a capital intensive industry, the proportion of fixed assets is much more than that of the current assets. Against it, the labour-intensive industries have lower proportion of fixed assets and higher percentage of assets is devoted to working capital in the form of current assets. Therefore, the position of the constituents of total assets should be interpreted in terms of the very nature of industry. In the above case the structure of assets in 2004 has substantially changed. The fixed assets which were 64.8% in 2003 had gone down to 53.1% despite additions to land and building and furniture. The decline seems due to decrease in the value of assets due to depreciation. The liquid position of the company has significantly improved from just 22.3% to 34.0% but this may be rightly interpreted-in relation to corresponding current liabilities.

As regards liabilities, the shareholders funds represented by capital and reserves accounted for 40.9% and 41.5% at the end of 2003 and 2004 respectively. The long-term liabilities were 51.8% and 51.3% at the same point of time. Current liabilities constituted 7.3% and 7.2% at the end of the same periods. Thus the liabilities structure in 2004 is not much different from that at the end of the year 2003. From this type of observation, one may be tempted to conclude that the company has not grown over a period of one year as the percentage constituents of different liabilities is more or less the same. This type of conclusion will be erroneous. It may be realized that the common size statements present vertical representation of facts at a point of time and the comparison in the above form may mislead the analyst. Therefore, the consideration of absolute figures of assets and liabilities alongwith their percentages is highly important before any conclusion is drawn.

Trend Analysis

The absolute figure of an activity is not much useful in decision-making. Therefore, a set of figures for purposes of comparison is necessary. The accounting figures relating to sales, production, profit, overheads, working capital, etc., for the last few years expressed as a percentage of some figure in a base period give trend which throw more light on the related problem. Generally, the figures for the last 3 to 5 years should be considered for better understanding of an economic phenomenon. The trend indicates general tendency or direction of change in which management is more interested, but the fact that a trend is more influenced by the base year figure, should always be borne in mind. The analysis and interpretation will not be fruitful if the base year figure is unusually high or low. Therefore, the selection of the base year should be done carefully. It should be the year of normal conditions. The trend can be rightly interpreted if the effect of inflation on different years figures of money income is neutralized. Another method of proper analysis would be to calculate the percentage of physical quantities, wherever possible, by the use of index numbers technique. The percentage of current year may be calculated as under:

$$\% \text{ for current year} = \frac{\text{Current year figure}}{\text{Base year figure}} \times 100$$

The trend analysis may be understood by perusing the following financial statement based on imaginary figures of few important items of Income and position statements of an hypothetical firm.

Items	2001		2002		2003		2004		2005	
	Amount	%	Amount	%	Amount	%	Amount	%	Amount	%
Sales	20,000	100	22,000	110	30,000	150	25,000	125	32,000	160
Direct Cost	8,000	100	10,000	125	14,000	175	11,000	137	13,000	163
Factory overheads	1,000	100	1,200	120	1,400	140	1,200	120	1,500	150
Administration	800	100	800	100	1,000	125	1,000	125	1,000	125
Selling overheads	200	100	250	125	300	150	250	125	350	175
Gross Margin	12,000	100	12,000	100	16,000	133	14,000	117	19,000	158
Profit before tax	10,000	100	9,750	97	13,300	133	11,550	115	16,150	161
Gross working Capital	40,000	100	45,000	112	45,000	112	50,000	125	80,000	200
Current Liabilities	20,000	100	25,000	125	25,000	125	30,000	150	35,000	175

Precautions in Financial Statement Analysis

The objective of analysis of financial statement is achieved only if the analysis is rightly done. In order to be successful the analyst should be well-versed in the art of analysis, he should take the following precautions in the analysis of financial statements:

1. He should see that the financial statements have been prepared by following the same concepts and conventions of book-keping and accounting. If there has been any change in the depreciation policy, inventory valuation method or any other variable affecting profit figure and assets and liabilities, the analyst should first make the data comparable by making necessary adjustments in the concerning items.

2. If two or more companies are being compared, it should be seen that their nature and size do not widely differ.

3. In the computation of trend the base year, with which the data of other years are compared should be selected carefully. The base year in any case should be a normal year.

4. Sometimes a percentage figure is misleading. Therefore, the analysis of statements submitted to management should contain absolute figures alongwith their percentages.

5. The relationship should be established only between the relevant figures. For example, the profitability should be interpreted only in terms of sales or capital employed.

❐

3

Inventory Valuation

Inventories in case of a manufacturing organisation may consist of raw materials, semi-manufactured goods and finished goods which are held for further processing and sales in the next production and sales budget period. The valuation of inventories possess a problem to the management as it can be valued in a number of ways. Different methods of inventory valuation give different values and this is the area where management may give colour to accounting information by following a method of inventory valuation which serve their purpose. The enterprise which is interested in the computation of true income and depicting correct financial position of its business affairs should rightly value the inventories and follow a consistent inventory valuation policy. Proper inventory valuation is absolutely necessary for correct income measurement and disclosure of financial position as inventories are recorded both in the Income Statement and Balance Sheet External financial analyst should note the method of inventory valuation which has been followed in the past 2-3 years. If there is any change in the method of valuation for the current year, then he should calculate the effect of such a change on the gross profit of the enterprise. Any change in the method of inventory valuation makes a lot of difference if the proportion of inventory is quite large.

We need two information to calculate the value of inventory:

(A) Physical Quantity. It is the quantity of raw materials, work-in progress and finished goods which remain unconsumed/ unsold on the date when final accounts are to be prepared. This quantity information can be gathered by physical counting of inventory items.

Physical verification will show the exitence of inventory items on the date of final accounts. Other sources of information regarding physical quantity is the costing records which are maintained on continuous basis. Costing records provide detailed information such as opening show purchases and issue of items from time to time and closing stock alongwith their values.

(b) Unit Price. It is the price/rate at which the inventory may be valued. The value of inventory can be arrived at by multiplying simply the physical quantities by the unit price.

The accuracy of the valuation of inventory largly depends upon the right calculation of unit-price which is determined by taking into accounts all costs related to purchases and dividing the same by the number of units brought. The actual cost of raw material inventory shall consist of its purchase price, freight charges, insurance in transit, octroi and cost of buying, receiving and storing. Similarly, the cost of finished goods shall include the cost of raw material and all costs increased in the conversion of raw materials into finished products. In actual practice, a firm may find some difficulties in the computation of cost per unit due to estimation of 'other costs' associated with the inventory items.

Methods of Inventory Valuation

There are different methods of valuing inventors for the purpose of showing the same in the final accounts. The management should clearly understand the implication of each method and follow the one which is most appropriate to its nature of enterprise. International Accounting standard 2 (IAS-2) recommends that the inventories should be valued at the lower of 'Historical cost' and 'net reliasable value.' This standard is based on the conservative principle of book-keeping which ignores expected gains but provides for possible losses. Thus there are primarily three methods of valuing inventories *(i)* Historical cost price *(ii)* Market Price and *(iii)* Lower of historical cost and market price. In order to facilitate the task of selection of a particular method, a brief explain of each one of them is provided hereunder:

1. Historical Cost Price. Historical cost of inventories is defined as the cost of purchases, cost of conversion and other costs, incurred in bringing the inventories to their present location and condition. It means the inventors of raw materials will not only be valued at the actual price of paid for the same but the price will also include the proportionate expenses incurred on acquisition such as freight charges, insurance in transit, octrio and other duties. In case of work-in-progress and finished goods inventories, the wages and other manufacturing cost related to such inventories will also be included. Since inventories an a given date may belong to a particular lot or different lots of purchases the assignment of historical cost to inventories may cause some confusion and difficulty. Following methods based on historical actual cost are used to assign values to material/goods issued or sold and the inventories.

(A) Specific Identification Method. According to this method, each item of inventory is identified with its cost and sum of such costs represent the value of inventory. In other words, the value of inventory on any date is the aggregate cost of all the inventory items valued at their actual cost. In this manner, it is a very simple method but it may cause a lots of problem to the valuer when the number of items is quite large. This method also provides scope for income manipulation when similar lots of items were purchased at different rates. Suppose a firm purchased 200 units of a particular item in four lots of 5050 units each at a price of Rs. 2, Rs. 3, Rs. 4 and Rs. 5 respectively and sold 100 units @ Rs. 6 per unit. In this case the inventory (unsold stock) of 100 units may be valued by the firm at any rate assuming that it pertain to that particular lot of items. If the firm desires to depict higher profits and show current valuation of inventory, then it will value 100 units @ Rs. 5 per unit. If its decides to show a depressed figure of profit and low valuation of assets, then it will certainly value 100 items at a value lesser than 5. This may be a suitable method in case the number of inventory items is few and nature of business is such where purchases are made to meet the specific requirements of the customers.

(B) First-in First-out (FIFO) Method. According to this method, the inventory is valued at the most recent cost value of the unsold stock. It is based on the assumption that the raw materials or goods purchased first are issued first. Thus the inventories constitute the last or most recent purchases. In actual practice, it is not essential that the oldest stock is sold first but it is assumed to have been sold first for the purpose of accounting. However, the general tendency on the part of the seller is to dispose off the old stock first and it is more true in case of less durable and perishable goods. Thus the method is more in true with the business practice. It places the current cost on the value of inventories and thus Balance Sheet of a firm pursuing this method would show current economic position in relation to stock-in-trade (inventory). Valuation of inventory according to FIFO method may be explained by a simple illustration as under:

Illustration-1

From the following information show the value of inventory after each receipt and issue of raw materials:

2004

Jan. 1 Balance 100 @ Rs. 15

Jan. 10 Purchased 500 @ Rs. 20

Jan. 12 Issued 200

Jan. 20 Purchased 200 @ Rs. 25

Jan. 31 Issued 400

Solution

STATEMENT OF INVENTORY

Date	*Receipts*			*Issues*			*Balance*		
	Quality	*Rate*	*Value*	*Quality*	*Rate*	*Value*	*Quality*	*Rate*	*Value*
Jan. 2004	—	—	—	—	—	—	100	15	1500
Jan. 10	500	20	10,000	—	—	—	100	15	1500
							500	20	10,000
Jan. 12		—	—	200 [100	15	1500	400	20	8,000
				100	20	2000			
20	200	25	5000	—	—	—	400	20	8000
							200	25	5000
31	—	—	—	400	20	8000	200	25	5000

The statement is self-explanatory. It is clear that the inventory of 200 units valued at Rs. 5000 is the same which was bought on 20th Jan. at the rate of Rs. 25.

(C) Highest in First-Out (HIFO) Method. According to this method the highest priced material in store is assumed to have been issued first. Accordingly the material issued is priced at the highest price till the quantity of the highest priced material is exhausted. Next issue is made at the next highest price if the quantity of the first highest price material is finished. Thus, the production absorbs the highest cost of materials and the inventory (stock in strode) is valued at lesser than its current cost is clear from the following statement:

STATEMENT OF INVENTORY
(HIFO METHOD)

Date	*Receipts*			*Issues*			*Balance*		
	Quality	*Rate*	*Value*	*Quality*	*Rate*	*Value*	*Quality*	*Rate*	*Value*
2005									
Jan. 1	—	—	—	—	—	—	100	15	1500
Jan. 10	500	20	10000	—	—	—	100	15	1500
							500	20	10,000
Jan. 12	—	—	—	200	20	4000	400		7500
Jan. 20	200	25	5000	—	—	—	600		12500
Jan. 31	—	—	—	200	25	5000	—		3500
				200	20	4000	200		

(D) Next-in First-out (NIFO) Method. Under this method the issue price is not the lost price of the materials/goods in store but it is the price at which the next delivery of material for which an order has been placed, is expected to the received. The issue price under conditions of rising prices will be higher whereas it will be lower than earlier costs when purchase price constantly declines. Accordingly, the book value of unsold stock will decrease and increase.

(E) Last-in First-out (LIFO) Method. This method of inventory valuation is based on the assumption that the materials goods purchased last are issued first for disposition. Obviously the assumption under this method is just opposite of the FIFO method.

Thus the inventory in a firm following this method is assumed to consist of old stock and hence valued at old or earliest rates.

Like FIFO method, it is not essential in LIFO method that the actual flow of materials/goods conferm to the assumption under which the method operates. The chief feature of this method is that it attempts to charge current cost plus profit from the customers but the inventory value is quite different firm its current or replacement cost. Under conditions of rising prices, the cost is in tune with the market condition but the inventory is under-valued which creates a sort of secret reserve and to that extent Balance Sheet gets window dressed.

Using the cost data of illustration-1, The valuation of inventory may be shown as below:

Statement of Inventory

Date	*Receipts*			*Issues*			*Balance*		
	Quality	*Rate*	*Value*	*Quality*	*Rate*	*Value*	*Quality*	*Rate*	*Value*
2004									
Jan. 1	—	—	—	—	—	—	100	15	1500
Jan. 10	500	20	10,000	—	—	—	100	15	1500
							500	20	10000
Jan. 12	—	—	—	200	20	4000	100	15	1500
							300	20	6000
Jan. 20	200	25	5000	—	—	—	100	15	1500
							300	20	6000
							200	25	5000
Jan. 31	—	—	—	200	25	5000	100	15	1500
				200	20	4000	100	20	2000

Thus the statement shows that the inventory of 200 items consists of 100 units purchased at Rs. 15 and another 100 units which were purchased at Rs. 20. The Last in purchases of 200 units purchased at Rs. 200 have already been issued to production.

A comparison of inventory value under the FIFO and LIFO methods shows that under the former method the value of 200 units is 5,000 whereas the value of the same inventory under the later method is Rs. 3,500. Value assigned to inventory under the LIFO method is much less than the value under the FIFO method due to the fact that the LIFO method takes into account the earliest cost for the purpose of valuation and the earliest cost under condition of raising prices is lesser than the current prices.

Average Cost Methods

The FIFO and LIFO methods of inventory valuation were based on the assumptions of a particular sequence of issue of materials. In fact, the physical flow of raw material hardly conform to the assumption made. Sometimes, it is, therefore, considered proper to issue raw materials/goods at average cost. For the purpose of issuing raw materials/goods, we may use either simple average cost or weighted average cost.

(F) Simple Average Cost Method. The closing inventory, value, as per this method, depends upon the issue price which is the simple average of prices, which is arrived of by adding the different prices and dividing the total by number of such prices. For instance, if 500 units are purchased at Rs. 20 and 200 units at Rs. 25, then the simple average of prices is 20 + 25 = 45 + 2 = 22.50. Issue price and inventory value based on simple average method is represented in the following statement:

Statement of Inventory

Date	*Receipts*			*Issues*			*Balance*		
	Quality	*Rate*	*Value*	*Quality*	*Rate*	*Value*	*Quality*	*Rate*	*Value*
2004									
Jan. 1	100	15	1,500	—	—	—	100	15	1500
Jan. 10	500	20	10,000	—	—	—	600	—	11500
Jan. 12	—	—	—	200	17.50	3500	400	—	8000
Jan. 20	200	25	5,000	—	—	—	600	—	13000
Jan. 31	—	—	—	400	22.50	9000	200	—	.4000

From the statement, it is clear that the cost of inventory on 10th Jan. 2004 of 600 units is Rs. 11500. On 12th Jan., 200 units at an average price of Rs.17.50(15+20/2) have been issued and the balance of inventory (400 units) valued at Rs. 8000. On the last day of the month 400 units at an average price of 22.50 (20 + 25/2) have been issued and thus leaving an inventory of 200 units at a cost value of Rs. 4000.

The average cost method is a very simple method of issue and valuation of inventory. But it suffers from all the limitations with which simple average suffers. Since a simple average is affected to great extent by extreme values, it is likely that in a certain case, the inventory may be shown at zero or a negative figure, which would be beyond imagination. Supper 100 units are purchased at Rs. 15 and 500 units are purchased at Rs. 5 and 400 units are issued at an average price of 10, then the closing inventory of 200 units would be reduced to zero which is an absurd valuation. Thus, this method is unscientific and generally gives unsatisfactory results.

(G) Weighted Average Method. The weighted average method of pricing and valuation of inventory duty recognises the weights or quantities of inventories in stock on the date of issue of raw materials or goods. Under this method, the average price is calculated by dividing the total cost by the total number of units. The materials are issued at the weighted average cost which is calculated after each fresh arrival of materials/goods. This method is a better method insofar as it gives due importance to quantities due to which the effect of large variations in prices is lessened and cost structure reflects true cost of materials/goods issued for production/sales. However, the inventory value under this method, may be very much different from its current value. The operation of the method is represented through the statement given below:

Statement of Inventory

Date	*Receipts*			*Issues*			*Balance*		
	Quality	*Rate*	*Value*	*Quality*	*Rate*	*Value*	*Quality*	*Rate*	*Value*
2004									
Jan. 1	—	—	—	—	—	—	100	15	1500
Jan. 10	500	20	10,000	—	—	—	600	19.17	11500
Jan. 12	—		—	200	19.17	3834	400	19.17	7666
Jan. 20	200	25	5,000	—	—	—	600	21.11	12666
Jan. 31	—	—	—	400	21.11	8444	200	21.11	4222

On 10th Jan the total inventory of 600 units is value at actual cost of Rs. 11500. The average price for a unit is 19.17 (11500+600). At this rate the issue of 200 units has been priced. On the ival of first 200 units, the stock of 600 units cost Rs. 12666 and the average weighted price is 21.11 (12666 + 600). At this rate, the next issue of 400 units has been made. This leaving the inventory of 200 units at a cost of 4222; the average price remaining the same.

(H) Replacement Cost Method. Replacement cost is the market price of materials/goods on the date of issue. It is the price at which the goods can be replaced by purchasing from the market. Under this method the cost of closing inventory will depend upon the replacement cost. In case of rising prices, the replacement cost is always higher than earlier costs. If the inventories are bought in large quantities and issues are made at replacement cost, then the cost of closing inventory will be lesser than the cost of acquisition.

The issues at replacement cost is meant to reflect the current cost of raw materials in the total cost of manufacture. But the valuation of closing inventory at book value arrived at in this manner for the propose of showing the same in the Balance Sheet, will represent unrealistic position as the stock valuation will be at a figure which will be either too low or too high depending upon the condition of rising prices and declining prices respectively. In case the replacement price is not available, then it is based on management's, best estimation which might be different from the real replacement cost and this affects the book value of closing inventory. This method is very simple to follow as issues are made an replacement cost for which information is gathered from the market, as shown below:

Statement of Inventory

Date	*Receipts*			*Issues*			*Balance*		
	Quality	*Rate*	*Value*	*Quality*	*Rate*	*Value*	*Quality*	*Rate*	*Value*
2004									
Jan. 1	—	—	—	—	—	—	100	—	1500
Jan.10	500	20	10,000	—	—	—	600	—	11500
Jan. 12	—	—	—	200	21	4200	400		7,300
Jan. 20	200	25	5000	—	—	—	600		12,300
Jan. 31	—	—	—	400	26	10,400	200		1,900

The above representation is based on the assumption that the replacement price on 12th January and 31st January was Rs. 21 and Rs. 26 respectively. On comparison with earlier methods, it will be observed that the book value of closing eventory of Rs. 1900 is much less then the book values of the same 200 units under other methods.

(I) Standard Price Method. Standard Price is a price which is pre-determined by the costing department for the purpose of issuing raw materials/goods from store to factory/sales depots. The standard pricing system is applied with a view to control cost and follow a realistic price policy. Standard price is neither too low nor too high a price. It is the price which is pre-determined after taking into account the prevailing rates and likely changes in future prices for a particular period of time and revised from time to time in accordanc with the changes in the market and other conditions. Thus standard price is not the actual cost price but notional price which is much affected by management's perception about future.

Under standard pricing method, the issues are made at the same standard price. The closing inventory value depends upon the standard issue price.

Using the same data and further assuming that the standard price is taken at Rs. 22, the issue and stock values are depicted in the following statement:

Statement of Inventory

Date	*Receipts*			*Issues*			*Balance*		
	Quality	*Rate*	*Value*	*Quality*	*Rate*	*Value*	*Quality*	*Rate*	*Value*
2004									
Jan. 1	—	—	—	—	—	—	100	—	1,500
Jan.10	500	20	10,000	—	—	—	600	—	11,500
Jan. 12	—	—	—	200	22	4400	400	—	7,100
Jan. 20	200	25	5,000	—	—	—	600	—	12,100
Jan. 31	—	—	—	400	22	8800	200	—	3,300

(J) Base Stock Method. Base-Stock is the minimum stock of materials/goods which is generally maintained in any firm. According to this method, the Basestock will be valued at a fixed cost which is generally the cost of the frist lot of materials/goods out of which the based stock is assumed to have been created. Any quantity of materials/goods in excess of the Base-stock will be valued by FIFO, LIFO or any other method. In this manner, the Base Stock Method is not an independent method as it is used with application of any other method.

The merits and demarits of this method depends upon the method used for pricing the issue of materials/goods in excess of the Base-stock.

The Base-Stock is valued at the historical cost and is shown at the same value in Balance Sheet, which is not in tune with showing the current economic position of an enterprise.

2. Market Price Method. Inventories may be valued at market price instead of cost price. Market price means the current market rate at which inventories can be disposed of. It would be appropriate to value inventories at market value if the market price for the inventory items is fairly stable. If the requirements of International Accounting Standard is to be satisfied, then the inventory should be valued at 'Net Realisable Value' which means the current selling price minus selling cost. According to International Accounting—Standard (IAS-2), the net realisable value means, "the estimated selling price in the ordinary course of business less costs of compilation and less costs necessarily to be incurred in order to make the sale." If the current market rate is not stable and the management foresee a change in the current rates, then the realisable value may be estimated accordingly. However, minor fluctuations in prices may be ignored. The valuation of inventories at current market price seems quite realistic as it contributes in showing the current economic position of the enterprise but such a valuation gives rise to the problem of unrealised profit/loss.

3. Lower of Cost or Net Realisable Value. It means the inventory should be valued at cost price if it is lesser than the net realisable value and valuation should be done at net realisable value if it is lesser than the cost price. This is based on the conservative principle of book-keeping according to which all expected losses should be provided for but all expected gain should be ignored. If this method of inventory valuation is to be adopted, then the question of comparison of cost price and net realizable value will arise. The comparison can be made in a number of ways. We can compute the total cost price of different items of inventories and compare the same by the aggregate net realisable value of all the items. We compute also divide the total inventory items into homogeneous group and find out the cost price and net realisable value of each group of items separately. It is also possible to compare the cost and realizable value of individual items. Inventory value under different methods is shown below:

Statement of Inventory Valuation under Different Methods

Item		*Cost*	*Market Price*	*Lower of Cost or Market Price*		
				Aggregate	*Group*	*Individual*
Group-I	A	500	750			500
Group-I	B	800	700			700
	(i)	1300	1450		1300	
Group-I	C	1200	1800			1200
	D	2900	1300			1300
	(ii)	3200	3100		3100	
Total Inventory (i + ii)		4500	4550	4500		
		Inventory	valuable	4500	4400	3700

Above statement shows different values of inventories under different methods. It may be pointed out that the value of inventories under all the methods will be the same if the market price for all the items shows either constantly increasing or decreasing trend. The fluctuations in the market price of individual items makes all the difference in the value of inventories. IAS-2 has recommended the valuation of inventories either by comparison of cost and market values of group items or the comparison of individual items for the purpose.

Selection of a Method

From the explanation of the different methods as provided above, it is clear that the income determination and asset (stock in trade) measurement is different under different methods of pricing the issue of materials/goods. Which one of the available methods is the best or ideal is a difficult question to answer. The choice of a methods is governed more by the situation faced by an firm. Number of factors such as the need to conform to the physical flow of goods, matching current cost with revenues, degree of price fluctuations nature of inventory items, management policy, etc. are to be taken into consideration while selecting a particular method of valuation. Whichever method the management of a firm chooses for the purpose, should be used consistently till the change has not become inevitable.

APPENDIX

Values of Inventories

The following is the text of the revised Accounting Standard (AS)2, 'Valuation of Inventories', issued by the Council of the Institute of Chartered Accountants of India. This revised Standard supersedes Accounting Standard (AS)2, Valuation of Inventories, issued in June, 1981. The revised standard comes into effect in the respect of accounting periods commencing on or after April 1, 1999 and is mondatory in nature.

Objective

A primary issue is accounting for inventories is the determination of the value at which inventories are carried in the financial statements until the related revenues are recognised. This Statement deals with the determination of such value, including the ascertainment of cost of inventories and any write-down thereof to net realisable value.

Scope

1. This Statement should be applied in accounting for inventories other than:

(a) work-in-progress arising under construction contracts, including directly related service contracts (see Accounting Standard (AS) 7, Accounting for Construction Contractrs);

(b) work-in-progress arising in the ordinary course of business of service providers;

(c) shares, debentures and other financial instruments held as stock-in-trades; and

(d) producers' inventories of livestock, agricultural and forest products, and mineral oils, ores and gases to the extent that they are measured at net realisable value in accordance with well established practices in those industries.

2. The inventories referred to in paragraph l(d) are measured at net realisable value at certain stages of production. This occurs, for example, when agricultural crops have been harvested or mineral oils, ores and gases have been extracted and sale is assured under a forward contract or a government guarantee, or when a homogenous market exists and there is a negligible risk of failure to sell. These inventories are excluded from the scope of this Statement.

Definitions

3. The following terms are used in this Statement with the meanings specified: inventories are assets:

(a) held for sale in the ordinary course of business;

(b) in the process of production for such sale; or

(c) in the form of materials or supplies to be consumed in the production process or in the rendering of services.

Net realisable value is the estimated selling price in the ordinary course of business less the estimated costs of completion and the estimated costs necessary to make the sale.

4. Inventories encompass goods purchased and held for resale, for example, merchandise purchased,by a retailer and held for resale, computer software held for resale, or land and other property held for resale. Inventories also encompass finished goods produced, or work-in-progress being produced, by the enterprise and include materials, maintenance supplies, consumables and loose tools awaiting use in the production process. Inventories do not include machinery spares which can be used only in connection with an item of fixed

asset and whose use in expected to be irregular, such machinery spares are accounted for in accordance with Accounting Standard (AS) 10, Accounting for Fixed Assets.

Measurements of Inventories

5. Inventories should be valued at the lower of cost and net realisable value.

Cost of Inventories

6. The cost of inventories should comprise all costs of purchase, costs of conversion and other costs incurred in bringing the inventories to their present location and condition.

Costs of Purchase

7. The costs of purchase consist of the purchase price including duties and taxes (other than those subsequently recoverable by the enterprise from the taxing authorities), freight inwards and other expenditure directly attributable to the acquisition. Trade discounts, rebates, duty drawbacks and other similar items are deducted in determining the costs of purchase.

Costs of Conversion

8. The costs of conversion of inventories include costs directly related to the units of production, such as direct labour. They also include a systematic allocation of fixed and variable production overheads that are incurred in converting materials into finished goods. Fixed produciton overheads are those indirect costs of production that remain relatively constant regardless of the volume of production, such as depreciation and maintenance of factory buildings and the cost of factory management and administration. Variable production overheads are those indirect costs of production that vary directly, or nearly directly, with the volume of production, such as indirect materials and indirect labour.

9. The allocation of fixed production overheads for the purpose of their inclusion in the costs of conversion is based on the normal capacity of the production facilities. Normal capacity is the production expected to be achieved on an average over a number of periods or seasons under normal circumstances, taking into account the loss of

capacity resulting from planned maintenance. The actual level of production may be used if it approximate normal capacity. The amount of fixed production overheads allocated to each unit of production is not increased as a consequence of low production or idel plant. Unallocated overheads are recognised as an expense in the period in which they are incurred. In periods of abnormally high production, the amount of fixed production overheads allocated to each unit of production is decreased so that inventories are not measured above cost. Variable production overheads are assigned to each unit of production on the basis of the actual use of the production facilities.

10. A production process may result in more than one product being produced simultaneously. This is the case, for example, when joint products are produced or when ther is a main product and a by-product. When the costs of conversion of each product are not separately identifiable, they are allocated between the products on a rational and consistent basis. The allocation may be based, for example, on the relative sales value of each product either at the stage in the production process when the products become separately identifiable, or at the completion of production. Most by-products as well as scrap or waste materials, by their nature, are immaterial. When this is a case, they are often measured at net realisable value and this value is deducted from the cost of the main product. As a result, the carrying amount of the main product is not materially different from its cost.

Other Costs

11. Other costs are included in the cost of inventories only to the extent that they are incurred in bringing the inventories to their present location and condition. For example, it may be appropriate to include overheads other than production over heads or the costs of designing products for specific customers in the cost of inventories.

12. Interest and other borrowing costs are usually considered as not relating to bringing the inventories to their present location and condition and are, therefore, usually not included in the cost of inventories. Exclusions from the Cost of Inventories.

13. In determining the cost of inventories in accordance with paragraph 6, it is appropriate to exclude certain costs and recognise them as expenses in the period in which they are incurred. Examples of such Costs are:

(a) abnormal amounts of wasted materials, labour, or other production costs;

(b) storage costs, unless those costs are necessary in the production process prior to a further production stage;

(c) administrative over heads that do not contribute to bringing the inventories to their present location and condition; and

(d) selling and distribution costs. Cost Formulas

14. The cost of inventories of items that are not ordinarily interchangeable and goods or services produced 'and segregated for specific projects should be assigned by specific identification of their individual costs.

15. Specific identification of cost means that specific costs are attributed to identified items of inventory. This is appropriate treatment for items that are segregated for a specific project, regardless of whether they have been purchased or produced. However, when there are large numbers of Herris of inventory which are ordinarily interchangeable, specified identification of costs is inappropriate since, in such circumstances, an enterprise could obtain predetermined effects on the net profit or loss for the period by selecting a particular method of ascertaining the items that remain in inventories.

16. The cost of inventories, other than those deals with in paragarph 14, should be assigned by using the first-in, first-out (FIFO), or weighted average cost formula. The formula used should reflect the fairest possible approximation to the cost incurred in bringing the items of inventory to their present location and condition.

17. A variety of costs formulas is used to determine the cost of inventories other than those for which specific identification of individual costs is appropriate. The formula used in determining the cost of an item of inventory needs to be selected with a view to providing the fairest possible approximation to the cost incurred in

bringing the item to its present location and condition. The FIDO formula assumes that the items of inventory which were purchased for produced first are consumed or sold first, and consequently the items remaining in inventory at the end of the period are those most recently purchased or produced. Under the weighted average cost formula, the cost of each item is determined from the weighted average of the cost of similar items at the beginning of a period and cost of similar items purchased or produced during the period. The average may be calculated on a periodic basis, or as each additional shipment is received, depending upon the circumstances of the enterprise.

Techniques for the Measurement of Cost

18. The techniques for the'measurement of the cost of inventories, such as the standard cost method or the retail method, may be used for convenience if the results approximate the actual cost. Standard costs take into account normal levels of consumption of materials and supplies, labour, efficiency and capacity utilisation. They are regularly reviewed and, if necessary, revised in the light of current conditions.

19. The retail method is often used in the retail trade for measuring inventories of large numbers of rapidly changing items that have similar margins and for which it is impracticable to use other costing methods. The cost of the inventory is determined by reducing from the sales value of the inventory the appropriate percentage gross margin. The percentage used takes into consideration inventory which has been marked down to below its original selling price. An average percentage for each retail department is often used.

Net Realisable Value

20. The cost of inventories may not be recoverable if those inventories are damaged, if they have become wholly or partially obsolete, or if their selling prices have declined. The cost of inventories may also not be recoverable if the estimated costs of completion or the estimated costs necessary to make the sale have increased. The practice of writing down inventories below cost of net realisable

value is consistent with the veiw that assets should not be carried in excess of amounts expected to be realised from their sale or use.

21. Inventories are usually written down to net realisable value of an item-by-item basis. In some circumstances, however, it may be appropriate to group similar or related items. This may be the case with items of inventory relating to the same product line that have similar purposes or end uses and are produced and marketed in the same geographical area and cannot be practicably evaluated separately from other items in that product line. It is not appropriate to write down inventories based on a classification of inventory, for example, finished goods, or all the inventories in a particular business segment.

22. Estimates of net realisable value are based on the most reliable evidence available at the time the estimates are made as to the amount the inventories are expected to realise. These estimates take into consideration-fluctuations of price or cost directly relating to events occurring after the balance sheet date to the extent that such events confirm the conditions existing at the balance sheet date.

23. Estimates of net realisable value also take into consideration the purpose for which the inventory is held. For example, the net realisable value of the quantity of inventory held to satisfy firm sales or service contracts is based on the contract price. If the sales contracts are for less than the inventory quantities held, the net realisable value of the excess inventory is based on general selling prices. Contingent losses on firm sales contracts in excess of inventory quantities held and contingent losses on firm purchase contracts are dealt with in accordance with the principles enunciated in Accounting Standard (AS) 4, Contingents And Events Occurring After The Balance Sheet Date.

24. Materials and other supplies held for use in the production of inventories are not written down below cost if the finished products in which they will be incorporated are expected to be sold at or above cost. However, when there has been a decline in the price of materials and it is estimated that the cost of the finished products will exceed net realiable value, the materials are written down to net realisable value. In such circumstances, the replacement cost of the

materials may be the best available measure of their net realisable value.

25. An assessment is made of net realisable value as at each balance sheet date.

Disclosure

26. The financial statements should disclose:

(a) the accounting policies adopted in measuring inventories, including the cost formula used; and

(b) the total carrying amount of inventories and its classification appropriate to the enterprise.

27. Information about the carrying amounts held in different classifications of inventories and the extent of the changes in these assets is useful to financial statement users. Common classifications of inventories are raw materials and components, work-in-progress, finished goods, stores and spares, and loose tools.

❑

4

Depreciation

Expenditure incurred in an enterprise may broadly be classified into two categories, namely capital expenditure and revenue expenditure. Capital expenditure is concerned with the acquisition of capital assets and other fixed equipments such as land, building, plant and machinery, furniture and fixtures, tools and implements, etc. Such an expenditure is not incurred every now and then but there are special occasions on which the heavy capital expenditure is incurred. On the other hand, revenue expenditure are is done in the usual course of business. The usual items of revenue expenditure the payment for purchase of raw materials, wages and other direct and indirect expenses of running the enterprise in the normal course of business. The whole of revenue expenditure is charged against the profit of the year in which it is incurred. But the capital expenditure needs special treatment in view of its very nature. As we know that a capital asset gives service for fairly long period of time and the amount involved in it is so heavy that whole of it cannot be charged against the profit of a particular year.

Depreciation is something which is concerned with the treatment of capital expenditure in the from of assets in the account books. There is a lot of confusion in so far the causes and method of charging depreciation are concerned. According to J.R. Batlib that term "depreciation represents loss or diminution in the value of an asset consequent upon wear and tear, obsolescence, effluxion of time or permanent fall in market value." In the opinion of L.C. Cropper. "Depreciation is the domination in the financial value of an asset owing to wear and tear, effluxion of time obsolescence, or similar causes the suggestion being rather that of gradual depreciation than sudden loss or diminition in value." The Institute of Chartered Accountants in England an Wales defines depreciation as "the measure of wearing out, consumption or other loss of value of a fixed asset, whether arising from use, effluxion of time or obsolescence through technology and market changes... "These definition emphasize on the causes of depreciation. The value of a machine goes down as a result of its constant use. The persistent usage also causes the production capacity to decline gradually and after few years it is observed that the machine has been rendered completely unproductive. This is indicative of the fact that every machine has a production or useful life after which the manufacturing concern has to replace it by a new one. Thus the whole value of the asset is to be charged gradually over its productive life. This change is nothing but, depreciation. Hence every kind of decrease in the value of an asset cannot be termed as depreciation. The loss of a machine due to accident or obsolescence can better be called capital loss but not depreciation. Depreciation is that fractional amount of an asset which is debited to the profit and loss account of a concern according to a pre-conceived plan or schedule of depreciation. It has rightly be recognised that the depreciation accounting is a process of allocation and not of valuation. In other words, the depreciation accounting of a firm is concerned with distributing the cost of assets over the useful life of the same according to a reasonable, method and debeting the Income Statement (Profit and Loss Account) each year with the amount allocated for that year. The accountant has nothing to do with ascertaining exact decrease in the value of the assets or valuing assets annually in order to knew the decrease in their values. In their efforts to show the current economic position, a firm may however, resort to revolution of its assets and show the resultant capital profit and revaluation through Revolution Reserve Account in the Balance Sheet.

How much amount may be charged by way of depreciation on an asset is a problem which may be solved by taking into account the cost value of the asset, residual or scrap value and the productive useful life of the asset. For example, if a machine costing Rs. 15000 has a productive life of 5 years and the scrap value is estimated to fatch Rs. 5000 after the end of its life. In this case the depreciable value is 45000-5000 = 40000. Depreciable value of 40000 divided by the number of years *i.e.* by 5 years an amount of Rs. 8000 (40000 + 5) what may he charged every year on account of depreciation. There are other methods to spread the cost of assets over their lives.

The fair value of depreciation will largely depend on the accuracy with which the scrap/ salvage value and the productive useful life are predetermined. Truely speaking, it is not possible to exactly forecast these two variables which considerably effect the amount of depreciation. However, the past experience and sound judgement of technical expert can contribute greatly in arriving at the productive life and scrap value and hence fair value of depreciation.

Objects of Providing Depreciation

Charging depreciation periodically throughout the life of an assets serves useful purpose. The managent try to achieve the following objectives through depreciation accounting:

1. Correct Income Determination. Like any other revenue expenditure, depreciation is a charge against profit. Therefore, it has to be debited to the Profit and Loss Account in order to determine correct profit for a year's time. If the depreciation charge is inadequate or no depreciation is provided for, then the Profit and Loss Account would show on inflated profit figure. Similarly excessive depreciation charge would reduce the profit unnecessarily. Thus, both the situation are bad. Reasonable depreciation charge consistently throughout the life of the machine enables us to determine fair profit for further appropriations. The object of showing correct operating performance of an enterprise is achieved only if all the operating expenses including depreciation is rightly calculated every year and shown in the Profit and Loss Account

2. Correct Economic Position. A Balance Sheet depicts correct economic position on a given date if all the assets and liabilities are brought in it at their correct and fair values. Fixed assets form quite a large proportion of total assets in acapital intensive industry. All the assets in a Balance Sheet should be shown at their book values minus depreciation. If the assets are not rightly depreciated, the Balance Sheet cannot be regarded as correct. If the depreciation is not provided or inadequately provided in any year, the Balance Sheet would fail to show the correct picture of the economic position as the assets would get over-valued. Thus the object of depreciation accounting is also to show the assets one their unexpired cost (book value minus depreciation) and thus depict the correct economic position of the enterprise.

3. Replacement of Assets. Every asset has a fixed productive useful life after which it needs to be replaced by the new one so that the production is continued without stoppage. Depreciation charge on a continuous basis during the life of assets enables an enterprise to replace the assets at the end of their lives without difficulty. The amount of depreciation may be invested outside the business or an insurance policy taken for generating adequate surplus to by new assets.

4. Depreciation as a Source of Finance. If the amount of depreciation is allowed to remain within the enterprise by not investing the same outside the business, it becomes a source of financing the working capital requirements.

5. Fulfilment of Legal Requirements. The companies Act 1956 requires that depreciation must be provided for before the declaration of dividend to shareholders. The provision of depreciation is important to ensure that the dividend is not declared out of capital.

6. Reduction of Tax Liability. Depreciation is allowed as a deduction from total income for the purpose of computing taxable income. If the corporate tax rate is 50%, then tax equal to half of the amount of depreciation can be saved. Thus depreciation can be used a tax-saving device. A company can maximise tax-savings by following a suitable depreciation policy.

Thus the depreciation serves many objects. An enterprise is generally not led by a single object of charging depreciation. A firm attempts to show true and fair view of its business operations and economic position by allowing appropriate depreciation charge but its effort is also to achieve other objectives such as enumerated above.

Methods of Charging Depreciation

We have already observed that depreciation is to be charged according to a pre-conceived plan schedule of depreciation. This implies a particular method which should be used for charging depreciation. There are a number of methods of charging depreciation and a firm can use anyone of them which is more suitable to its nature of business and other condition in which it is operating. We shall examine the question of suitability of a method a little later. Let us study the different methods of charging depreciate, which are available to any business concern. The object of explanation is to understand the nature of the methods and their merits and limitation and not the accounting of depreciation.

1. Straight Line Method or Fixed Instalant Method. According to this methods, the depreciation charge is the same for all the years over the life of an asset. If the data of depreciation are plotted on a graph paper, a straight line is obtained, hence the method is known as stright line method. The amount of depreciate is estimated after taking into consideration the cost value of asset, the scrap value and the estimated life of the asset. Cost value minus scrap value divided by the number of years the asset will last give the amount of depreciation. A rate percent can also be fixed for calculating depreciation on original cost value of the asset. Since the instalment of depreciation charge remains fixed, this method is also known as 'Fixed instalment Method' of charging depreciation.

Example: Suppose on 1st Jan. 2000, an asset has been purchased for Rs. 50,000. According to an estimation the asset will last for 5 years with scrap value of Rs. 5,000. *(i)* Determine the amount of depreciation according to straight line method *(ii)* Also compute the rate of depreciation, and *(iii)* Show the treatment of depreciation in the Income Statement and Balance Sheet.

$$\text{(i) Amount of depreciation} = \frac{\text{Cost Value} - \text{Scrap Value}}{\text{Life of asset in years}}$$

$$= \frac{50{,}000 - 5{,}000}{10} = \frac{45{,}000}{5}$$

$$= 9{,}000$$

(ii) Rate of depreciate $= \dfrac{\text{Amount of depreciation}}{\text{Cost value of Asset}} \times 100$

$= \dfrac{9{,}000 \times 100}{50{,}000} = 18\%$ p.a.

(iii) The profit and Loss account will be debited with Rs.4,000 every year for 5 years and the Balance Sheet would show at the end of each year the asset at cost less depreciation as shown below. At the end of the 5th year the asset will be reduced to its scrap value.

BALANCE SHEET

31st Dec. 2000		
Asset	50,000	41,000
Less dep.	9,000	
31st Dec. 2001		
Asset	41,000	
Less dep.	9.000	32,000
31st Dec. 2002		
Asset	32,000	23,000
Less dep.	9,000	
31st Dec. 2003		
Asset	23,000	23,000
Less dep.	9,000	14,000
31st Dee 2004		
Asset	14,000	
Less dep	9,000	5,000

Merits

(i) The main merit of straight line method is at it is simple to understand and easy to apply.

(ii) Full value of the asset is written off over the life of the asset. The asset is reduced to zero or scrap value at the end of life of the asset.

(iii) The method is more suitable in case of those assets which loose their value with the passage of time. Leasehold property and patents can be depreciated reasonably by the application of this method.

Demerits

The straight line method suffers for the serious limitations such as *(i)* It does not take into account the physical use of the assets. The amount of depreciation remains the same irrespective of the use of an asset. According to this method, depreciation at the same rate has to be charged even if the asset has not been in use for a single day but such is a rare situation: *(ii)* The Profit and Loss Account is not uniformly charged with depreciation plus expenditure on repairs and renewals of the asset. The expenditure on maintenance of assets is heavy in the later life of on asset due to high cost of repairs and renewals. Thus the Profit and Loss A/C is over-burdened in the later years which is not fair. *(iii)* The method does not consider the productivity or operating efficiancy of machine which does not remain the same for all the years during the life of Machine.

(2) Diminishing Instalment Method. Under this method the depreciation is calculated at a particular rate on the Balance of the cost value of the asset standing in the accounts books at the beginning of each year. In this way, the depreciation goes on diminishing or declining year after year. Therefore, the method is also known by the name of reducing or declining instalment method. If an asset costing Rs. 1,000 is depreciated at 10% p.a. according to Diminishing Balance Method, then the depreciation for the first few years would be as under:

I—year on 1000	@ 10% = 100
II—year on 900 (1000–100)	@ 10% = 90
III—year on 810 (90–90)	@ 10% = 81
IV—year on 729 (810–81)	@ 10% = 72.90

Depreciation rate determination under this method is a little difficult problem which can be solved by the application of the following formula:

$$\text{Rate} = 1-\left(\frac{\text{Scrap Value}}{\text{Cost Value}}\right)^{\frac{I}{N}}$$

$$\text{Or } 1 - N\sqrt{\frac{\text{Scrap Value}}{\text{Cost Value}}}$$

Where n stands for the estimated life of the asset in years.

Merits

(i) The method is simple to understand and easy to apply.

(ii) It is equitable and fair in the sense that it attempts to uniformly burden the Profit and Loss Account for various years by recognising the expenditure on repairs and renewals as an important part of depreciation. The burden of depreciation plus cost of repairs in various years is likely to be uniform because the depreciation charge in the initial years is relatively more but the expenditure on repairs is less. As the asset advance in age, the depreciation charge declines but the expenditure on repairs and renewals increases. This is testified by the experience of practioners.

(iii) The method is advantageous from tax point of view. Higher depreciation in initial years saves higher tax also and the amount so saved is used throughout the life of the asset.

(iv) The method is useful in cases where the production capacity of asset declines rapidly and the asset produces more income in the early part of the life of the asset.

Demerits

(i) The value of asset cannot be reduced to zero as the depreciation is charged on the written down value. The method will not be suitable for assets with zero scrap value.

(ii) The determination of rate of interest is somewhat difficult.

(3) Machine Hour Rate Method

According to this method the depreciation is charged according to the number of hours the machine is put to use in a year. For this purpose an hourly rate is estimated by estimating the life of the machine in term of hours. Depreciation on all articular machine is calculated by multiplying the number of hours by machine hour rate.

This method seems satisfactory as it correlates depreciation with the working time of the machine but its use in actual practice is limited. Actually speaking, reasonable depreciation has to be changed despite the fact that an asset has remained idle for most of the time in a year. In actual practice it may be found difficult to translate the life of an asset in terms of hours.

Example. Suppose an asset has been purchased for Rs. 5000. It is estimated that the asset will enjoy working time of 12000 hours with scrap value of Rs. 5000. Determine the amount of depreciate in anyone year the machine worked for 2000 hours.

Solution

$$\text{Hourly Depreciation Rate} = \frac{\text{Cost Value} - \text{Scrape Value}}{\text{Life of Machine in Hours}}$$

$$= \frac{50,000 - 5,000}{12,000} = 3.75$$

Amount of depreciation = No of working hours X hourly rate

$$2000 \times 3.75 = 7500$$

(4) Production Units Method. This method takes into account the Production Units instead of operating time as the basis for calculating the amount of depreciation. It is considered to be the most suitable method to writ off the wasting assets such as mines, quarris, oil-wells, etc. which have fixed production capacity and it is possible to estimate total production content with fair degree of accurracy. The cost paid for the acquisition of such assets is spread over the number of production units the asset is estimated to yield in under to calculate depreciation cost per unit of output. Depreciation charge for a year will be calculated by multiplying the number of units produced in that year by the depreciation cost per unit of output.

Like Machine Hours rate method, the chief characteristic feature and advantage of the Production Units method is that it correlates the amount depreciation with the total estimated production capacity of the working asset. But the correctness of the depreciation is directly governed by the accuracy of the estimation of total production to be yielded by the asset.

Example

A mine is acquired for a value of Rs. 15,00,000. It is estimated value of the mine contains 10,00,000 tons of minerals. In an year 1,50,000 tons of minerals was extracted. How much depreciation be charged in that year.

Solution

Depreciation per unit (Ton) of output

$$= \frac{\text{Cost of Asset}}{\text{Total estimated Producton (Ton)}}$$

$$= \frac{15,00,000}{10,00,000} = 1.50$$

Amount of Depreciation = Production of the year × Rate per-ton

= 1,50,000 × 1.50 = 2,25,000

It will be observed that the amount of depreciation to be charged during the life of the assets remain fixed or uniform in case of the above three methods of straight line, Machine Hours and Production Units methods. Therefore, these methods may be put under one group of methods which may called by the name of 'Uniform Charge Method.'

(5) Sum of Years Digit Method. According to this method, the calculation of depreciation is very simple. The annual depreciation is in proportion to the ratio of the digit for the years of life remaining divided by the sum of this digits for the total life. It means, the numerator is equal to the number of years including the current year for which the asset will enjoy productive life and the denominator is equal to the sum of the digits of the life of the asset. For example, if an asset enjoy a life of 5 years, then fration for the purpose of depreciation in various years would be as under:

Sum of years digits – 1 + 2 +3 + 4 + 5 = 15

1st year's fraction $= \frac{5}{15}$

2nd years fraction $= \frac{4}{15}$

3rd years fraction $= \frac{3}{15}$

4th years fraction $= \frac{2}{15}$

5th years fraction $= \frac{1}{15}$

If an asset cost Rs. 50,000 with salvage value of Rs. 5,000, then the depreciation to be charged for various years as per the sum of Years Digits method would be as shown below:

1st Year Depreciation $= 45000 \times \frac{5}{15} = 15000$

2nd Year Depreciation $= 45000 \times \frac{4}{15} = 12000$

3rd Year Depreciation $= 45000 \times \frac{3}{15} = 9000$

4th Year Depreciation $= 45000 \times \frac{2}{15} = 6000$

5th Year Depreciation $= 45000 \times \frac{1}{15} = 3000$

Total Depreciation = 45000

It will be observed that the depreciation charge in the early years of the life of asset is more than in the later year. In other words, the depreciation declines with the passage of time. The method suggests the recovery of cost of asset as early as possible. This will be a suitable method if the management desire speedy recovery of capital cost in fixed assets. It may also be noted that the asset can be reduced to its residual value by tfie application of this method.

(6) Double Decling Balance Method. Under this method the depreciation is charged according to the Diminishing Balance method by the application of the rate which is twice the rate charged under the straight line ethod. The depreciation is charged on the cost value of asset without givirig any consideration to the scrap value but adjustment in depreciation in the final year of the life of the asset is made so that the asset is not reduced below the scrap value.

Illustration-I

Given: Cost value of asset = 50,000

Life of asset = 5 years

Scrap value = 5,000

Solution

The annual charge of depreciation without considering the scrap value, as per straight line method would be 50000 + 5 = 10000; and the % rate of depreciation would be $\left(\frac{1000 \times 100}{5000}\right) = 20\%$

This rate of 20% will be doubled under Double Declining Balance Method. Thus a rate of 40% will be used for calculating depreciation as shown below:

Year	*Cost value at the beginning of each year*	*Amount of depreciation @ 40% on Diminishing Balance*
(1)	*(2)*	*(3)*
I	50000	20000
II	30000	12000

(1)	*(2)*	*(3)*
III	18000	7200
IV	10800	4320
V	6480	1480*
		45000

* In this year, the depreciation at 40% of 6480 comes to Rs. 2592 but a depreciation of 1480 will be charged because asset cannot be reduced below scrap value of Rs. 5000.

The Double Declaning Method is permitted in the U.S.A. under the federal tax laws. Since the depreciation is charged at double the rate, the depreciation in charge in the initial year is quite high. The method provides a speedy recovery of capital cost and attempts to burden the Profit and Loss Account Uniformly over the different years by recognising the fact that the expenditure on repairs in the initial years is low and it goes an increasing with the use of machine in the succeeding years. This method may not find forever with those organisations who want to show a better economic performance in the initial years for which they prefer to show low depreciation charge deliberately.

(7) Inventory System of Depreciation. The usual methods of changirg depreciation are not considered convenient and economical in case of low cost items such as small tools and implements. Such items may be depreciated easily by following .the inventory system of depreciation. According to this method the cost value of assets in good working condition at the end of each year is computed and compared with the cost value of all the assets at the beginning of the year. The difference in cost value is treated an depreciation. Thus, it is a method which is concerned with the revaluation of assets. The loss in the value of assets during the year's time due to usage is termed as depreciation. This method may also be used to depreciate the assets such as live-stock whose life cannot be ascertained with certainly.

(8) Annuity Method. The methods of charging depreciation as explained above recognised the loss in the value of assets due to usage (depreciation) but did not consider the loss of interest on the amount invested in the assets. The enterprise could have earned interest on the amount invested in asset by investing the same in some other form of investment and thus looses interest by commiting the investment in the present form (asset). Therefore, the interest at some reasonable rate should be taken into account. The annuity Method duly considers the interest on balance of amount standing in the asset account at the beginning of the year. The depreciation is calculated with reference to annuity table which gives the annual amount necessary to write off Re 1 at a desired interest rate after a specified time. Total amount of depreciation is arrival at by the multiplication of the annuity factor and the cost value of asset.

(9) Depreciation Fund or Sinking Fund Method. The amount of depreciation charged annually may either be allowed to remain within the enterprise and use it as a resource of financing working capital or other requirements or invested outside the business in some kind of interest-bearing securities. According to Depreciation or sinking Fund method, the instalment of depreciation is invested in outside securities and the interest received on such an investment is also invested alongwith the instalment of depreciation in the subsequent years. The accounting process of charging depreciation and creating the depreciation' fund with the amount of depreciation and interest amount and making investments in outside securities is continued till the last year of the productive life of the asset. At the end of the last year, the depreciation is charged but the investment is not made because in this very year the investment have to be sold to realize money for purchase of the new machine.

Depreciation Fund Method is a useful method as it ensures provision of necessary amount which is needed to replace old asset by a new one at the end of a particular period. The only limitation of this method is that it provides for a fixed amount of depreciation whereas the need for money for repairs increases with the passage of time. Thus the Profit and Loss Account is not uniformly burdened with the cost of machine used in the process of manufacture.

(10) Insurance Policy Method. In order to be more certain about the receipt of amount necessary for replacing the old asset by a new one, the management may prefer to take on insurance policy for the required amount instead of making investment in outside securities and selling them at the end of last year of the useful life of the asset. The amount equal to depreciation is paid in the fonn of insurance premium to the insurance company which is obliged to pay a certain sum at the end of the specified period.

The Insurance Policy method is almost similar to the Depreciation Fund method. The added advantage of the former method is that an undertaking is relieved of the problem of making investment every year and maintaining accounts of interests, etc. There is also no risk which might arise due to decrease in the value of investments when they are sold.

(11) Replacement Cost Method. One of the objectives of charging depreciation is the provision of adequate funds to buy a new asset when the old one becomes unproductive. The traditional methods of charging depreciation simply provide for the recovery of the original cost of an asset and no cognisance is taken of the falt that the replacement requires more money than the cost of the original asset. This is true in a period of rising prices. Under conditions of continued inflation, the replacement of asset is not possible if a firm is absolutely dependent on the recovery of original cost of asset by following any traditional method of charging depreciation. The replacement cost is much higher than the historical cost, therefore, depreciation should be charged on replacement cost if the replacement is to be made without any financial difficulty. The amount of depreciation would be higher than the depreciation on historical cost. Thus, it will put more burden on the Profit and Loss Accounts. It may be pointed out that the depreciation charge on replacement cost is not required under any Act but the business firms may provide for extra depreciation in their own interest of replacement of assets. Since the extra depreciation charge is not permitted for tax purposes, therefore, the industry in general, do not follow the Replacement Cost method of charging depreciation. The management of some undertakings may not like it when they desires to show better performance as reflected by the profit figure. There are some practical difficulties in following this method. The 'replacement cost' is not certain and a rough estimate can only be made about it and the asset to be acquired in future is different in many respect due to technological changes. The tax authorities do not allow depreciation more than at the specified rates. Owing to these problems the use of the method has got limited application.

Suitable Method

After having stutied so many methods, a pertinent question which arises is — which method of charging depreciation is more suitable to write off an asset and provide funds for its replacement? It is very difficult to answer this question in an unequivocal terms in view of the fact that every method has its own merits and limitations. The question of the suitability or choice of method may be solved after careful consideration of the nature of depreciable asset and the type of industry in which the asset is in use. It may be noted that freehold land is not regarded as a depreciable asset and as such no depreciation is required to be charged on such an asset. Plant and machinery may be depreciated according to Machine Hour Rate method as this method reduces the machines to their scrap values at the end of their productiye life. The depreciation on buildings may be charged either by the application of Fixed Instalment method or Diminishing Instalment method. Items such as Loose tools, and live-stock can be depreciated by Revolution Method. Wasting assets such as mines, quarries, oil welb etc. may be written off by Production Units method. The selection of the method of depreciation should be governed by the criterion that the asset is equitably reduced to written down value at the end of its productive life.

Other creterion to be followed in the selection of a method are: *(a)* Early recovery of the cost value of asset for which accelerated method or depreciation at a higher rate is considered desirable. *(b)* Deriving maximum tax benefit in the early years of the life of asset for which depreciation at higher rate or Double Declining method is suggested. *(c)* Generating sufficient funds for the replacement of asset under conditions of inflation the depreciation on the estimated replacement cost is recommended. *(d)* Earning a uniform rate of return on investment for which a fair matching of expired cost against related income is always desirable. *(e)* Measurement of true and fair profit for which a reasonable method which avoids under or over-charging of depreciation is to be specified.

There are practical difficulties in the selection of an appropriate method of charging depreciation. There is no particular method which might lead to the achievements of all the objectives of the depreciation policy. For example, the object of early recovery of cost of asset and deriving maximum tax benefit is better served by accelerated depreciation method but it would be against the object of the mesurement of true and fair profit.

The sound management practice suggests that the method of charging depreciation should be reviewed periodically and it should be ensured that the assets are being depreciated rightly and the enterprise would be able to replace the existing assets by the new ones. If at any stage, the method of charging depreciation is found unsatisfactory or inadequate and the change has become inevitable, the management is free to switch over to any other suitable method but the effect of such a charge on the final accounts may be calculated and properly reported through the published accounts. Under conditions of rapid rise in price level, the cost of replacement of assets is obviously quite high and the management will have to think of providing for accelerated depreciation on making extra provision for replacement of asset. Similarly, the changes in laws regarding the provision of depreciation will have to be incorporated in the final accounts.

APPENDIX

DEPRECIATION ACCOUNTING

The following is the text of the revised Accounting Standard (AS) 6. Depreciation Accounting, issued by the Institute of Charatered Accountants of India.

Introduction

1. This Statement deals with depreciation accounting and applies to all depreciable assets, except the following items to which special considerations apply:

(i) forests, plantations and similar regenerative natural resources;

(ii) wasting assets including expenditure on the exploration for and extraction of minerals, oils, natural gas and similar non-regenerative resources;

(iii) expenditure on research and development;

(iv) goodwill;

(v) live-stock.

This statement also does not apply to land unless it has a limited useful life for the enterprise.

2. Different accounting policies for depreciation are adopted by different enterprises. Disclosure of accounting policies for depreciation followed by an enterprise is necessary to appreciate the view presented in the financial statements of the enterprise.

Definitions

3. The following terms are used in the statement with the meanings specified:

3.1. **'Depreciation'** is a measure of the wearing out, consumption or other loss of value of a depreciable asset arising from use, effluxion of time or obsolescence through technology and market changes. Depreciation is allocated so as to charge a fair proportion of the depreciable amount in each accounting period during the expected useful life of the asset. Depreciation includes amoritisation of assets whose useful life is predetermined.

3.2. **'Depreciable assets'** are assets which

(i) are expected to be used during more than one accounting period;

(ii) have a limited useful life; and

(iii) are held by an enterprise for use in the production or supply of goods and services, for rental to others, or for administrative purposes and not for the purpose of sale in the ordinary course of business.

3.3. **'Useful life'** is either *(i)* the period over which a depreciable asset is expected to be used by the enterprise; or *(ii)* the number of production or similar units expected to be obtained from the use of the asset by the enterprise.

3.4. **'Depreciable amount'** of a depreciable asset is its historical cost, or other amount substituted for historical costs in the financial statements, less the estimated residual value.

Explanation

4. Depreciation has a significant effect in determining and presenting the financial position and results of operations of an enterprise. Depreciation is charged in each accounting period by reference to the extent of the depreciable amount, irrespective of an increase in the market value of the assets.

5. Assessment of depreciation and the amount to be charged in respect thereof in an accounting period are usually based on the following three factors:

(i) historical cost or other amount substituted for the historical cost of the depreciable asset when the asset had been revalued;

(ii) expected useful life of the depreciable asset; and

(iii) estimated residual value of the depreciable, asset.

6. Historical cost of a depreciable asset represents its money outlay or its equivalent in connection with its acquisition, installation and commissioning as well as for additions to or improvement thereof. The historical cost of a depreciable asset may undergo subsequent changes arising as a result of increase or decrease in long term liability on account of exchange fluctuations, price adjustments, changes in duties or similar factors.

7. The useful life of a depreciable asset is shorter than its physical life and is:

(i) pre-determined by legal or contractual limits, such as the expiry dates of related leases;

(ii) directly governed by extraction or consumption;

(iii) dependent on the extent of use and physical deterioration on account of wear and tear which again depends on operational factors, such as, the number of shifts for which the asset is to be used, repair and maintenance policy of the enterprise etc; and

(iv) reduced by obsolescence arising from such factors as:

(a) technological changes;

(b) improvement in production methods;

(c) change in market demand for the product or service output of the asset;

or

(d) legal or other restrictions.

8. Determination of the useful life of a depreciable asset is a matter of estimation and is normally based on various factors including experience with similar types of assets. Such estimation is more difficult for an asset using new technology or used in the production of a new product or in the provision of a new service but is nevertheless required on some reasonable basis.

9. Any addition or extension to an existing asset which is of a capital nature and which becomes an integral part of the existing asset is depreciated over the remaining useful life of that asset. As a practical measure, however, depreciation is sometimes provided on such addition or extension at the rate which is applied to an existing asset. Any addition or extension which retains a separate identity and is capable of being used after the existing asset is disposed of, is depreciated independently on the basis of an estimate of its own useful life.

10. Determination of residual value of an asset is normally a difficult matter. If such value is considered as insignificant, it is normally regarded as nil. On the contrary, iftheresidual value is likely to be significant, it is estimated at the time of acquisition/installation, or at the time of subsequent revaluation of the asset. One of the basis for determining the residual value would be the realisable value of similar assets which have reached the end of their useful lives and

have operated under conditions similar to those in which the asset will be used.

11. The quantum of depreciation to be provided in an accounting period involves the exercise of judgement by management in the light of technical, commercial, accounting and legal requirements and accordingly may need periodical review. If it is considered that the original estimate useful life of an asset requires any revision, the unamortised depreciable amount of the asset is charged to revenue over the revised remaining useful life.

12. There are several methods of allocating depreciation over the useful life of the assets. Those most commonly employed in industrial and commercial enterprises are the straightline method and the reducing balance method. The management of a business selects the most appropriate method(s) based on various important factors *e.g.* *(i)* type of asset, *(ii)* the nature of the use of such asset and *(iii)* circumstances prevailing in the business. A combination of more than one method is sometimes used. In respect of depreciable assets which do not have material value depreciation is often allocated fully in the accounting period in which they are acquired.

13. The statute governing an enterprise may provide the basis for computation of the depreciation. For example, the Companies Act, 1956 lays down the rates of depreciation in respect of various assets. Where the management's estimate of the useful life of an asset of the enterprise is shorter than that envisaged under the provision of the relevant statute, the depreciation provision is appropriately computed by applying a higher rate. If the management's estimate of the useful life of the asset is longer than that envisaged under the statute, depreciation rate lower than that envisaged by the statute can be applied only in accordance with requirements of the statute.

14. Where depreciable assets are disposed of, discarded, demolished or destroyed, the net surplus or deficiency, if material, is disclosed separately.

15. The method of depreciation is applied consistently to provide comparability of the results of the operations of the enterprise

from period to period. A change from one method or providing depreciation to another is made only if the adoption of the new method is required by statute or for compliance with an accounting standard or if it is considered that the change would result in a more appropriate preparation or presentation of the financial statements of the enterprise. When such a change in the method of depreciation is made, depreciation is recalculated in accordance with the new method from the date of the asset coming into use. The deficiercy or surplus arising from retrospective recomputation of depreciation in accordance with the new method is adjusted in the accounts in the year in which the method of depreciation is changed. In case the change in the method results in deficiency in depreciation in respect of past years, the deficiency is charged in the statement of profit and loss. In case the change in the method results in surplus, the surplus is credited to the statement of profit and loss. Such a change is treated as a change in accounting policy and its effect is quantified and disclosed.

16. Where the historical cost of an asset has undergone a change due to specific circumstances, the depreciation on the revised unamortlsed depreciable amount is provided prospectively over the residual useful life of the asset.

17. The depreciation methods used, the total depreciation for the period for each class of assets, the gross amount of each class of depreciable assets and the related accumulated depreciation are disclosed in the financial statement along with the disclosure of other accounting policies. The depreciation rates or the useful lives of the assets are disclosed only if they are different from the principal rates specified in the statute governing the enterprise.

18. In case the depreciable assets are revalued, the provision for depreciation is based on the revalued amount on the estimate of the remaining useful life of such assets. In case the revaluation has a material effect on the amount of depreciation, the same is disclosed separately in the year in which revaluation is carried out.

19. A change in the method of depreciation is treated as a change in an accounting policy and is disclosed accordingly.

Accounting Standard

(The Accounting Standard comprises paragraphs 20-29 of this Statement. The Standard should be read in the context of paragraphs 1-19 of this Statement and of the Preface to the Statement of Accounting Standards.)

20. The depreciable amount of a depreciable asset should be allocated on a systematic basis to each accounting period during the useful life of the asset.

21. The depreciation method selected should be applied consistently from period to period. A change from one method of providing depreciation to another should be made only if the adoption of the new method is required by statute or for compliance with an accounting standard or if it is considered that the change would result in a more appropriate preparation or presentation of the financial statements of the enterprise. When such a change in the method of depreciation is made, depreciation should be recalculated in accordance with the new method from the date of the asset corning into use. The deficiency or surplus arising from retrospective recomputation of depreciation in accordance with the new method should be adjusted in the accounts in the year in which the method of depreciation is changed. In case the change in the method results in deficiency in depreciation in respect of past years, the deficiency should be charged in the statement of profit and loss. In case the change in the method results in surplus, the surplus should be created to the statement of profit and loss. Such a change should be treated as a change in accounting policy and its effect should be quantified and disclosed.

22. The useful life of a depreciable asset should be estimated after considering the following factors:

(i) expected physical wear and tear;

(ii) obsolescence;

(iii) legal or other limits on the use of the asset.

23. The useful lives of a major depreciable assets or classes of depreciable assets may be reviewed periodically. Where there is a

revision of the estimated useful life of an asset, the unamortised depreciable amount should be charged over the revised remaining useful life.

24. Any addition or extension which becomes an integral part of the existing asset should be depreciated over the remaining useful life of that asset. The depreciation on such addition or extension may also be provided at the rate applied to the existing asset. Where an addition or extension retains a separate identity and is capable of being used after the existing asset is disposed of, depreciation should be provided independently on the basis of an estimate of its own useful life.

25. Where the historical cost of a depreciable asset has undergone a change due to increase or decrease in long term liability on accountof exchange fluctuations, price adjustments, changes in duties or similar factors, the depreciation on the revised anamortised depreciable amount should be provided prospectively over the residual useful life of the asset.

26. Where the depreciable assets are revalued, the provision for depreciation should be based on the revalued amount and on the estimate of the remaining useful lives of such assets. In case the revaluation has a material effect on the amount of depreciation, the same should be disclosed separately in the year in which revaluation is carried out.

27. If any depreciable asset is disposed of, discarded, demolished or destroyed, the net surplus or deficiency, if material, should be disclosed separately.

28. The following information should be disclosed in the financial statements:

(i) the historical cost or other amount substituted for historical cost of each class of depreciable assets;

(ii) total depreciation for the period for each class of assets; and

(iii) the related accumulated depreciation.

29. The following information should also be disclosed in the financial statements alongwith the disclosure of other accounting policies:

(i) depreciation methods used; and

(ii) depreciation rates or the useful lives of the assets, if they are different from the principal rates specified in the statute governing the enterprise.

Depreciation in the Indian Context

In India, 'Section 350' of 'The Companies Act of 1956' deals with depreciation. It states that:

> 'The amount of depreciation to be deducted in pursuance of clause (k) of sub-section (4) of section 349 shall be the amount calculated with reference to the written down value of the assets as shown by the books of the company at the end of the financial year expiring at the commencement of this Act or immediately thereafter and at the end of each subsequent financial year at the rate specified in Schedule XIV:
>
> Provided that if any asset is sold, discarded, demolished or destroyed for any reason before depreciation has been provided for n full, the excess if any, of the written down value, shall be written off in the financial year in which the asset is sold, discarded, demolished or destroyed'.

Section 205 of the Act dealing with dividends also provides for depreciation before paying dividends. It is done in accordance with sub-section (2) of Section 205. It states that:

Depreciation shall be provided either:

(a) to the extent specified in Section 350; or

(b) in respect of each item of the depreciable asset, for such an amount as is arrived at by dividing ninety five per cent, of the original cost thereof to the company specified by the period in respect of such asset; or

(c) on any other basis approved by the central government which has the effect of writing off by way of depreciation ninety-five per cent of the original cost to the company of each such depreciable asset on the expiry of the specified period; or

(d) as regards any other depreciable asset for which no rate of depreciation has been laid down by this act or the rules made thereunder on such basis as may be approved by the Central Government by any general order published in the Official Gazette or by any special order in any particular case.'

Rates of Depreciation

Nature of Assets	Single Shift		Double Shift		Triple Shift	
	WDV	SLM	WDV	SLM	WDV	SLM
(1)	*(2)*	*(3)*	*(4)*	*(5)*	*(6)*	*(7)*
Buildings (other than factory buildings) NESD	5%	1.63%				
Factory buildings	10%	3.34%				
Purely Temporary structures	100%	100%				
Plant and Machinery	15%	5.15%	22.5%	8.09%	30%	11.31%
Cycles (NESD)	20%	7.07%				
Glass Melting Furnaces	20%	7.07%	30%	11.31%	40%	16.21%
Aeroplanes - Aircraft, aerial photographic apparatus (NESD)	30%	11.31%				
Dies and Moulds (NESD)	30%	11.31%				
Shoes and Leather goods factories	30%	11.31%	45%	18.96%	60%	29.05%
Data Processing Machines including computers (NESD)	40%	16.21%				

(1)	*(2)*	*(3)*	*(4)*	*(5)*	*(6)*	*(7)*
Motor Vehicles used in business on run on hire. (NESD)	40%	16.21 %				
Iron and Steel Industries - Rolling Mill rolls	100%	100%				
Equipment used in Mines and Quarries	100%	100%				
Furniture and Fittings (NESD)	10%	3.34%				
F&F in commercial use (NESD)	15%	5.15%				

❑

5

Fund Flow Analysis

The word fund here means net working capital. Working capital is ordinarily understood as excess of current assets over current liabilities, some persons call total of current assets as Gross Working Capital and current assets minus current liabilities as Net Working Capital or Net Current Assets. The word flow here means movements of this working capital *i.e.*, either increase in working capital or decrease in working capital in comparison to previous year. Fund really speaking is transfer of cost or cash equivalent *(A)* from one equity to another equity, or *(B)* from one assets to another assets, or *(C)* from assets to equity. Fund Flow Statement is a statement which shows changes in net working capital of an enterprise over a period of time which is mostly one year.

Fund Flow Statement shows sources and application of funds in a summary from over a period of time and indicates increase or decrease in net working capital of the enterprise during the period.

According to Smith and Brown, "A fund flow statement is prepared in a summary form to indicate charges (and trends if prepared regularly) occurring in items of financial condition between two balance sheet dates."

Fund Flow Statement is a Statement which shows sources of funds and their application during a prescribed period. Excess of sources over application indicates increase in working capital and excess of application of funds over sources indicates decrease in working capital. Here working capital and net working capital both are treated as the same. In whole of this chapter the word working capital has been used.

Ratio analysis and other analysis indicate the static aspects of financial statements, its dynamic aspect is shown by Fund Flow Statement. It indicates the comparative position of working capital of two balance sheets' dates.

In a business there is always inflow and outflow of funds. At the date of balance sheet both inflows and outflows of funds are stopped for a while. Therefore, on the basis of two balance sheets one tries to know the inflow and outflow of funds which are technically known as sources and application of funds.

This statement analyses the items which result in sources of funds and application of funds. Items resulting in non-flow of funds are not used in this balance sheet and if necessary some other particular are required to prepare their statements.

Various Names of Fund Flow Statement

(i) Sources and application of funds, *(ii)* Where got and where gone statements, *(iii)* Statement of inflow and outflow of funds, *(iv)* Statement of funds supplied and funds applied etc.

OBJECT AND USES OF FUND FLOW STATEMENT

The main object of this statement is to find out increase or decrease in working capital during a period by showing sources and uses of working capital.

Working Capital is most important for the business. It should be raised and used properly. Proper control of working capital is the keystone for the success of a business. This statement helps in achieving this purpose. Following are the uses of this statement which show its importance:

(i) It indicates the financing policies of the enterprise in respect of capital structure and expansion of assets.

(ii) It is used as basis for future planning.

(iii) It points out the sound or weak financial position of the enterprise.

(iv) Amounts of funds required for future develpment can be estimated on its basis.

(v) An idea about various sources of funds can be made by comparing these sources with the sources of previous years, it can be concluded whether the company is doing well or not.

(vi) Various uses of funds can be known and after comparing them with the uses of previous years, improvements or downfall in the company can be assessed.

(vii) It helps in improving the rate of income on assets.

(viii) It points out the causes for changes in working capital.

(ix) It explains the current area of business.

(x) Banks and other financial institutions get information regarding power of generating sources of funds and their uses with the help of this statement. These days this statement is regarded as a modern tool of assessing financial position of an enterprise.

(xi) Previous year's financial position can be compared on its basis.

(xii) It can also be found whether sources of funds are increasing or decreasing or are constant.

(xiii) It helps in knowing whether uses of fund are increasing or decreasing.

(xiv) It points out why income is more even when current assets have decreased.

(xv) It shows the method of financing of increase in working capital.

(xvi) It states income from operation and throws light on increase or decrease in dividends.

Whatever information regarding financial matters is not found out in other financial statements like Balance Sheet and Profit and Loss Account, is found out by this statement. During modern period everybody is flowing in some way or the other and is flowing very fast, why not funds too should flow. It is the flow of funds, that tells the current financial position of the enterprises and the standard of managerial policies and foresight.

LIMITATIONS OF FUNDS FLOW STATEMENT

1. It does not provide information about variations in cash position.
2. This statement lacks originality because it is only rearrangement of the matter of financial statement.
3. When both the aspects of a transaction are current, they are not included in this statement.
4. When both the aspects of a transaction are non-current, even then they are not inlcuded in this statement.
5. It does not show various changes which take place continuously. It only indicates fund flow in a summary form.
6. It indicates only past position and not future, through projects fund flow may serve this purpose but it is based only on estimates.
7. It gives some additional information only and cannot be regarded as an ideal tool for furnishing full financial position.
8. Possession of intensive and deep-rooted knowledge of accountancy and financial management is a prerequisite to make its intepretation.

WORKING CAPITAL

As the main aim of fund flow statement is to indicate changes in working capital, it is desirable to understand working capital.

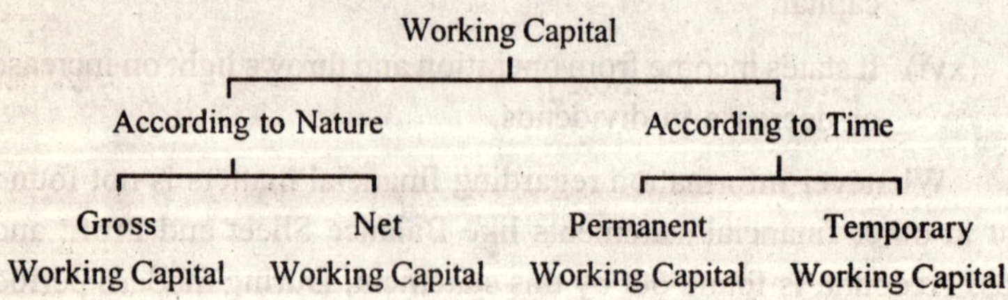

Working Capital According to Nature

Grass Working Capital. Working capital means funds invested in total current assets which are required in day-to-day running of the business. It is called Gross Working Capital. This capital is very important because fixed assets cannot work without it. For example, without raw material, machine is useless, and money invested in raw materials is working capital.

Net Working Capital. It is the excess of current asset over current liabilities.

Working Capital According to Time

Working capital is divided into two parts from the point of time, namely, permanent working capital and temporary working capital.

Permanent Working Capital. Minimum level of investment in current assets is called permanent working capital. To carry out minimum level of activity at all times, some minimum amount of captial is required which is permanent working capital.Characteristics of Permanent Working Capital are as follows:

(i) It always remains in the business in the one form or the other.

(ii) It constantly changes its form from cash to stock and from stock to debtors and from debtors to cash again and so on.

(iii) The suppliers of permanent working capital need not expect any return during the lifetime of the enterprise.

(iv) It is financed by long-term sources. It is the beginning when business is commenced with capital, nearly 2/3 portion of it is used for fixed asset and about 1/3 is used as working capital. Thus, it is financed by long-term source.

(v) Its amount increases with increase in business.

(vi) It is like fixed capital because it is permanently needed in business.

(vii) As it is financed by long-term finance, hence current ratio should always be more than one.

Temporary Working Capital. Capital required over minimum level of working capital is called temporary working capital. Its size is not fixed because it increases or decreases according to increase or decrease in business. In seasonal industries during season, temporary working capital required is too much. It is generally financed by short-term funds. Characteristics of Temporary Working Capital are as follows:

1. It is required in addition to permanent working capital.
2. It is needed for meeting additional day-to-day requirements due to increase in business.
3. It is financed by short-term debt.
4. In seasonal industries during season its requirements is abnormally hight.
5. It meets short period liquidity requirements of the enterprise.

Both permanent and temporary working capitals in adequate amount are required for smooth running of the enterprise. Changes in this working capital are measures through fund flow statement.

STEPS AND RULES RELATING TO PREPARATION OF FUND FLOW STATEMENT

1. Transactions Affecting Non-current Accounts Only. If there is a transaction which affects non-current accounts only it is not considered for flow of funds. Any account which is not current is treated as non-current as in the case of cloth business Building A/c, Machinery A/c, Furniture A/c and Vehicles A/c etc. are non-current.

When both aspects of transaction are non-current, no flow of fund takes place. Only that items can affect fund flow which either increases the working capital or decreases it and working capital is the excess of current assets over current liabilities. Therefore, the transaction must affect any one of the current assets or current liabilities in order to influence fund flow. The conclusion is that transactions affecting only non-current assets and non-current liabilities are ignored for the purpose of preparing fund flow statement.

2. Transactions Affecting Current Account Only. If both the aspects of a transaction are affecting current account only, no flow of fund takes palce. Flow of fund is related with working capital and working capital is the result of excess of current assets over current liabilities. Fund flow statement should either increase or decrease in working capital. It can happen only when current assets and current liabilities are disproportionately increases or decreases.

(A) Decreases in both Current Assets and Current Liabilities by the Same Amount. If current assets is decreased and current liabilities are also decreased by the same amount there is no changes in working capital.

(B) Increase and Decrease in Current Assets Only by the Same Amount. If one current assets decreases and other current assets increases by the same amount there is no working capital hence no effect on fund flow.

C. Increase in Current Assets and Current Liabilities by the Same Amount. This even does not effect the working capital therefore there will no flow of fund.

(D) Increase and Decrease in Current Liabilities Only by the Same Amount. In this situation working capital will not be effected or the amount of current liabilities will remain the same. There will be no flow of fund.

3. Transactions Affecting Current and Non-Current Liabilities. If a transaction is such that one aspect of it affects current account and its other aspect affects non-current account. There will be effect on working capital and fund will flow. Such transactions are considered for fund flow statement. The following situation may raise flow of funds:

(A) Increase in current assets and non-current liabilities.

(B) Decrease in non-current liabilities and current assets.

(C) Increase in non-current assets and decrease in current assets.

(C) Decrease in non-current and increase in current assets.

Steps and Rules

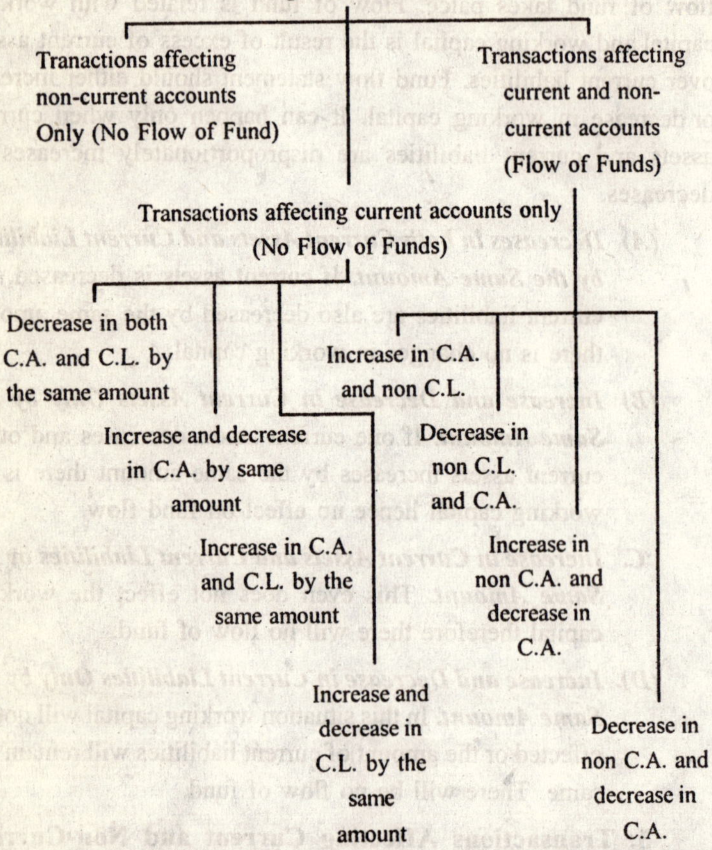

PROFIT AND LOSS ACCOUNT AND FUND FLOW

1. Sales and closing stock are treated as source.
2. Opening stock, purchases, and all expenses, and all expenses of revenue nature are treated as application of fund.
3. It is better to show the excess of sales and closing stock over opening stock, purchases and all revenue expenses as source of fund as it is net profit.

4. If total of sales and closing stock is less than total of opening stock, purchases and all revenue expenses, the deficiency is net loss. It is treated as application of fund.

Source from Operation by Preparing a Statement. (i) Following items are added in the net profit of the year which is given in the question in order to find out source from operation:

(a) Amount of goodwill written off

(b) Amount of preliminary expenses written off

(c) Depreciation

(d) Discount on issue of shares written off

(e) Discount on issue of debentures etc. written off

(f) Loss on sale of fixed assets

(g) Non-cash charges

(ii) After adding the above items in net profit, profit on sale of fixed assets should be deducted. The result after this deduction will be income from operation.

Source from Operation by Preparing Adjusted Profit and Loss Account. Sometimes it is necessary to prepare adjusted Profit and Loss Account in order to find out source from operation when both opening balance of profit and closing balance of profit are already given in the question. In order to explain the items which should be taken to credit and debit side of this account, following form is given for the sake of convenience:

Adjusted Profit and Loss Account

	Rs.		*Rs.*
To General Reserve (increase)		By Opening balance of profit (already given in the question)	
To Debenture Sinking Fund (increase)		By Decrease in revenue reserve	
To Other revenue reserve (increase)		By Profit of sale of fixed assets	

Contd.

	Rs.		*Rs.*
To Depreciation on various fixed assets		By Source from operation (excess of debit total over credit total)	
To Decrease in discount of issue of debentures			
To Decrease in discount of issue of shares			
To Loss on sale of fixed assets			
To Goodwill (amount written off)			
To Preliminary Exps. (amount written off)			
To Dividend Equalisation A/c (increase)			
To Proposed dividend during the year			
To Provision for tax during the year			
To Balance c/d (closing Balance of profit already given in the question) Rs.		Rs.	

If credit total is more than debit total, excess of credit over debit is regarded as application from operation.

CURRENT AND NON-CURRENT ITEMS

Preparation of fund flow statement is based on the distinction of current and non-current itmes, hence following are some of the headings about which information regarding treating them as current or non-current is given:

1. Proposed Dividend. It may be treated both as current or non-current.

(a) ***As Current.*** If proposed dividend is treated as current liability, actual payment of this dividend is not treated as application of fund.

(b) ***As Non-current.*** If it is treated as non-current, its actual payment is treated as application of fund.

2. Depreciation. It is treated as non-current because it relates to non-current assets.

3. Dividend. Devidend is treated as non-current because it relates with non-current liability, *i.e.*, share capital.

4. Provision for Bad and Doubtful Debts. It is treated as current because it relates with current assets *i.e.*, debtors.

5. Relationship. It is a general rule that if an item relates to non-current, it should be treated as non-current and if an item relates to current, it should be treated as current.

6. Provision for Tax. It may be treated either as current or as non-current.

(a) ***As Current.*** If it is treated as current liability, tax payment is not regarded as an items of application of fund and provision for tax is not adjusted to profit or loss for finding out income from operation.

(b) ***As Non-current.*** If provision for tax is treated as non-current, payment of tax is treated as application of fund and it is treated for adjustment of profit or loss.

7. Capital. Capital of all types is non-current liability whether it is equity or preference.

8. Debentures. Debentures are non-current liabilities.

9. Share Premium. It is non-current liability because it relates with non-current item share capital.

10. Profit and Loss. It is non-current.

11. Forfeited Shares. It is non-current liability because it relates with non-current *i.e.*, shares.

12. Capital Reserve. It is non-current liability.

13. Transfer to Dividend Equalisation Fund. It is non-current.

14. Debentures Sinking Fund. Transfer to debentures sinking fund is non-current.

15. Transfer to General Reserve. It is treated as non-current.

16. Transfer to Compensation Fund. It is treated as non-current.

17. Long Period Loans. They are treated as non-current. If only loan is given, it is treated as long period loan.

NON-CURRENT ASSETS

Following are treated as non-current assets:

1. All fixed assets which are given in Schedue VI of the Companies Act, 1956, namely:

(i) Good will,

(ii) Land,

(iii) Buildings,

(iv) Leaseholds,

(v) Railway sidings,

(vi) Plant and machinery,

(vii) Furniture and fittings,

(viii) Development of property

(ix) Patents, Trade-marks and Designs,

(x) Live-Stock,

(xi) Vehicles etc.

2. All Deferred Expenditures like:

(a) Preliminary expenses.

(b) Abnormally heavy advertisement expenses.

(c) Discount on issue of Debentures.

(d) Discount on issue of shares.

(e) Commission and Brokerage on shares and debentures

(f) Interest paid out of capital during construction.

(g) Development expenditure not adjusted.

3. Profit and Loss Account debit balance which is treated as net loss.

CURRENT ASSETS

Following are generally treated as current assets:

1. Cash in Hand,
2. Cash at Bank,
3. Bills Receivable,
4. Closing Stock,
5. Debtors,
6. Income earned but not yet received,
7. Prepaid expenses,
8. Any other amount which is receivable within short period *i.e.*, a period of one year.

CURRENT LIABILITIES

Following items are treated as current liabilities:

1. Creditors,
2. Bills Payable,
3. Outstanding Expenses,
4. Instalment of long period loan falling due for payment during current year,
5. Provision for taxation (it may also be treated as non-current as has been explained earlier),
6. Provision from dividend (it may also be treated as non-current as has been explained earlier),
7. Bank overdraft if it is of casual nature (if it is of continuous nature, it is treated as non-current.)

Treatment of Current and Non-current in Fund Flow Statement at a Glance

Particulars	*Use in Fund Flow Statement*
1. Both aspects of a transaction are current.	No flow of fund, hence not used in Fund Flow Statement.
2. Both aspects of a transaction are non-current.	No flow of fund, hence not used in Fund Flow Statement.
3. One aspect of a transaction is current other aspect is non-current.	Fund flows, hence used in Fund Flow Statement.

Additional Information

If additional information is given in addition of balance sheets of two different dates, concerned account related with this information should be prepared. In case it is not necessary to prepare an account, treatement on the basis of source or application of fund should be made.

Hidden Information

With the help of above-mentioned additional information and balance sheets, hidden information is derived which is very essential for preparation of Fund Flow Statement. For this purpose concerned account is prepared and the balance of this account gives the hidden information which is used as source or application of fund as the case may be.

Example. Amount of machinery in Balance Sheet of December 31, 1985 is Rs. 1,80,000 and the amount of same machinery in Balance Sheet of December 31, 1984 is Rs. 1,50,000. Arrangement for depreciation on machinery has been made to the extent of Rs. 25,000 in 1985. Find out hidden information for Fund Flow Solution.

By preparing Machinery Account, hidden information can be found out.

Machinery Account

	Rs.		Rs.
To Balance b/d	1,50,000	By Depreciation A/c	25,000
To Purchase (Balancing figure)	55,000	By Balance c/d	1,80,000
	Rs. 2,05,000		Rs. 2,05,000

Above machinery Account indicates the balance of Rs. 55,000. This amount shows that a machinery of R. 55,000 has been purchased, hence it is application of fund.

PROVISION FOR TAXATION ACCOUNT

Missing figure about transfer to provision for Taxation Account can be found out by preparing Provision for Taxation Account.

Example.

Provision for taxation at the end of December 31, 1985 is Rs. 70,000 and at the end of December 31, 1984 is Rs. 56,000 Income-tax paid Rs. 40,000 during the year 1985. Prepare provision for taxation account and find out hidden figure for Fund Flow Statement.

Solution.

Provision for Taxaton Account

	Rs.		Rs.
To Bank A/c	40,000	By Balance b/d (Opening balance)	56,000
To Balance c/d (closing balance)	70,000	By Profit and Loss A/c (Balancing amount)	54,000
	Rs. 1,10,000		Rs. 1,10,000

Rs. 54,000 must have been transferred from Profit and Loss Account to Provision for Taxation Account.

PROJECTED PROFIT AND LOSS ACCOUNT V/S PROJECTED FUND FLOW STATEMENT

When Balance Sheet of current year and projected Profit and Loss Account of next year and some additional information are given, a projected Fund Flow Statement is prepared. For this purpose projected Balance Sheet of next year is prepared with the help of given information. Comparison of amounts of projected Balance Sheet is made with the Balance Sheet of current year which is already given, and on the basis of the comparsion and additional information, a Fund Flow Satement is prepared for the period for which projected Balance Sheet has been prepared. This Fund Flow Statement is called projected Fund Flow Statement.

Fund flow Statement may be prepared in any one of the following two methods:

1. Vertial Method.
2. Horizontal Method.

VERTICAL METHOD

Its specimen is given below:

Statement of Sources and Applications

Sources:	*Rs.*
Issue of Capital	....
Issue of Debentures	....
Long-term Borrowings	....
Fortfieited Shares	....
Provision for Taxation (if treated non-current)	....
Provision for Dividend (if treated non-current)	....
Sales of Fixed Assets	....
Non-trading Receipts	....
Capital Reserve	....
Sale of Investments	....
Share Premium	....
Source from Operation	....
Total of Sources or Total Fund Provided	....

Contd.

Application:	***Rs.***	
Purchase of Fixed Assets	....	
Purchase of Investments	....	
Repayment of Pref Shares Capital	....	
Repayment of Debentures	....	
Repayment of long period loans	....	
Payment of Dividend (if treated non-current)	....	
Payment of Tax (if treated non-current)	....	
Non-trading Expenses	....	
Loss from operations	....	
Total Applications	....	
Increase/Decrease in working capital		....

HORIZONTAL FORM

Fund Flow Statement can be prepared in horizontal form also. Its specimen is given below:

Fund Flow Statement

Or

Statement of Sources and Application of Funds

	Rs.		*Rs.*
Issue of Capital	....	Purchase of Fixed Assets	....
Issue of Debentures	....	Purchase of Investments	....
Long-term Borrowings	....	Repayment of Pref. Share Capital	....
Share Premium	....		
Sale of Fixed Assets	....	Repayment of Debentures	....
Sale of Investment	....	Payment of Dividend (if treated non-current)	....
Forfeited Shares	....		
Non-trading Receipts	....	Payment of Taxes (If treated non current)	....
Provision for Taxation (If treated non-current)	....		
		Non-trading Expenses	....

Contd.

	Rs.		Rs.
Provision for dividend (If treated non-current)	....	Loss from operations	....
Capital Reserve	....	Excess of Sources of Funds over Application of Funds (Increase Balances in Working Capital	
Source from Operation	....		
Excess of Application over Sources, if any (Decrease in Working Capital)	....		
Total	....	Total	....

SCHEDULE OF CHANGES IN WORKING CAPITAL

Schedule of changes in working capital is a schedule which shows increase or decrease in working capital in detail by indicating changes in individual items of working capital. It is also called Statement of Change in Working Capital.

It is mostly prepared on the basis of current assets and current liabilities but now items of non-current assets and non-current liabilities are also used for it. Thus, there are two methods of its preparation:

1. Use of Current Assets and current liabilities only.
2. Use of both current and non-current assets and liabilities.

USE OF CURRENT ASSETS AND CURRENT LIABILITIES

A Current Assets

(i) The amount of every current assets of the current year is compared with its amount of previous year. If the amount of current asset of the current year is more than its amount of previous year, the excess is recorded in debit column.

(ii) If the amount of current asset of the current year is less than its amount of the previous year, the deficiency is recorded in credit column.

(iii) It must be noted that the difference of each current assets are recorded separately.

(iv) If the amount of current liability of current year is less than its amount of previous year, the deficit is recorded in debit columns.

(v) The difference of each individual current liability is recorded separately.

(vi) If the amount of current liability of current year is more than its amount of previous year, the excess is recorded in the credit column.

(vii) Total of all debit amounts and all credit amounts which have been recorded on the basis of above are found out.

(viii) If debit of total of current is more than credit total the excess is called net increase in working capital.

(ix) Two additional columns for the purpose of writing above-mentioned accounts are made in the Schedule of changes in working capital. Its specimen form is given below :

(x) If credit total of current is more than debit total of current, the deficiency is called net decrease in working capital.

Schedule of Changes in Working Capital

Particulars	*Amount of the prev. year*	*Amounts of the current year*	*Changes in current assets and current liabilities*	
			Dr.	*Cr.*
	Rs.	Rs.		
Total	....	....		
Net Increase in working capital				

USE OF BOTH CURRENT AND NON-CURRENT ASSETS AND LIABILITIES

The form of this schedule is just like the above schedule with only one difference that two more columns *i.e.*, one for debit and other for credit are also made for writing increase or decrease in non-current assets and liabilities. Specimen form is given below:

Schedule of Changes in Working Capital

Particulars	*Amount of the prev. year*	*Amounts of the current year*	*Changes in current assets and current liabilities*		*Changes in non-current assets and non-current liabilities*	
			Dr.	*Cr.*	*Dr.*	*Cr.*
	Rs.	Rs.				
Total	....	....				
Net Income or decrease in working capital						

RULES FOR PREPARATION OF CHANGES IN WORKING CAPITAL SCHEDULE

The amounts of every current and non-current assets of the current year are compared with the amounts of such assets of the previous year and increases or decreases are recorded as per following particulars:

(i) Rules for recording increase and decrease in current assets and current liabilities are the same as have been discussed earlier.

(ii) If the amount of non-ccurent asset of the current year is more than its amount of previous year the excess is recorded in debit column.

(iii) If the amount of non-current assets of the current year is less than its amount of previous year, the deficiency is recorded in credit column.

(iv) Differences of each non-current assets are recorded separately.

(v) If the amount of non-current liability of the current year is more than its amount of previous year, the excess is recorded in credit column.

(vi) If the amount of non-current liability of the current year is less than its amount of previous year, the deficiency is recorded in debit column.

(vii) Total of all debit and credit balances are made.

(viii) If the total of debit balances of non-current is less than total of credit balances of non-current, the excess is treated as decrease in working capital.

(ix) Depreciation is treated as non-current liability.

(x) Differences of each non-current liability are recorded separately.

(xi) If the total of debit balances of non-current is less than total of credit balances of non-current, the deficiency is treated as net increase in working capital.

Equal Balances. It is worth nothing that the difference in total of debit amounts and credit amounts of current assets and current liabilities will be the same as that of the balance of the total of debit and credit amounts of non-current assets and liabilities. If current assets and liabilities will show credit balance, then non-current assets and liabilities will show debit balance of the same amount and vice versa.

Record of debit and credit of current and non-current assets and liabilities for schedule of changes in Working Capital at a Glance

Assets	Treatment	
Increase in Current Assets	Debit	Increase in assets is recorded in debit column
Increase in Non-current Assets	Debit	
Decrease in Current Assets	Credit	Decrease in liabilities is recorded in credit column
Decrease in Non-current Assets	Credit	
Liabilities		
Increase in Current Liabilities	Debit	Increase in liabilities is recorded in debit column
Increase in Non-current Liabilities	Credit	
Decrease in Current Liabilities	Debit	Decrease in liabilities is recorded in credit column
Decrease in Non-current Liabilities	Debit	

Balance Equal

Total of debit of C.A. and C.L. — Total of credits of C.A. and C.L. = Total of credits of non C.A. and non C.L.—Total of debits of non C.A. and non C.L.

BASIS OF PREPARATION OF SCHEDULE OF CHANGES IN WORKING CAPITAL

This schedule is prepared only on the basis of two balance sheets, *i.e.*, amounts of the balance sheet of one year and the amounts of the balance sheet of other years. If any other information in addition to balance sheets is given, such informations are not made use of in preparing this schedule. It must be carefully noted that all such additional informations are ignored for the purpose of this schedule, but are used for preparing Fund Flow Statement . Answer of changes in working capital will be the same in this Schedule and Fund Flow Statement hence it is advisable to prepare schedule of changes in working capital to know the amount of changes in working capital without in the least incurring the labour of going in the complexities of additional information.

Example I.

Find out flow of fund from operation on the basis of the following:

Profit and Loss Account
(For the year ended on Dec. 31, 1985)

	Rs.		*Rs.*
To Opening Stock	8,000	By Sales	40,000
To Purchases	12,000	By Closing Stock	5,000
To Wages	5,000		
To Carriage inward	5,000		
To Gross Profit	15,000		
Rs.	45,000	Rs.	45,000
To Salaries	5,000	By Gross Profit	15,000

Contd.

	Rs.		*Rs.*
To Depreciation on machinery	100	By gain on sale of Furniture	150
To Depreciation on Furniture	50		
To Preliaminary expenses	100		
To Goodwill (written off)	50		
To Loss on sale of Machinery	50		
To Net Profit	9,800		
Rs.	15,150	Rs.	15,150
To General Reserve	4,800	By Balance b/d	10,000
To Dividend Equalisation Fund	2,000	By Net Profit of current year	9,800
To Proposed Dividend	1,00		
To Interim Dividend	1,000		
To Debenture Redemption Fund	2,000		
To Balance c/d	9,000		
Rs.	19,800	Rs.	19,800

Solution.

First method

			Rs.
Balance of Profit and Loss Account			9,000
Add :	Items not forming part of fund flow:	Rs.	
	Depreciation on Machinery	100	
	Depreiation on Furniture	50	
	Preliminary Expenses	100	
	Goodwill	50	
	Loss on sale of Machinery	50	
	General Reserve	4,800	
	Dividend Equalisation Reserve	2,000	

Proposed Dividend	1,000	
Interim Dividend	1,000	
Deb. Redemption Fund	2,000	11,150
		99,150
Less: Items not forming part of fund flow :		
Gain on sale of furniture		150
		20,000
Less: Opening balance of Profit		10,000
Source form Operation		Rs. 10,000

Second Method

Adjusted Profit and Loss Account

	Rs.		*Rs.*
Depreciation of machinery	100	Balance b/d (Jan. 1,1985)	10,000
Depreciation on Furniture	50	Profit and sale of Furniture	150
Preliminary Expenses	100	Source from Operation	10,000
Goodwill	50		
Loss on sale of Machinery	50		
General Reserve	4,800		
Dividend Equalisation Reserve	2,000		
Proposed Dividend	1,000		
Interim Dividend	1,000		
Debentures Redemption Fund	2,000		
Balance c/d (closing balance on Dec., 31, 1985)	9,000		
Rs.	20,150	Rs.	20,150

Example II.

The following are the summarised Trial Balances of a limited company as on 31st March, 1984 and 1985:

	1984		1985	
	Dr.	*Cr.*	*Dr.*	*Cr.*
	Rs.	Rs.	Rs.	Rs.
Fixed Assets	23,36,960	—	24,60,500	—
Current Assets	9,60.540	—	7.91,800	—
Debenture Discount	30,000	—	25,000	—
Issued Capital :				
Equity	—	15,00,000	—	15,00,000
Preference	—	3,00,000	—	4,00,000
Share Premium	—	30,000	—	40,000
Debentures	—	5,00,000	—	5,00,000
Current Liabilities	—	6,20,000	—	4,40,000
Provision for Depreciation	—	1,80,000	—	1,95,000
Dividend for 1983-84	—	—	1,50,000	
Provision for Doubtful Debts	—	6,000	—	5,000
Profit and Loss A/c:				
Previous year balance	—	24,400	—	1,91,500
Net Profit	—	1.67,100	—	1,55,800
Total Rs.	33.27.500	33.27.500	24,27,300	34.27.300

(a) During the year ended 31st March, 1985 machinery costing Rs. 2,00,000 (accumulated provision for depreciation Rs. 60,000) was sold for Rs. 1,50,000.

(b) Rs. 1,00,000 Preference Share Capital was issued during 1984-85 at a premium of Rs. 10,000.

(c) The net profit for 1984-85 has been arrived at after taking credit for the profit on sale of machinery, reduction in the provision for doubtful debts and writing off the discount on issue of debentures.

You are required to prepare:

(a) a statement showing the net increase in the working capital during the year 1984-85; and

(b) a statement showing the sources of the increase in the working capital and application therefore during the year.

Solution.

Statement of Sources and Application of Funds
(For the year 1984-85)

Sources of Funds	*Rs.*	*Application of Funds*	*Rs.*
Sale of Machinery	1,50,000	Purchase of Fixed Assets	3,23,540[8]
Issue of Pref. Shares	1,00,000	Dividend Paid (1983-84)	1,50,000
Premiumun on Pref. Share	10,000	Increase in Working Capital	12,260
Sources from Operation	2,25,800[1]		
	Rs. 4,85,800		Rs. 4,85,800

[1]Profit and Loss Account
(Adjusted)

	Rs.		*Rs.*
To Discount on Debentures	5,000[4]	By Balance b/d	1,91,500[2]
To Provision for Depreciation	75,000[5]	By Profit on Sale of Machinery	1,0,000[3]
To Closing Profit	3,47,300[6]	By Sources from Operation	2,25,800[7]
	Rs. 4,27,300		Rs. 4,27,300

[2] Rs. 24,400 + 1,67,100 = Rs. 1,91,500;

[3] Rs. 2,00,000 – 60,000 = Rs. 1,40,000; Rs. 1,50,000 – 1,40,000 = Rs. 10,000;

[4] Rs. 3,00,000 – 25,000 = Rs. 5,000;

[5] Rs. (60,000 + 1,95,000) – 1,80,000 = Rs. 75,000;

[6] Rs. 1,91,500 + 1,55,800 = Rs. 3,47,300;

[7] This amount is balancing figure.

[8] Fixed Assets Account

	Rs.		Rs.
To Balance b/d	23,36,960	By Provision for Depreciation	80,000
To Profit on Sale of Machinery	10,000	By Cash (Sale of Machinery)	1,50,000
To Cash (Purchase of Machinery)	3,23,540[9]	By Balance c/d	24,60,500
Rs.	26,70,500	Rs.	26,70,500

[9] This amount is balancing figure.

Statement of Change in Working Capital

Particulars	*1983-84*	*1984-85*	*Effect on Working Capital* *Dr.*	*Cr.*
	Rs.	Rs.	Rs.	Rs.
Current Assets	9,60,540	7,91,800		
Less : Provision for D. Debts	6,000	5,000		
	9,54,540	7,86,800		1,67,740
Current Liabilities	6,20,000	4,40,000	1,80,000	
Working Capital	3,34,540	3,46,800		
Increase in Working Capital	12,260			
Rs	3,46,800	3,46,800	1,80,000	12,260

Example III.

From the following Balance Sheets of A Ltd. make out: (i) Statement of changes in the Working Capital, and (ii) Fund Flow Statement:

Balance Sheet of A Ltd.

	1984	*1985*		*1984*	*1985*
	Rs.	*Rs.*		*Rs.*	*Rs.*
Share capital	2,00,000	2,50,000	Land and Buildings	2,00,000	1,90,000
General Reserve	50,000	2,50,000	Machinery and Plant	1,50,000	1,69,000
Profit and Loss A/c	30,500	30,600	Stocks	1,00,00	74,000
Short Period Bank					
Loans	70,000	—	Debtors	80,000	64,200
Crditors	1,50,00	1,35,200	Cash	500	600
Provision for		Bank	—	8,000	
Taxation	30,000	35,000	Goodwill	—	5,000
Rs.	5,30,500	5,10,800	Rs.	5,30,500	5,10,800

During the year ended 31st December, 1985:

(i) Dividend of Rs. 23,000 was paid;

(ii) Assets of another company were purchased for a consideration of Rs. 50,000 payable in shares. The following assets were purchased: Stocks Rs. 20,000; machinery Rs.25,000;

(iii) Machinery was purchased for Rs. 8,000;

(iv) The net profit of the year was Rs. 66,100;

(v) Depreciation written off : Building Rs. 10,000, Machinery Rs. 14,000;

(vi) Income-tax paid during the year was Rs. 28,000; Provision of Rs. 33,000 was made for taxation.

Solution.

Fund Flow Statement

Sources of Funds	*Rs.*	*Application of funds*	*Rs.*
Share Capital	20,000[1]	Purcahses of Machinery	8,000[6]
Source from Operation	90,100[2]	Dividend Paid	23,000
Income-tax-paid	28,000		
Increase in Working Capital	51,100		
Rs.	1,10,100	Rs.	1,10,100

[1] Closing Capital Rs. 2,50,000 - (Opening Capital Rs. 2,00,000 + Machinery Rs. 25,000 + Goodwill R. 5,000) = Rs. 20,000 Here Goodwill of Rs. 5,000 has been found out as : Rs. 50,000 - (20,000 + 25,000) = Rs. 5,000. Only that portion of capital has been treated as source here which represent current stock and that is Rs. 20,000.

[1] Profit and Loss Account
(Adjusted)

	Rs.		*Rs.*
To Depreciation on Machinery	14,000[3]	By Balance b/d	30,500
To Depreication on Building	10,000[4]	By Sources from Operation	90,100
To Dividend	23,000		
To Provision for Taxation	23,000		
To General Reserve	10,000[5]		
To Balance c/d	30,600		
Rs.	1,20,600	Rs.	1,20,600

[3] (Opening balance Rs. 1,50,000 + Cash purchases Rs. 8,000 + Purchase by shares Rs. 25,000) – Closing balance Rs. 1,69,000 = 14,000.

[4] Rs. 2,00,000 – Rs. 1,90,000 = Rs. 10,000;

[5] Rs. 60,000 – Rs. 50,000) = Rs. 10,000;

[6] Purchase of machinery in shares has not been considered because it affects current assets, *i.e.*, cash but purchase of machinery in shares has not been considered because it affects fixed liability, *i.e.*, capital.

Statement Showing Changes in Working Capital

Particulars		*1984*		*1985*	*Effect on Working Capital* *Dr.*	*Cr.*
	Rs.	Rs.	Rs.	Rs.	Rs.	Rs.
Current Assets:						
Stock		1,00,000		74,000		26,000
Debtors		80,000		64,200		15,800

Cash		500		600	100	
Bank		—		8,000	8,000	
Total		1,80,500		1,46,800		
Current Liabilities :						
Bank Loans	70,000				70,000	
Creditors	1,50,000		1,35,200		14,800	
	2,20,000	2,20,000		1,35,2000		
		-39,500		+11,600		
Increase in Working Capital		+ 51,100[1]				51,100
		11,600		11,600	92,900	92,900

1 Rs. 39,500 + 11,600 = Rs. 51,100

Alternative Method

Statement Showing Changes in Working Capital

Partuiculars	*1984*	*1985*	*Changes in current assets and current liabilities*		*Changes in non-current assets and non-current liabilities*	
			Dr.	*Cr.*	*Dr.*	*Cr.*
	Rs.	*Rs.*	*Rs*	*Rs*	*Rs.*	*Rs.*
Land & Buildings	2,00,000	1,90,000	—	—	—	10.000
Machinery & Plant	1,50,000	1,69,000	—	—	19,000	—
Stocks	1,00,000	74,000	—	26,000	—	—
	1,00,000	74,000	—	26,000	—	—
Debtors	80,000	64,200	—	15,800	—	—
Cash	500	600	100	—	—	—
Bank	—	8,000	8,000	—	—	—
Goowill	—	5,000	—	—	5,000	—
	5,30,500	5,10,800				

Share Capital	2,00,000	2,50,000	—	—	—	50,000
General Reserve	50,000	60,000	—	—	—	10,000
P. & L. A/c	30,500	30,600	—	—	—	100
Bank Loan	70,000	—	70,0000	—	—	—
Creditors	1,50,000	1,35,200	14,800	—	—	—
Provision for Taxation	30,000	35,000	—	—	—	5,000
	5,30,500	5,10,800				
Net Increase in W.C.				51,100	51,100	
			92,900	92,900	75,100	75,100

Example IV.

From the following Balance Sheet of Sudhir Ltd. make schedule of changes in Working Capital and Funds Flow Statement :

Balance Sheet of A Ltd.

	1984	*1985*		*1984*	*1985*
	Rs.	*Rs.*		*Rs.*	*Rs.*
Share Capital	3,00,000	4,00,000	Goodwill	—	20,000
Reserve	50,000	50,000	Fixed Assets	3,75,000	3,94,000
Profit and Loss A/c	40,000	45,000	Stocks	1,20,000	1,12,00
Bank Overdraft	60,000	—	Advance	3,000	1,000
Creditors	50,000	52,000	Debtors	92,000	87,000
B/P	45,000	23,000	Cash at Bank	5,000	6,000
Provision for Tax	50,000	50,000			
Rs.	5,95,000	6,20,000	Rs.	5,95,000	6,20,000

Additional information obtained from the General Ledger is as follows:

During the year 1985 a dividend of Rs. 15,000 was paid. The assets of another company were purchased at Rs.1,00,000 payable in fully paid shares of the company. The assets consisted of Stock Rs. 45,000, fixed assets Rs. 35,000 and Goodwill Rs. 20,000.

Income-tax paid during the year was Rs. 35,000. The net profit for the year was Rs. 55,000 before charging tax.

Solution.

Fund Flow Statement
(For the Year 1985)

Sources of Funds	*Rs.*	*Application of funds*	*Rs.*
Share Capital	45,000[1]	Income-tax	35,000
Source from Operation	71,1000[2]	Dividend	15,000
		Increase in Working Capital	66,000
Rs.	1,16,000	Rs.	1,16,000

[1] Rs. 4,00,000 – Rs. 3,00,000 = Increase in share capital Rs. 1,00,000. That portion of share capital which is equal to current assets = Rs. 1,00,000 - (Fixed assets Rs. 35,000 + Good will Rs. 20,000) = Rs. 45,000.

[2] Profit and Loss Account
(Adjusted)

	Rs.		*Rs.*
To Depreciation	16,000	By Balance b/d	40,000
To Dividend	15,000	By Source from Operation	71,000[2]
To Income-tax	35,000		
To Balance c/d	45,000		
Rs.	1,11,000	Rs.	1,11,000

[1] (Opening balance of fixed assets Rs. 3,75,000 + Purchase of fixed assets Rs. 35,000) - Closing balance Rs. 3,94,000 = Rs. 16,000 depreciation.

[2] This amount is balancing figure.

Schedule of Changes in Working Capital

Particulars	*1984*		*1985*		*Effect on Working Capital*	
					Dr.	*Cr.*
	Rs.	Rs.	Rs.	Rs.	Rs.	Rs.
Current Assets:						
Cash at Bank		5,000		6,000	1,000	—
Debetors		92,000		87,000	—	5,000
Advances		3,000		1,000	—	2,000
Stock	1,20,000		1,12,000	—	8,000	
Total	2.20,000		2,06,000			
Current Liabilities:						
Creditrors	50,000		52,000		—	2,000
B/P 45,000		23,000		22,000	—	
Bank Overdraft	60,000	-1,55,000	—	75,000	60,000	—
Net Working Capital	65,000		1,31,000			
Increase Working Capital		66,000				66,000
		1,31,000		1,31,000	83,000	83,000

Note : Provision for Taxation has not been treated as current liability here because additional information for payment of income-tax is given in it.

Example V.

Find out flow of fund from operations on the basis of following Profit and Loss Account:

Profit and Loss Account
(For the year ended on Dec. 31, 1985)

		Rs.			Rs.
To Opening Stock		10,000	By Sales	1,50,000	
To Purchases	80,000		Less : Returns	5,000	1,45,000
Less: Returns	10,000	70,000			
To Carriage		5,000	By Closing Stock		35,000
To Wages		10,000			
To Outstanding Wages		5,000			
To Gross Profit		80,000			
		Rs. 1,80,000		Rs.	1,80,000
To Salaries		18,000	By Gross Profit		80,000
To Insurance	1,800		By Gain on sale of machinery		2,250
Less : Prepaid	100	1,700			
To Depreciation on plant		700			
To Dep. on machinery		300			
To Dep. on furniture		50			
To Loss on sale of furntiture		100			
To Preliminary Exps.		400			
To Goodwill (written off)		1,000			
To Provision for Taxation		4,000			
To Net Profit		56,000			
	Rs.	82,250		Rs.	82,250

Solution.

First method (Statement Form)

		Rs.
Net Profit as per Profit and Loss Account		56,000
Add : Items not forming part of fund flow:	Rs.	
Depreciation on Plant	700	
Deprecation on Machinery	300	
Depreciation on Furniture	50	
Loss on sale of Furniture	100	
Preliminary Expenses	4,00	
Goodwill	1,000	
Provision for Taxation	4,000	6,550
		62,550
Less:		
Items not forming part of fund flow :		
Gain on sale of furniture		2,250
	Rs.	60,300

Alternative Method (Account Form)
Adjusted Profit and Loss Account

	Rs.		*Rs.*
Opening Stock	10,000	Sales (Net)	1,45,000
Purchases (Net)	70,000	Closing Stock	35,000
Carriage	5,000		
Wages	10,000		
Outstanding Wages	5,000		
Salaries	18,000		
Insurance	1,700		
Sources from Operation	60,300		
	Rs. 1,80,000		Rs. 1,80,000

Example VI.

A Ltd. has been in operation for several years but suffered a set back in its operations about three years back. It expects to show better results in future and has plans to expand rapidly. The summarised Balance Sheet and Profit and Loss Accounts of the company are given below:

Balance Sheet

(Rs. in lakhs)

	1984 *Rs.*	*1985* *Rs.*	*1986* *Rs.*
Fixed Assets (Gross)	365	350	360
Less: Depreciation to date	100	125	160
Net Fixed Assets	265	225	200
Debtors	325	335	380
Stock of Raw Materials	100	75	120
Stock of finished and semi-finished goods	280	250	350
Other Current Assets	10	10	15
Total Asset;	980	895	1,065
Share Capital	60	60	60
Reserves	1	3	90
Term Loans	—	—	155
Bank Overdraft	650	650	475
Current Liabilities and Provisions	269	182	285
Total Liabilities	980	895	1,065

Profit and Loss Account

(Rs. in lakhs)

	1984	*1985*	*1986*
Sales	880	1,000	1,225
Materials	50	725	850

Contd.

	1984	*1985*	*1986*
Salaries and Wages	125	130	140
Other Expenses	60	70	65
Depreciation	25	30	35
Interest	60	50	50
	920	1,005	1,140
Net Operating Profit (Loss)	(40)	(5)	85
Non-Operating Profit	Nil	7	2

Prepare a statement showing sources and uses of funds.

Solution.

Statement of Sources and Uses of Funds

(For the year ending on Dec. 31, 1984, 1985 & 1988)

	1985 (Rs.in lakhs)	*1988 Rs. in lakhs)*
Sources of Funds:		
Operating profits before depreciation	25[1]	120[2]
Not-Operating Profit	7	2
Loss on sale of fixed assets written off	10[3]	—
Term Loan	—	155
Total	42	277
Application of Funds:		
Purchase of Fixed Assets	—	10[4]
Increase in Working Capital	42	267

Statement of Changes in Working Capital

	1984 (Rs.in lakhs)	*1985 (Rs.in lakhs)*	*1986 Rs. in lakhs)*
Current Assets	715[1]	670[2]	865[7]
Current Liabilities including bank overdraft	919[8]	832[6]	760[10]
Net Working Capital	-204	-162	+105
Increase in Working Capital	—	42[11]	267[12]

[1] 1985 : Net loss Rs. 5 lakhs + Depreciation Rs. 30 lakhs = Profit Rs. 25 lakhs.

[2] 1986 : Net Profit Rs. 85 lakhs + Depreciation Rs. 35 lakhs = Rs. 120 lakhs.

[3] In 1984 Fixed Assets Rs. 385 lakhs - in 1985 Fixed Assets Rs. 350 lakhs = Reduction in Fixed Assets Rs. 15 lakhs

Depreciation in 1985 Rs. 30 lakh while cumulative depreciation increases by (Rs. 125 lakhs - Rs. 100 lakhs) - Rs. 25 lakhs only, hence Rs. 5 lakhs written off. Above-mentioned Rs. 15 lakhs - Rs. 5 lakhs = Rs. 10 lakhs loss.

[4] 1986 Fixed Assets Rs. 380 lakhs - 1985 Fixed Assets Rs. 350 lakhs = Rs. 10 lakhs.

[5] Rs. in lakhs 325 + 100 + 280 +10 = Rs. 715 lakhs.

[6] Rs. in lakhs 335 + 75 + 250 + 10 = Rs. 670 lakhs.

[7] Rs. in lakhs 380 + 120 + 350 + 15 = Rs. 865 lakhs.

[8] Rs. in lakhs 650 + 369 = Rs. 919 lakhs.

[9] Rs. in lakhs 650 + 182 = Rs. 832 lakhs.

[10] Rs. in lakhs 475 + 285 = Rs. 760 lakhs.

[11] Deficit of Rs. 204 lakhs is reduced to Rs. 162 lakhs hence 204 - 162 = 42 lakhs indicate increase in working capital.

[12] Deficit of Rs. 162 lakhs is wiped out and excess of Rs. 105 lakhs is there, hence total increase is Rs. 162 + 105 = Rs. 267 lakhs.

Example VII.

From the following Balance Sheet of A Ltd., make out (I) Statement of Changes in Working Capital, and (2) Funds Flow Statement.

Balance Sheet of A Ltd.

	1984	*1985*		*1984*	*1985*
	Rs.	*Rs.*		*Rs.*	*Rs.*
Equity Share			Goodwill	1,10,000	80,000
Capital	3,00,000	4,00,000	Land and Buildings	2,00,000	17,000
8% Redeemable Pref.			Plant	80,000	2,00,000
Share Capital	1,50,000	1,00,000	Investment	20,000	30,000
Capital Reserve	—	20,000	Sunday Debtors	1,40,000	1,70,000
General Reserve	40,000	50,000	stock	77,000	1,09,000
P & L. A/c	30,000	48,000	Bills Receivable	20,000	30,000
Proposed Dividend	42,000	50,000	Cash in Hand	15,000	10,000
Sundry Creditors	25,000	47,000	Cash at Bank	10,000	8,000
Bils Payable	20,000	16,000	Preliminary Expenses	15,000	10,000
Liabilities for Expenses	30,000	36,000			
Provisions for Taxation	40,000	50,000			
Rs.	6.77,000	8,17,0000	Rs.	6,77,000	8,17,000

(i) A piece of land has been sold out in 1985 and the profit on sale has been credited to capital reserve.

(ii) A machine has been sold for Rs. 10,000. The written down value of the machine was Rs. 12,000. Depreciation of Rs. 10,000 is charged on Plant Account in 1985.

(iii) The investments are trade investments. Rs. 3,000 by way of dividend is received including Rs. 1,000 from pre-acquisition profit has been credited to Investment Acccount.

(iv) An interim dividend of Rs. 20,000 has been paid in 1985.

Solution.

Fund Flow Statement
(For the Year 1985)

Sources of Funds	*Rs.*	*Application of funds*	*Rs.*
Issue of Equity Capital	1,00,000[1]	Purchase of Plant	1,42,000[10]
Sale of Machine	10,000	Investment	11,000[11]
Sale of Land	50,000[2]	Repayment of Preference	
Dividend Received	3,000	Capital	50,000[12]
Source from operation	1,43,000[3]	Proposed Dividend Paid	42,000
		Interim Dividend Paid	20,000
		Increase in Working Capital	41,000
	Rs. 3,06,000		Rs. 3,06,000

[1] Rs. 4,00,000 - 3,00,000 = Rs. 1,00,000.

[2] Land and Buildings Account

	Rs.		*Rs.*
To Balance b/d	2,00,000	By Cash (Sale)	50,000*
To Profit transferred to capital Reserve	20,000	By Balance c/d	1,70,000
	Rs. 2,20,000		Rs. 2,20,000

This is balancing figure.

[3] Adjusted Profit and Loss Account

	Rs.		*Rs.*
To Proposed Dividend	50,000	By Balance b/d	30,000
To General Reserve	10,000[4]	By Dividend	2,000[9]
To Interim Dividend	20,000	By Source from Operation	1,43,000
To Goodwill	20,000[5]		
To Provision for Taxation	10,000[5]		
To Depreciation on Plant	10,000		

To Loss or Sale of Plant	2,000[7]		
To Preliminary Expenses	5,000[8]		
To Balance c/d	48,000		
Rs.	1,75,000	Rs.	1,75,000

[4] Rs. 50,000 – 40,000 = Rs. 10,000;

[5] Rs. 1,00,000 – 80,000 = Rs. 20,000;

[6] Rs. 50,000 – 40,000 = Rs. 10,000;

[7] Rs. 12,000 – 10,000 = Rs. 2,000;

[8] Rs. 15,000 – 10,000 = Rs. 5,000;

[9] Rs. 3,000 – 1,000 = Rs. 2,000.

[10] Plant Account

	Rs.		*Rs.*
To Balance b/d	80,000	By Depreciation	10,000
To Cash (Purchase)	1,42,000	By Cash (Sale)	10,000
		By Profit and Loss	2,000
		By Balance c/d	2,00,000
Rs.	2,22,000	Rs.	2,22,000

* This is balancing amount.

[11] Investment Account

	Rs.		Rs.
To Balance b/d	20,000	By Depreciation A/c	1,000
To Cash (Purchase)	11,000*	By Balance c/d	30,000
Rs.	31,000	Rs.	31,000

* This is balancing amount.

[12] Rs. 1,50,000 – 1,00,000 = Rs. 50,000.

Note: Investments have been considered for Funds Flow Statement here because they are trade investments.

Statement Showing Changes in Working Capital

Particulars	*1984*		*1985*		*Effect on Working Capital* Dr.	Cr.
	Rs.	Rs.	Rs.	Rs.	Rs.	Rs.
Current Assets:						
Debtors		1,40,000		1,70,000	30,000	
Stocks		77,000		1,09,000	32,000	
B/R		20,000		30,000	10,000	
Cash in Hand		15,000		10,000		5,000
Cash at Bank		10,000		8,000		2,000
Total		2,62,000		3,27,000		
Current Liabilities:						
Creditors	25,000		47,000			22,000
B/P	20,000		16,000		4,000	
Liability for Expenses	30,000		36,000			6,000
Total	75,000	-75,000	99,000	– 99,000		
Working Capital		1,87,000		2,28,000		
Increse in Working Capital		41,000				41,000
		2,28,000		2,28,000	76,000	76,000

❑

6

Statement of Cash Flow

CASH FLOW ANALYSIS

A cash flow statement shows the sources of cash receipt and the purposes for which payments are made thus explaining the changes in the cash balances of the business. This statement summarise the changes in cash position of the firm. The transactions which increase the cash position of the concern are treated as inflow of cash and which decreases the cash flow statement traces the various sources which bring in cash such as cash from operations, sale of current and fixed assets, issue of share capital and debentures etc. and applications which causes outflow of cash such as loss from operation, purchase of current and fixed assets; redemption of debentures and preference shares and other long term debts for cash. Cash statement shows the cash receipts and disbursement during the period. For example if the cash balance of a business concern shows by the balance sheet on 31st December, 1992 at Rs. 40,000 which the cash balance as per its balance sheet on 31 st December, 1993 is Rs. 55,000/-. It means that there has been an inflow of cash of Rs. 15,000/- in the year 1993 as compared to the year 1992. The cash flow statement explains the reasons for such inflows or outflows of cash, as the case may be. A cash flow statement is not very much different from a fund flow statement. During preparing the fund flow statement the sources and uses of all 'funds' (working capital) are taken into account while in preparation of cash flow statement, the sources and uses of cash alone are taken into account. The focus is on 'cash' rather than on 'net working capital'. Cash flow statement is prepared to show the impact of various transactions on the cash position of firm. It takes into account the transactions resulting in cash in flow only. A cash flow statement is a statement which summaries sources of cash inflows and uses of cash outflows of a firm during particular period of time, *i.e.*, months or a year.

Objectives of Cash Flow Statement

In cash flow there are number of objectives of financial management.

(a) The object of cash flow statement is to summarise the cause of changes in cash position between the two different years, months, dates of balance sheets. It shows the sources of and uses of cash. This statement analyses changes in non-current account as well as current accounts to determine the flow of cash.

(b) It indicates a comparison of the cash flow statement for the previous year with the budget for the year which indicate to what extent the resources of the concern were generated and applied to the plan. It is specially useful to management while preparing cash budget.

(c) A business concern may earn large profits yet it may run out of cash or when it suffered a loss and still has plenty of cash at bank. The cash flow analysis would unable the financial manager to account for such state of affair.

(d) This statement is useful in evaluating financial policies and current cash portion of a concern. Analysis of cash flow is useful for short-term planning. The fund flow statement is particularly useful for long term planning, cash flow statement provides information for planning the short range needs of the firm. It is very helpful to analyse the pattern of cash inflow and outflow. A business concern needs sufficient cash to pay debt maturing in the near future, to pay interest and other expenses, to pay dividends to the shareholders and to plan purchases of fixed assets. It may, thus, plan out the investment or surplus or meeting the deficit, if any.

The following are 'sources' and 'applications' of cash, as used for preparing a cash flow statement.

Sources of Cash. Cash from operations is the main internal source. The net profit shown by the Profit and Loss Account will have to be adjusted for non-cash items for finding out cash from operations. The items are as follows:

(a) Good will, preliminary expenses, etc. when written off against profits, reduce the net profits without affecting the cash balance. The amounts written off should, therefore, be added back to profits to find out cash from operations.

(b) Sale of fixed assets is taken as a separate source of cash, it should be deducted from the profits.

(c) If the profit for the year has been arrived at after charging transfers to reserves, such transfers should be added back to profits. In case operation shows a net loss, such net loss after making adjustments for non-cash items will be as an application of cash.

(d) Loss on sale of fixed assets does not result in outflow of cash and, therefore, should be added back to profits.

(e) Gains from sale of fixed assets is taken as a separate source of cash, it should be deducted from net profit.

(f) Depreciation does not result in outflow of cash and therefore, net profit will have to be increased by the amount of depreciation or development rebate charged, in order to find out the real cash generated from operations.

To find out real cash from operations, adjustments will have to be made for 'changes' in current assets and current liabilities arising out on account of operations *viz.*, trade debtors, trade creditors, bills receivable, bills payable etc. This may be done by applying the general rules:

Increase in current asset or decrease in current liability results in decrease in cash and decrease in a current asset or increase in a current liability results in increase in cash.

Applications of Cash. It may take any of the following terms:

(a) Payment of tax will result in decrease of cash, hence, it is as application of cash.

(b) The decrease in unsecured loans, deposits etc. denotes that they have been paid off to that extent. It results therefore in outflow of cash.

(c) Loss suffered on account of business operations will result in outflow of cash.

(d) The payment of long term loan such as loans from financial institutions or debentures results in decrease in cash. It is, therefore, application of cash.

(e) Cash may be utilised for purchase of additional fixed assets or renewals or replacement of existing fixed assets.

(f) Payments for plant and machinery purchased on deferred payment basis has to be made as per agreement. It is, therefore, an application of cash.

(g) Payment of dividend decreases the cash for business and hence it is application of cash.

CONSTRUCTION OF CASH FLOW STATEMENT

Cash Flow Statement (CFS) is prepared with the help of balance sheet, Profit and Loss Account and other additional information. The calculation and measurement of cash flow is primarily based on P & L A/c or Income Statement. It should be noted that items in an Income Statement are shown on accrual basis while items are shown on cash basis in Cash Flow Statement. Cash flow measurement depends primarily on determining cash receipts and cash payments over a given period, whereas income is determined by matching revenue and expenses in a given period. Therefore, a number of items appear on either the Cash Flow Statement or the Income Statement but not on both. For instance, depreciation and bad debts written off are recognised in determining the net income, hence they are debited to the Income Statement/P. & L. A./c, but they are excluded from the Cash Flow Satements as they don't require any cash outlay or in other words, they are non-cash items.

There are two parts of Cash Flow Statement *i.e.*, cash inflow and cash outflow. Cash inflow means sources of cash and cash outflow means uses of cash. The items of cash inflow and outflow are computed separately.

The main items of cash flow are as follows—

I. SOURCES OF CASH/CASH INFLOW

The following are the items of cash inflow:

1. Cash From Operation. There are two methods to calculate cash from operation—

(A) Cash Sales Methods. Cash from operation can be calculated on this method as—

Cash from operation (CFO) = Cash Sales (Cash purchase + Cash operating expenses)

Where, Cash Sales = Total Sales – Credit Sales

or, Cash Sales = total Sales – Increase in Debtors and B/R

Note. It should be noted that decrease in the amounts of debtors and bills receivable (B/R) should not be added to total sales. Such decreases should be shown separately as collections from debtors/bill receivable under sources of cash because it represents the amount collected from previous year's debtors or B/R.

Cash Purchase = Total Purchase – Credit Purchases

or Cash Purchase = Total Purchase – Increase in Trade Creditors and Bills payable (B/P)

Where, Total Purchases = Cost of Goods Sold + Increase in Stocks (or minus decrease in stock)

Cash Operating Expenses are determined as follows—

(Amount in Rs.)

Total operating expenses for the period		----
Less : Non – Cash items (*e.g.* Depreciation)		----
	Rs.	----
Add : Decrease in outstanding expenses	----	
Increase in prepaid expenses	----	----

Less : Increase in outstanding expenses	----	
Decrease in prepaid expenses	----	----
Cash Operating Expenses	Rs.	---

Format of Determining Cash from Operations

(Amount in Rs.)

Total Sales		----
Less : Credit Sales		----
Cash Sales		----
Less : Cash Purcahses—		
Total Purchase	----	
Less : Credit Purchases	----	----
(or increase in Account Payable)	----	----
Less : Cash operating expenses (after adjusting non-cash items, accruals and pre-payments)		----
Cash From Operation		----

Note—Cash Sales method is the best method.

(B) Net Profit Method. Cash From Operation (CFO) can be determined by this second method *i.e.*, net profit method. In this method, in the amount of net profit depreciation, loss on the sale of fixed assets, intangible assets written off and other non-cash items are added. On the other hand, all non-business income, increase in receivables, stock-in-trade, prepaid expenses, reduction in deferred credit and decrease in payables should be deducted from it.

Format of Calculating Cash from Operation on the Basis of Net Profit Method

(Amount in Rs.)

Net profit as per Income Statement		----
Add: (A) Non-Cash items:		
(i) Depreciation	----	
(ii) Loss on the sale of fixed assets written off		
(iii) Goodwill written off	----	
(iv) Advertising Suspense a/c written off	----	

	(B) Non-business expenses Dividend paid	----	
	(C) Increase in Current Liabilities (Account payable outstanding expenses etc.)	----	
	(D) Decrease in Current Assets	----	----
Less :	(A) Non-business Income Income from investment	----	----
	(B) Decrease in current liabilities (A/c payable outstanding expenses etc.)	----	
	(C) Increase in current assets (Prepaid expenses A/C Receivable etc.)	----	----
	Cash From Operation	Rs.	----

Tutorial Notes About Treating Operating Profit as Cash From Operations (CFO)

Some authorities opine to show operating profit (as determined under FFS) instead of cash from operations. If this procedure is adopted, changes in Current Assets and Current Liabilities will not be adjusted in net profit (as in (A) and (B) methods) but will be shown directly in the Cash Flow Statement. Accordingly the increase in stock, debtors and B/R and decrease in creditors, B/P etc. will be shown as application of cash, and increase in creditors and B/P and decrease in stock, debtors and B/R as sources of cash.

2. Increase in Share Capital. If Equity share capital or Preference share capital is increased during the concerned period then it will be the part of cash inflow or sources of cash. The net effect (add premium on share and less discount on issue of share) of issue of share capital should be taken into account. However, an increase in share capital happens due to purchase of fixed assets (*i.e.*, shares are issued in consideration other than cash) or shares are issued in conversion of debentures or long-term loans, it would not be inflow of cash.

3. Issue of Debentures, Loans etc. If debentures are issued or loans are taken in cash, it will form a source of cash. However, if debentures are issued or loans raised for consideration other than cash, it will not constitute inflow of cash.

4. Reduction in or sale of assets. If fixed assets are sold and long term investments are reduced by receipt of cash, these proceeds will form part of the source of cash or cash inflow.

5. Other Receipts. There may also be some other sources of cash inflow such as sale proceeds of by-products or waste materials, cash receipts of dividend and interest, income tax refund, compensation received etc.

II. APPLICATION OR USES OF CASH OR CASH OUTFLOWS

The items are as follows—

1. Operating Loss. The procedure of calculation of operating loss is the same as Cash From Operation. Operating loss is shown under application of cash flow.

2. Redemption of Preference Shares/Debentures. Cash actually paid for redemption of share/debentures (*i.e.*, adding premium or deducting discount on the redemption of shares/debentures) constitutes outflow of cash. Arrears of dividend are also shown as outflow of cash. However, if equity shares are given for repayment of preference share capital or debentures, it will not constitute cash outflow.

3. Decrease in or Repayment of Loans. Decrease in loans or repayment of long-term or short-term loans, creditors or B/P, these will form outflow of cash.

4. Increase in or Purchase of Fixed Assets. The acquisition of fixed assets and investments constitutes cash outflow. However, if the acquisition is made on credit or by the issue of shares or debentures, it will not involve outflow of cash.

5. Other Payments. Payment of dividend (interim or final but not stock dividend), income tax, interest compensation etc., will constitute outflow of cash.

FORMS OF CASH FLOW STATEMENT (CFS)

CFS may be prepared in the following types:

(a) ***Reminder Type.*** Under this method, the Cash Flow Statement is divided into two parts—sources of cash and applications of cash. The difference of the total of both the sides shows the surplus deficiency of cash at the end of the year.

(b) ***Self-Balance Type.*** Under this method, the cash flow statement is prepared in the same manner—sources and uses of cash as the Reminder Type. But the short side of the statement is balanced with the figure of variation in the balance of cash and then both sides are closed.

(c) ***Reconciling Type.*** In this method one starts with the opening balance of cash. To the opening balance all items for the inflow of cash are added and outflows of cash are deducted; the net figure must be cash in hand *i.e.*, closing balance of cash at the end of the specific period. This method is more popular and widely used.

Specimen of Report Form Reconciling Type Cash Flow Statement

(Amount in Rs.)

Opening Cash Balance		- - - -
Add: Sources of Cach/Cash inflows		
1. Cash from operation	- - - -	
2. Collection from Debtors or Decrease in Debtors	- - - -	
3. Sale of Investments	- - - -	
4. Issue of Share Capital Debentures	- - - -	
5. Increase in Loans	- - - -	- - - -
Total Cash Available		- - - -

Less: Application of Cash/Cash Outflows

1. Purchase of Machinery	- - - -	
2. Dividend paid	- - - -	
3. Decrease in Accounts Payable	- - - -	
4. Repayment of Bank Loan	- - - -	
5. Redemption of Debentures	- - - -	- - - -
Cash balance at the end		- - - -

Account Form Reconciling Type Cash Flow Statement

Sources of Cash	Amount Rs.	Application of Cash	Amount Rs.
Opening Cash Balance	—	Loss from Operation	—
Other Sources of Cash:	—	Purchase of Machinery	—
Cash from Operation	—	Repayment of Bank Loans	--
Sale of Investment	—	Redemption of Preference	—
Issue of Shares/Debentures	—	Share Capital/Debentures	—
Loans	—	Decrease in Accounts Payable	---
Collection from Debtors	—	Closing balance of Cash	—
Total (Rs.)	—	Total (Rs.)	—

DIFFERENCE BETWEEN CASH FLOW AND FUND FLOW STATEMENT

Both the statements shows the changes in the financial position of concern yet there are many points which show the difference between Fund Flow and Cash Flow Statement. The following are the main points:

(a) Cash is the part of working capital and, therefore, an improvement in the cash position results in improvement in the funds position but the reserve is not true. So the inflow of cash results, the inflow of funds but inflow of funds may not necessarily results in flow of cash.

(b) Cash Flow Statement is merely a record of cash receipts and disbursement. It is valuable in its own way but it fails to bring to light many important changes involving the disposition of resources. While studying the short term solvency of a business one is interested not only in cash balance but also in the assets which may easily be converted into cash.

(c) Cash Flow Statement is useful for short terms financial planning where as Fund Flow Statement is useful for long term financial planning.

(d) In Cash Flow Statement an increase in a current liability or decrease in a current asset (other than cash) results in increase in cash or vice versa whereas in case of Fund Flow statement an increase in current liability or decrease in a current asset results in working capitals and vice versa.

(e) Funds from operations are calculated by making adjusted profit and loss account taking into consideration all adjustments which are made at the end of the accounting period. Cash Flow Statement deals with only actual receipts and payments of income and expenses. In order to calculate cash from operation further adjustments are required to be made for increase and decreases in current assets and current liabilities.

(f) Cash Flow Statement is more useful to the management as a tool of financial analysis in short period as compared to Fund Flow Statement. It has rightly been said that shorter the period covered by analysis, greater is the importance of cash flow statement. Example, if it is to be found out whether the business can meet its obligations maturing after 10 years from now, a good estimate can be made about firms capacity to meet its long term obligations if changes in working capital position on account of operations are observed.

Utility to Cash Flow Statement

A cash flow statement, is an important, financial tool for the management. Its utility can be discussed as follows:

(a) Cash flow statement discloses the complete story of cash movement. The increase in or decrease of, cash and the reason therefore can be known. It discloses the reasons for low cash balance inspite of heavy operating profits or for heavy cash balance inspite of low operating profits.

(b) The extent of success or failure of cash planning can be known by comparing the projected cash flow statement with the actual cash flow statement and necessary remedial measures can be taken.

(c) Cash flow analysis helps in evaluating financial policies and cash position. Cash in the basis for all operations and hence a projected cash flow statement will enable the management to plan and contribute the financial operations properly. The management can know how much cash is needed, from which source it will be derived, how much can be generated internally and how much could be obtained from outside.

(d) Cash flow statement provides information about funds which will be available from operations. This will help the management in determining policies regarding internal financial management *e.g.* possibility of repayment of long term debt, dividend policies, planning replacement of plant and machinery etc.

METHOD ADOPTED FOR CASH FLOW STATEMENT

Cash flow statement shows the impact of various transactions on cash position of a firm. It is prepared with the help of financial statement *i.e.* balance sheet and profit and loss account and some additional information. A cash flow statement starts with the opening balance of cash and balance at bank, all the inflows of cash are added to the opening balance and outflow of cash are deducted from total. The balance *i.e.* opening balance at bank, all the inflows of cash are added to the opening balance and outflow of cash are deducted from total. The balance *i.e.* opening balance of cash and bank balance plus inflow of cash minus outflows of cash is reconciled with the closing of cash. The cash flow statement involves the determining of:

(a) Inflows of Cash

(b) Outflows of Cash

(a) Sources of Cash Inflows

(i) Cash flow from operations

(ii) Increase in existing liabilities or creation of new liabilities

(iii) Reduction in or sale of Assets

(iv) Non-trading receipts

(b) Cash Outflows

(i) Cash lost in operation

(ii) Decrease in or discharge of liabilities

(iii) Increase in or purchase of assets

(iv) Non-trading payments

In order to prepare cash flow statement the following two methods are used:

(1) Statement Form

(2) Account Form

(1) Statement Form. Under this form cash statement begins with the opening cash and bank balances. The sources of cash are added to it and applications of cash deducted out of it. Proforma of the same is given below :

Cash Flow Statement

		Rs.
Cash balance in the beginning		
Add:	Cash inflows:	
	Cash from operations	
	Issue of share or bonds	
	Sale of fixed assets	
	Raising of Loans or accepting public deposits	
	Refund of Income-tax	
	Dividend received	
Less:	Outflows of Cash	
	Purchase of fixed assets	
	Repayment of Loans	
	Redemption of debentures bonds or preference shares	
	Payment of taxes	
	Payment of dividend	
	Purchase of long term investments	
	Drawings	
	Loss of Cash by embezzlement	
	Cash lost in operations	—

(2) Account Form or 'T' Form. Under this method, opening cash and bank balances are shown on the debit side; sources of cash are debited and applications of cash credited. The account is balanced by putting the closing balance on the credit side. A proforma of this form is given below:

	Rs.		Rs.
Cash Balance in the beginning		*Outflows of Cash:*	
Add: Cash inflows		Purchase of fixed assets	
Cash from operations		Payment of loans	
Issue of Shares		Redemption of debentures	
Issue of Debentures		and preference shares	
Sale of fixed assets		Payment of taxes	
Raising of Loans		Payment of dividends	
Refund of tax		Drawings	
Dividend received		Loss of cash by embezzlement	
		Cash lost in operations	
	——	Cash/bank balance at close	——

The major difference between a fund flow statement and cash flow statement lies in the amount shown as 'resources provided by business operations.' Most of the other items relating to non-current assets and liabilities appear in the cash flow statement with the same figure as they appear in the cash flow statement with the same figure as they appear in the funds flow statement. Therefore, funds from operations are to be adjusted so as to get the figure of cash from operations for preparing a cash flow statement.

CASH FROM OPERATIONS

'Funds From Operations' are based on Accrual Accounting system *i.e.*, sales, whether cash or credit and purchase, whether cash or credit are considered as cash items. Similarly, outstanding expenses are considered as the use of working capital and pre-payments of such expenses as source of working capital. But, under a cash concept of funds we are concerned with the 'cash basis of accounting.' Only cash sales and cash receipts from debtors against credit sales are recongnised as a source of cash. Similarly, cash purchases and cash payments to suppliers for credit purchases are regarded as the use of cash. The same holds true for other expenses and incomes. No consideration is to be given for outstanding and prepaid expenses and incomes.

Cash generated from trading operations will not be equal to the net profit as reported in the profit and loss account. It is so because of certain non-cash items (*e.g.*, depreciation on fixed assets, fictitious assets amortization) and non-operating items (*e.g.* loss or profit on sale of fixed assets, dividend received or paid, amount transferred to general reserve, provision for taxation and so on) changed to the profit and loss account. Non-cash and non-operating items are adjusted to the figure of profit or loss in the same way as these were adjusted for getting the figure of 'funds from operations' as we have already seen somewhere else.

Thus figure of profit is further adjusted for changes in current assets except cash and current liabilities except bank-overdraft to get the amount of 'cash from operations'. The following tables show the procedure for determining 'cash from operations.'

Format of Statement of Changes in Financial Position

		Amount (Rs.)
(A)	Working capital from business operation *i.e.* : funds from operation (as per Funds Flow Statement)	....
(B)	Adjustment to convert to cash basis:	
	Add: Decrease in Current assets and increase in current liabilities (other than cash) 'itemwise'	....
	Less: Increase in Current assets and decrease in current liabilities (other than cash) 'itemwise'	....
(C)	Cash inflow from business operations	....

The same can be restated in the 'formula manner' as below:

Cash from operation = Net profit (*i.e.*, funds from operations) (+) Decrease in current assets and increase in current liabilties

&

(–) Increase in current assets and decrease in current liabilities

Cash is only one of the current assets and is part of net working capital. Therefore, the change in all of the other current assets and in the current liabilities must be analysed in relation to their effect in cash.

It may be remembered that changes in current assets and current liabilities only have been adjusted to the profit to get the figure of cash from operations. Changes in fixed assets and fixed liabilities have not been adjusted as these are shown separately in the cash flow statement. It is so because current assets (*i.e.*, debtors as a result of credit sales, inventories as a result of purchases and sales and prepaid expenses caused by operating expenses) and current liabilties (*i.e.* Creditors because of credit purchase and outstanding expenses caused by non-payment of some of the expenses of the current period) are directly related to operations.

CALCULATION OF OPERATING PROFIT

The figure of net profit shown in the Profit and Loss Account includes items which do not increase or decrease cash. Such items should be adjusted to net profit to determine the net increase in profit from operations. To ascertain profit from operations one should :

(a) take the profit as disclosed by P & L A/c,

(b) add those items that represent mere book entries without any payment or loss of cash.

(c) deduct profit arising out of special transactions such as sale of fixed asset or redemption of liability.

FORMULA FOR CASH FROM OPERATION

Cash from operation can be calculated with help of following formula.

+ Decrease in stock
+ Decrease in debtors
+ Decrease in prepared expenses
+ Decrease in accrued income
+ Increase in debtors
+ Increase in outstanding expenses
+ Increase in income-in-advance

Cash from operation =

Net Operating profit *Or*

– Increase in debtors
– Increase in stock
– Increase in prepaid expenses
– Decrease in creditors
– Decrease in outstanding expenses
– Decrease in income-in-advance

Cash from operation = + Decrease in current Assets

Net Operating Profit – Increase in current liabilities

Or

– Increase in current Assets

– Decrease in current liabilities

Cash from operation may be calculated as follows:

	Rs.
Net profit for the period	....
Add: Non-cash items:	....
(individually be shown)	....

Less:	Net operating incomes		————
	Net operating profit		....
Add:	(Item-wise)	....	....
	Decrease in current Assets		
	(Except cash)		
	Increase in current liabilities	....	....
Less:	(Item-wise)	....	....
	Increase in current assets:		
	(Except cash)		
	Decrease in current liabilities:		
	Cash from operation	....	....

SOME ILLUSTRATIONS

Illustration.

Compute cash from operations from Profit and Loss Account

Profit and Loss Account

(year ending 31st Dec. 1991)

	Rs.		Rs.
To Rent	1,000	By Gross Profit	25,000
To Salaries	5,000	By Profit on sale of land	5,000
To Depreciation	2,000	By Income Tax Refurd	3,000
To Loss on Sale on plant	1,000		
To Goodwill written off	4,000		
To Proposed Dividends	5,000		
To Provision for Taxation	5,000		
To Net Profit	10,000		
	33,000		33,000

Solution.

Computation of Cash from operations
(year ending 31st Dec., 1991)

		Rs.	*Rs.*
Net profit as per P & L Account			10,000
Add:	Non-cash items (which do not result in outflow of cash)		
	Depreciation	2,000	
	Less on sale of plant	1,000	
	Goodwill written off	4,000	
	Proposed dividends	5,000	
	Provision for Tax	5,000	17,000
			27,000
Less:	Non-cash items (which do not result in flow of cash from operations)		
	Profit on sale of land	5,000	
	Refund of Tax	3,000	8,000
	Cash from operations		19,000

Illustration.

Prepare Cash Flow Statement from the following Balance Sheets as on 31st Dec. 1990 and 31st Dec. 1991.

Liabilities	*1990*	*1991*	*Assets*	*1990*	*1991*
Share Capital	1,00,000	1,50,000	Fixed Assets	1,00,000	1,50,000
Profit & Loss A/c	50,000	80,000	Goodwill	50,000	40,000
General Reserve	30,000	40,000	Inventories	50,000	80,000
12% Bonds	50,000	60,000	Debtors	50,000	80,000
Sundry Creditors	30,000	40,000	Bills Receivable	10,000	20,000
Outstanding Exps.	10,000	15,000	Bank	10,000	15,000
	2,70,000	3,85,000		2,70,000	3,85,000

Solution.

Cash Flow Statement
(year ending 31st Dec., 1991)

	Rs.	*Rs.*
Bank Balance as on 1.1.1990		10,000
Add: Sources		
Issue of shares	50,000	
Issue of bonds	10,000	60,000
Total Sources		70,000
Less: Applications	5,000	
Operations	50,000	55,000
Bank Balance as on 1991		15,000

Woking Notes : Adjusted Profit and Loss Account

	Rs.		Rs.
To Goodwill written off	10,000	By Balance c/d	50,000
To General Reserve	10,000	By Funds from operations	50,000
To Balance c/d	80,000		
	1,00,000		1,00,000

Cash From Operations

	Rs.	*Rs.*
Funds from operations		50,000
Add: Increase in creditors		10,000
Increase in outstanding expenses		5,000
		65,000
Less: Increase in inventories	30,000	
Increase in Debtors	30,000	
Increase in B/R	10,000	70,000
Cash outflow from operations		5,000

Illustration.

Following are the comparative balance sheets of M/s Golden Ind. Ltd.

Liabilities	*Dec. 31 1990*	*Dec. 31 1990*	*Assets*	*Dec. 31 1990*	*Dec. 31 1990*
	Rs.	*Rs.*		*Rs.*	*Rs.*
Share Capital	70,000	74,000	Cash	9,000	7,800
Debentures	12,000	6,000	Trade debtors (good)	14,900	17,700
Trade creditors	10,360	11,840	Stock in Trade	49,200	42,700
Provision for doubtful debts	700	800	Land	20,000	30,000
Prof & Loss A/c	10,040	10,560	Goodwill	10,000	5,000
	1,03,100	1,03,200		1,03,100	1,03,200

Additional Information:

(a) Dividends were paid totalling Rs. 3,500.

(b) Land was purchased for Rs. 10,000 and amount provided for the amortization of goodwill Rs. 5,000.

(c) Debentures loan was redeemed Rs. 6,000.

Prepare cash flow statement from the above balance sheet and additional information.

Solution.

Profit & Loss Appropriation A/c

	Rs.		*Rs.*
To provision for doubtful debt (800-700)	100	By Balance b/d	10,040
To Goodwill written off (10,000 – 5,000)	5,000	By Profit during the year (balance figure)	50,000
To Balance B/d	10,560		
	15,660		15,660

Cash From Operations

	Rs.
Profit during the year	5,620
Add: Decrease in stock-in-Trade	6,500
Increase in Trade Creditors	1,480
	13,600
Less: Increase in Book-debts	2,800
Cash from operations	10,800

Cash From Statement

	Rs.	Rs.
Cash balance in the beginning		9,000
Add: Cash from operations		10,800
Shares issued		4,000
		23,800
Less: Debentures repaid	6,000	
Land purchased	10,000	16,000
Cash balance in the end		7,800

Illustration.

Prepare the cash flow from the Balance Sheets of M/s Lucky International Ltd.

Liabilities	*1991* *Rs.*	*1992* *Rs.*	*Assets*	*1991* *Rs.*	*1992* *Rs.*
1			2		
Equity share capital	3,00,000	4,00,000	Goodwill	1,15,000	90,000
10% Redeemable Pref shares	1,50,000	1,00,000	Land & Building	2,00,000	1,70,000
General Reserves	40,000	70,000	Plant	80,000	2,00,000
Profit & Loss A/c	30,000	48,000	Debtors	1,60,000	2,00,000

Contd.

	1			2	
Proposed Dividend	42,000	50,000	Stock	77,000	1,09,000
Creditors	55,000	83,000	Bills Receivable	20,000	30,000
Bills Payable	20,000	16,000	Cash in hand	15,000	10,000
Provision for taxation	40,000	50,000	Cash at bank	10,000	8,000
	6,77,000	8,17,000		6,77,000	8,17,000

Additional Information:

(i) Depreciation of Rs. 10,000 and Rs. 20,000 have been charged on plant account and land and building account respectively in 1992.

(ii) An interim dividend of Rs. 20,000 has been paid in 1992.

(iii) Income tax during the year in 1992 was paid Rs. 35,000.

Solution.

(i) Calculation of profit made during the year:

Adjusted Profit and Loss A/C

	Rs.		Rs.
To Goodwill	25,000	By Balance b/d	30,000
To Depr. plant	10,000	By Profit from operation	2,18,000
To Dep. Bldg.	20,000		
To Proposed dividend	50,000		
To Interim dividend	20,000		
To Provision for tax	45,000		
To General Reserve	30,000		
To Balance B/d	48,000		
	2,48,000		2,48,000

(ii) Calculation of cash from operation:

		Rs.	Rs.
Profit from operations			2,18,000
Add:	Increase in current liabilities	28,000	
	Creditors	Nil	
	Decrease in current assets		28,000
			2,46,000
Less:	Increase in current assets:		
	Debtors	40,000	
	Stock	32,000	
	Bill Receivable	10,000	
Less:	Decrease in current liabilities	4,000	
	Bills payable		86,000
	Cash from operation		1,60,000

Statement of Cash Flow

		Rs.	Rs.
Cash in hand and at bank as on Dec. 31, 1991			
	(Rs. 15,000 + 10,000)		25,000
Add:	Inflow of cash:		
	Cash from operations	1,60,000	
	Sale of land and building	10,000	
	Issue of Shares	1,00,000	2,70,000
	Total cash available for use		2,95,000
Less:	Outflow of cash:		
	Purchase of plant	1,30,000	
	Payment of Final dividend for the last year	42,000	
	Payment of interim dividend	20,000	
	Payment of tax	35,000	
	Redemption of Pref. shares	50,000	2,77,000
	Cash in hand and bank as on Dec. 1992		18,000

Illustration.

From the following information you are required to calculate Cash From Operation (CFO):

	31st March	
	1995	*1996*
	Rs.	*Rs.*
Debtors	50,000	47,000
Bills Receivable	10,000	12,500
Creditors	20,000	25,000
Bills Payable	8,000	6,000
Outstanding expenses	1,000	1,200
Prepaid expenses	800	700
Accrued Income	600	750
Income Received in advance	300	250
Profit made during the year	—	1,30,000

Solution.

Cash From Operation

		Rs.	Rs.
Profit made during the year			1,30,000
Add:	Decrease in Debtors	3,000	
	Increase in Creditors	5,000	
	Increase in Outstanding Expenses	200	
	Decrease in Prepaid Expenses	100	8,300
			1,38,300
Less:	Increase in Bills Receivable	2,500	
	Increase in Accrued Income	150	
	Decrease in Bills Payable	2,000	
	Decrease in Income received in advance	50	4,700
	CFO		1,33,600

Illustration.

The following information is in respect of M/s S.K.Y. Ltd. as on 1st Jan. 1996.

	Rs.
Fixed Assets	6,00,000
Less: Depreciation	2,10,000
	3,90,000
Bank balance	35,000
Current Assets other than Bank balance	2,50,000
Share Capital (Rs. 100 each)	3,00,000
Current Liabilities	1,00,000

The Company made the following estimate for 1996—

(a) The profit would be Rs. 55,000 after depreciation of Rs. 60,000.

(b) The company will acquire fixed assets costing Rs. 10,00,000 after selling one machine for Rs. 20,000 costing Rs. 50,000 and one on which depreciation provided amounted to Rs. 35,000.

(c) Current assets and current liabilities other than bank balance at the end of 1996 are expected to be Rs. 2,95,000 and Rs. 1,30,000 respectively.

(d) The Company will pay free of tax dividend of 10%, the rate of tax being 25%.

Ascertain the Bank balance (overdraft of SKY Ltd. at the end of 1996).

Solution.

Cash Flow Statement

Source of Cash	*Rs.*	*Application of Cash*	*Rs.*
Opening Cash Balance (1.1.96)	35,000	Purchase of Fixed Assets	1,00,000
Cash from Operation	95,000	Closing balance of Cash on	
Sale of Machinery	20,000	(31.12.96)	50,000
	1,50,000		1,50,000

Working Notes—

Cash From Operation

		Rs.	Rs.
Profit for the year			55,000
Add:	Depreciation	60,000	
	Increase in Current Liabilities	30,000	90,000
			1,45,000
Less:	Profit on sale of machinery	5,000	
	Increase in Current Assets	45,000	50,000
	Cash from Operation		95,000

Illustration.

The Statement of the Financial Position of M/s A.K.Y. Brothers for the year 1996 is given below. Prepare the firm's Cash Flow Statement.

Liabilities	1-1-96	31-12-96	Assets	1-1-96	31-12-96
	Rs.	Rs.		Rs.	Rs.
Capital	14,78,000	12,30,000	Buildings and Other		
Bills Payable	58,000	50,000	Fixed Assets	2,00,000	1,60,000
			Cash	12,00,000	10,00,000
			Debtors	40,000	34,000
			Stock	16,000	26,000
	15,36,000	12,80,000		14,56,000	12,80,000

The additional information for the firm is:

(i) There was no drawing.

(ii) There were no purchases or sales of either building or other fixed assets.

Solution.

Statement of Cash Flow

(for the year ended 31st December, 1996)

Sources of Cash	Amount Rs.	Application of Cash	Amount Rs.
Opening Cash Balance	80,000	Loss from Trading Operation	8,000
Add: Cash in flow		Addition of Stock	10,000
Decrease in Debtors	6,000	Decrease in Bills Payable	8,000
Sale of Machinery		Closing balance of Cash	60,000
	86,000		86,000

Working Notes—

1. Net loss for the year 1996

	Rs.
Capital at the end	12,30,000
Capital at the beginning	14,78,000
	2,48,000

2. Cash lost in Operation/Trading loss from Operation

	Rs.	Rs.
Net loss for 1996		2,48,000
Less: Non-Cash Charges		
(i) Depreciation on Building (2,00,000 – 1,60,000)	40,000	
(ii) Depreciation on Other Fixed Assets (12,00,000 – 10,00,000)	2,00,000	2,40,000
		8,000

Illustration.

The following are two balance sheets relating to the years 1992 and 1993 and Profit and Loss Appropriation Account for 1993 of M/s Golden Jaipur Ltd. Prepare the Cash Flow Statement for the year ended 31st Dec. 1993.

Balance Sheet of Golden Jaipur as on 31st March

Liabilities	*1992*	*1993*	*Assets*	*1992*	*1993*
	Rs.	*Rs.*		*Rs.*	*Rs.*
Share capital	5,00,000	6,00,000	Fixed Assets	10,00,000	11,20,000
Reserves	1,50,000	1,80,000	Less dep.	3,70,000	4,60,000
Profit & Loss A/c	40,000	65,000	Written off	6,30,000	6,60,000
Debentures	3,00,000	2,50,000	Stock in trade	2,40,000	3,70,000
Creditors for goods	1,70,000	1,60,000	Book Debts	2,50,000	3,30,000
Provision for Income-tax	60,000	80,000	Cash in hand and at bank	80,000	60,000
			Preliminary Exp.	20,000	15,000
	12,20,000	13,35,000		12,20,000	13,35,000

Profit & Loss Appropriation Account

	Rs.		Rs.
To Transfer to Reserves	30,000	By Balance b/d	40,000
To Dividend paid	80,000	By Net profit	1,35,000
To Balance c/d	65,000		
	1,75,000		1,75,000

Solution.

(i) Calculation of profit from operations:

	Rs.
Result of Trading operations	1,35,000
Add: Non cash changes:	
Depreciation written off during the year	90,000
Preliminary Expenses written off	5,000
Provision of tax	80,000
Profit from operations	3,10,000

(ii) Calculation of cash from opoerations:

	Rs.	Rs.
Profit from operations		3,10,000
Add: Decrease in current Assets:		
Sundry debtors		20,000
		3,30,000
Less: Decrease in current liabilities:		
Sundry creditors	10,000	
Less: Increase in current Assets:		
Stock-in-trade	1,30,000	1,40,000
Cash from Operation		1,90,000

Statement of Cash Flow

	Rs.	Rs.
Cash Balance, March 31, 1991		80,000
Add: Inflow of cash:		
Cash from operations	1,90,000	
Issue of shares	1,00,000	2,90,000
Total cash available for use		3,70,000
Less: Outflows of cash:		
Repayment of Debentures	50,000	
Fixed Assets acquired	1,20,000	
Dividend paid	80,000	
Income Tax paid	60,000	3,10,000
Cash Balance, March 31, 1993		60,000

Illustration.

The following are the Balance Sheets of M/s Usha Fibers Private Ltd. as on March 31, 1993 and 1994. Prepare a statement of cash flow.

Liabilities	*1993*	*1994*	*Assets*	*1993*	*1994*
	Rs.	*Rs.*		*Rs.*	*Rs.*
12% Redeemable preference shares	—	1,000	Fixed Assets	4,100	4,000
Equity shares	4,000	4,000	*Less:* Depreciation	1,100	1,500
General Reserve	200	200		3,000	2,500
P & L A/c	100	120	Debtors	2,000	2,400
Debentures	600	700	Stock	3,000	3,500
Creditors	1,200	1,100	Prepaid Expenses	30	50
Provision for Taxation	300	420	Cash	120	350
Proposed Dividend	500	580			
Bank overdraft	1,250	680			
	8,150	8,800		8,150	8,800

Solution.

Cash Flow Statement
(year ending 31st March, 1994)

		Rs.	*Rs.*	*Rs.*
Opening Balance as on 1/1/1993			120	
Bank ovderdraft			(–) 1,250	(–) 1,130
Add:	Sources of Cash			
	Issue of Preference Shares			1,000
	Issue of Debentures			100
	Sale of Fixed Assets			100
	Cash from operations:			
Less:	Increase in Debtors	400	1,420	
	Increase in Stock	500		
	Increase in pre-paid expenses	20		

	Decrease in creditors	100	1,020	400
				470
Less:	Applications			
	Payments of tax	300		
	Payment of dividend	500		(–) 800
	Cash Balance			(–) 330
	Represented by:			
	Cash in Hand	350		
	Bank overdraft	(–) 680		(–) 330

Working Notes:

Dr. Adjusted P & L Account Cr.

	Rs.		Rs.
To Depreciation	400	By Balance b/d	100
To Proposed dividend	580	By Funds from operations	1,420
To Provision for Tax	420	(Balance Figure)	
To Balance c/d	120		
	1,5,200		1,5,200

Illustration.

From the following information you are required to prepare a cash flow statement of J.P. Cement Ltd. for the year ended 31st Dec. 1993:

Balance Sheet

Liabilities	*1992*	*1993*	*Assets*	*1992*	*1993*
	Rs.	*Rs.*		*Rs.*	*Rs.*
1			*2*		
Share Capital	70,000	70,000	Plant & Mach.	50,000	91,000
Secured loans	—	40,000	Inventory	15,000	40,000
(Repayable in 1997)					

Contd.

	1			2	
Creditors	14,000	39,000	Debtors	5,000	20,000
Tax payable	1,000	3,000	Cash	20,000	7,000
P & L A/c	7,000	10,000	Prepaid Gen. Exps.	2,000	4,000
	92,000	1,62,000		92,000	1,62,000

Profit and Loss Account

(year ended 31st Dec. 1993)

	Rs.		*Rs.*
To opening Inventory	15,000	By closing inventory	40,000
To purchases	98,000	By Sales	1,00,000
To Gross profit c/d	27,000		
	1,40,000		1,40,000
To General Expenses	11,000	By Gross Profit b/d	27,000
To Depreciation	8,000		
To Taxes	4,000		
To Net profit c/d	4,000		
	27,000		27,000
To Dividend	1,000	By Balance b/d	7,000
To Balance c/d	10,000	By Net profit b/d	
	11,000		11,000

Solution.

Cash Flow Statement

	Rs.	*Rs.*
Cash Balance as on 1.1.1993		20,000
Add: Sources		
Raising of loans		40,000
Less: Applications:		
Plant & Machinery purchased	49,000	

Dividend paid	1,000	
Operations	1,000	
Tax paid	2,000	53,000
Cash Balance as on 31.12.1993		7,000

Working Notes:

(1) Cash From Operations

	Rs.	*Rs.*
Net profit as per P & L A/c		4,000
Add: Provision for Tax		4,000
Increase in creditors		25,000
Depreciation		8,000
		41,000
Less: Increase in inventory	25,000	
Increase in Debtors	15,000	
Increase in Prepaid Expenses	2,000	42,000
Cash outflow on account of operation		1,000

(2) Tax Payable Account

	Rs.		*Rs.*
To Bank	2,000	By Balance b/d	1,000
To Balance c/d	3,000	By P & L Account	4,000
	5,000		5,000

(3) Plant & Machinery Account

	Rs.		*Rs.*
To Balance b/d	50,000	By Depreciation	8,000
To Balance (Purchase)	3,000	By Balance c/d	91,000
	99,000		99,000

Illustration.

Following are the comparative balance sheets of M/s Gopal Ram Co. Ltd. on 31st Dec.

Liabilities	*1994*	*1995*	*Assets*	*1994*	*1995*
	Rs.	*Rs.*		*Rs.*	*Rs.*
Share Capital	10,00,000	11,00,000	Goodwill	50,000	40,000
Debentures	5,00,000	3,00,000	Land & Building	4,20,000	6,60,000
General Reserves	2,00,000	2,00,000	Plant & Machinery	6,00,000	8,00,000
Profit & Loss A/c	1,10,000	1,90,000	Closing Stock	2,50,000	2,10,000
Trade creditors	50,000	49,000	Debtors	3,00,000	2,40,000
Bills Payable	20,000	30,000	Cash	3,00,000	24,000
Provisions for b/d	30,000	24,000	Preliminary Exps.	30,000	20,000
	19,50,000	19,94,000		19,50,000	19,94,000

Additional Information:

(a) During the year, a part of machinery costing Rs. 7,500 (accumulated depreciation thereon being Rs. 2,500) was sold for Rs. 3,000.

(b) Dividend of Rs. 1,00,000 was paid during the year ended 31st Dec. 1995.

(c) Income-tax Rs. 50,000 was paid during the year 1995.

(d) Depreciation for year 1995 was provided as follows:

Land and Building	Rs. 10,000
Plant & Machinery	Rs. 50,000

You have to prepare

(i) Schedule of changes in working capital,

(ii) Fund Flow Statement,

(iii) Cash Flow Statement.

Solution.

Schedule of Change in working capital

	1994	*1995*	*Increase*	*Decrease*
		in w.c.	*in w.c.*	
	Rs.	*Rs.*	*Rs.*	*Rs.*
Current Assets				
Debtors	3,00,000	2,40,000		60,000
Stock	2,50,000	2,10,000		40,000
Cash	3,00,000	24,000		2,76,000
Current Liabilities				
Trade creditors	50,000	40,000	10,000	
Bills payable	20,000	30,000		10,000
Prov. for Bad Debts	30,000	24,000	6,000	
			16,000	3,86,000
Decrease in W.C.			3,70,000	
			3,86,000	3,86,000

Profit & Loss A/c (Adjusted)

		Rs.		Rs.
To Loss on sale on machine		2,000	By Balance b/d	1,10,000
To Preliminary Expenses written off		3,000	By Profit during the year (Funds from operation)	3,82,000
To Goodwill written off		10,000		
To Dividends		1,00,000		
To Provision for tax*		1,20,000		
To Depreciation				
Land & Building	10,000			
Plant & Machinery	50,000	60,000		
To Balance c/d		1,90,000		
		4,92,000		4,92,000

Provision for Taxation A/c*

	Rs.		*Rs.*
To Tax paid	50,000	By Balance b/d	40,000
To Balance c/d	3,000	By P & L A/c	1,20,000
		(Balance of figure)	
	1,60,000		1,60,000

Plant & Machinery A/c

	Rs.		*Rs.*
To Balance b/d	6,00,000	By Cash A/c	3,000
To Cash A/c (Purchases	2,55,000	By P & L A/c	2,000
during the year)		By Depreciation A/c	50,000
		By Balance c/d	8,00,000
	8,55,000		8,55,000

Land & Building A/c

	Rs.		*Rs.*
To Balance b/d	4,20,000	By Depreciation A/c	10,000
To Cash A/c	2,50,000	By Balance A/c	6,60,000
(Purchases during the year)			
	6,70,000		6,70,000

Goodwill A/c

	Rs.		*Rs.*
To Balance b/d	50,000	By P & L A/c	10,000
		(Balancing figure)	
		By Balance c/d	40,000
	50,000		50,000

Fund Flow Statement

(Year ended 1st December, 1995)

Sources	*Rs.*	*Uses*	*Rs.*
Issue of Shares	1,00,000	Redemption of Debenture	2,00,000
Sale of Machinery	3,000	Income tax paid	50,000
Funds from operation	3,82,000	Dividend paid	1,00,000
Decrease in working capital	3,70,000	Purchase of Land & Building	2,50,000
		Purchase of Machines	2,55,000
	8,55,000		8,55,000

(c) For Cash Flow Statement, first calculate cash from operations.

Cash from Operations

	Rs.	*Rs.*
Profit during the year		3,82,000
Add: Decrease in current Assets & increase in current Liabilities:		
Closing stock	40,000	
Debtors	60,000	
Bills Payable	10,000	1,10,000
		4,92,000
Less: Increase in current Assets & decrease in current liabilities		
Provision for Bad Debts	6,000	
Trade Creditors	10,000	16,000
Cash from operations		4,76,000

Cash Flow Statement

	Rs.		Rs.
Cash Balance on 31.12.94	3,00,000	Payment of dividends	1,00,000
Add: Cash from operations	4,76,000	Payment of tax	50,000
Issue of shares	1,00,000	Repayment of Debentures	2,00,000
Sale of Machinery	3,000	Purchase of Land & Building	2,50,000
		Purcahse of Plant of Mach.	2,55,000
			8,55,000
		Closing balance on 31.12.95	24,000
	8,79,000		8,79,000

Illustration.

Balance sheets of M/c A and B as on 1st January, 1991 and on 31st December, 1991 are as follows:

Liabilities	*1.1.91*	*31.12.91*	*Assets*	*1.1.91*	*31.12.91*
	Rs.	*Rs.*		*Rs.*	*Rs.*
Capital	1,50,000	1,90,000	Cash	20,000	26,000
MRs B's Loan	30,000	—	Debtors	54,000	76,000
Loan from SBI	60,000	80,000	Stock	48,000	42,000
Sundry Creditors	50,000	56,000	Furniture	2,000	2,000
			Machinery	90,000	65,000
			Land	36,000	45,000
			Building	40,000	70,000
	2,90,000	3,26,000		2,90,000	3,26,000

During the year a machine costing Rs. 12,00 (accumulated depreciation Rs. 4000) was sold for Rs. 5,500. The provision of depreciation against machinery as on 1st Jan. 1991 was Rs. 24,000 and on 31st Dec. 1991 Rs. 37,000. Net profit for the year 1991 amonuted to Rs. 60,000. You are required to prepare:

(i) Cash Flow Statement

(ii) Funds Flow Statements

Solution.

(a) Cash Flow Statement

(year ended 31st Dec. 1991)

	Rs.		*Rs.*
Opening Balance of Cash on 1.1.1991	20,000	Outflow of Cash:	
		Repayment of Mrs. B's loan	30,000
Sources of Cash in flow:			
Loan from SBI	20,000	Increase in Debtors	22,000
Increase in Sundry Creditors	6,000	Purchase of Land	9,000
Decrease in Stock	6,000	Purchase of building	30,000
Sale of machine	5,000	Drawings	20,000
Operating profit (including cash items)	79,500	Cash Balance 31.12.1991	26,000
	1,37,000		1,37,000

Workings Notes:

	Rs.
Operating Profit (including non-fund/cash items)	
Net profit for the year (as given)	60,000
Add: Non fund/Cash & non-operating items:	
Depreciation on machinery	17,000
Loss on sale of machinery	2,500
	79,500

Deprecation on Machinery

Accumulated depreciation on 1.1.1991	24,000

Less: Depreciation on machinery	4,000
Sold during year	20,000
Accumulated depreciation at the end *i.e.* 31.12.1991	37,000
Depreciation provided during the year	17,000

Drawings:

Capital on 1.1.1991	1,50,000
Add: Profit for the year	60,000
	2,10,000
Less: Capital at the end of the year 31.12.1991	1,90,000
Drawings	20,000

(b) Schedule of Change in Working Capital

	1.1.91 *Rs.*	*31.12.91* *Rs.*	*Increase in work cap.* *Rs.*	*Decrease in work cap.* *Rs.*
Current Assets				
Cash	20,000	24,000	6,000	—
Debtors	54,000	76,000	22,000	—
Stock	48,00	42,000	—	6,000
	1,24,00	1,44,00		
Current Liabilities				
Sundry creditors	50,000	56,000		6,000
	50,000	56,000		
Working Capital	72,000	88,000		
Net increase in working capital	16,000			
	88,000	80,000	28,000	28,000

Fund Flow Statement

Sources	*Amount Rs.*	*Application*	*Amount Rs.*
Loan from SBI	20,000	Repayment of Mrs. B's loan	30,000
Sale of machine	5,500	Purchase of land	9,000
Funds from operation	79,500	Puchase of Building	30,000
		Drawings	21,000
		Net increase in W.C.	16,000
	1,05,000		1,05,000

□

7

Concept of Management Accounting

In order to understand this, it is appropriate to analyse a more traditional but commonly accepted definition of accounting given in the *Accounting Terminology Bulletin No.1 of the American Institute of Certified Public Accountants, viz*:

"Accounting is the art of recording, classifying and summarising in a significant manner and in terms of money, transactions and events, which are in part at least, of a financial changes and interpreting the results thereof."

Explanation

(A) Transactions. Recordable happenings or events (usually exchanges) that affect the assets, liabilities, capital, revenues or expenses of an entity.

(B) Event. A process or a part of a process having a particular moment and place of occurrence. A typical event is a transaction with an outsider.

Thus the accounting must be viewed in its fundamental processes of recording classifying and reporting the transactions and interpreting the financial data, thereof. It aims at revealing the financial conditions of an organisation and financial changes which take place in it from time to time. Following basic features of are accounting function may be explained as under:

1. Recording. It means that the transactions of financial character must be written down reasonably soon after occurrence in the books of the organisation *e.g.*, cash book, sales and purchase books, journals, and so on, so that a complete record is available about different phases of business activities of the organisation. In addition, it must also be made certain that all of financial transactions are recorded in an orderly manner that is under appropriate account titles. Such records would be of great assistance for presentation and interpretation of business results, that is, the extent to which the business is successful or whether its finances are in good order. Timely and orderly recording of transactions makes it possible to obtain whatever information which is necessary.

2. Summarising. The art of summarising in a significant manner involves the preparation of statements such as income statement, balance sheet and other reports from the classified data in a manner useful to the internal management and external users of accounting information. In this way all important and material accounting information is disclosed.

3. Classifying. It is concerned with the systematic analysis of the recorded data so that the items of same type or like nature are grouped under appropriate accounts. This accounting classification is accomplished in an orderly fashion by maintaining ledgers with individual account heads under which all financial transactions of similar nature are collected. For example, all transactions relating to cash/bank would be recorded in the cash book while the credit purchases and sales in the purchases and sales books respectively and so on.

4. Interpreting. Finally, the accountants are required to interpret the contents of their statements and reports in a manner beneficial to the users and enable them to make meaningful judgements about the operational efficiency or and financial position of the business enterprises. "The emergence of mechanised and electronic data processing devices has freed accountants from the routine aspects of recording and classifying data, enabling them to concentrate more on the analytical and interpretation aspects of the accounting function. These are the areas most affected by the new demands for accounting function."

Interpretation may involve explanation of the uses, meaning and limitations of 'accounting information. The past figures are important for future guidance. "Consequently the accountant must be able to .explain not only what did happen but also why it happened and most important what is likely to happen under certain conditions in future". He must be able to interpret correctly the meaning of data recorded so as to use the same for future projections. Comparison of past and present statements and reports, use of ratio analysis and long term trends are the important tools for this purpose. His very largely the ability to weave a living, dynamic pattern from a mass of inert figures that makes the accountant worth his salt.

NATURE OF ACCOUNTING

The definition of accounting includes such important phrases as: "in a significant manner" and "transactions and events". These phrases raise important questions like 'significant for whom?' and what son of transactions and events?' Though the definition clarifies that the recording is carried out in terms of money, a layman can hardly appreciate the nature and scope of accounting in this manner. While accounting is many things to many people, its nature is essentially described as follows:

1. **An Intellectual Discipline.** The commonly recognised fields of specialised study are philosophy, physics, chemistry, mathematics, political science, economics and biology, space research etc. These are often called intellectual disciplines or simply disciplines. Most people agree that accounting is a separate discipline. It is in a way a dynamic discipline in which new procedures and principles are constantly evolving. Other disciplines are also concerned with measurements and information. Thus the boundaries of accounting merge readily and significantly with the boundaries of economics, engineering, psychology, law, statistics etc. When accounting is related to and combined with other disciplines, it tends to be more useful than when it stands alone. The many practical uses to which accounting knowledge can be put serve as a 'primary attraction to the field.

2. **A Social Force.** A third pan of accounting is its thrust as a social force. The expansion of large scale modern business

or public organisations would have been impossible without an adequate financial information system. The separation of ownership and management, a characteristic feature of corporate form of business organisation, is feasible only if reliable periodic financial upon are supplied by professional managers to the owners. In a sense, accounting facilitates ownership by remote control. Accounting information is also helpful in the fields of price determination of products monopoly and restrictive trade practices legislation, the regulation of stock markets, the fixation of rates in public utilities and lot of other similar issues. Accounting information directly influences decisions in these areas. This influence arises from the way in which the accounting records the transactions, classifies and summarises them and later reports to various interested users.

3. **A Profession.** Although modem accounting dates back to 1494 when an Italian monk named Fr. Luca Paciolo described a double-entry accounting procedure that forms the basis for accounting practice today, the development of accounting as a profession is relatively new. It was stimulated primarily by new forms of economic activity resulting from industrial revolution. The development of the corporation form of business organisation, the product of industrial revolution, also created a new social need—the need for an independent audit to provide some assurance that management's financial representations were reliable. In fact this audit function, often referred to as the "attest function" was chiefly responsible for the development of accounting as a profession. Other functions are management consultants and tax services. Professional accountants are recognised by different names in different countries of the world *e.g.* Chartered Accountants in India, Certified Public Accountants in U.S.A. The phenomenal growth in commerce education and rapid increase in the number of chartered accountants, cost and works accountants etc.,

provide an adequate evidence for the growth of accounting as a profession.

4. **A Tool of Social Welfare.** The nature of accounting should not be analysed in a way that it is confined only to private use of information which has limited scope and which is concerned with the effect of accounting information on the welfare of individuals as such. The social welfare concept of accounting is related to the impact of information on all the individuals making the society. As we shall discuss later that accounting information is used by a number of groups having vested interest in the activities of the business enterprise *e.g.*, managers, owners, creditors, employees etc. It is clear that the supply of information to one group may give them unfair advantage over the other groups in the decisions which they subsequently make, resulting in the changes in the allocation of social benefits. "The social welfare theory of accounting requires that the interests of employees, trade unions and consumers ought to be taken into account and the traditional imbalance existing in the supply of information should be corrected.

OBJECTIVES OF ACCOUNTING

1. Resource Allocation Decisions And Accounting Information. One of the central economic problems of every economy is the allocation of limited resources among competing alternative uses. Considering it at the micro level, this problem affects the decisions of business entities, individuals and even the Government. The primary purpose of any business activity is to earn profit. Due to scarcity of almost every type of resources, the business entities must decide whether to invest in stock of goods (or raw materials) plant and machinery, advertising, research and development or other alternatives. Managers of these entities are responsible for obtaining maximum advantage from the use of resources placed at their disposal. Thus they need accounting it formation to help them make decisions regarding the use of firm's limited resources. For example, a business enterprise engaged in the production of more than one kind of product must be aware of the cost of producing each type of product. The financial information would enable the management to decide whether or not certain products should be continued or whether certain products should be manufactured in greater quantities. Management can also determine from financial information when certain machinery is to be replaced; whether additional labour force be employed or some employees should be dismissed. In addition to business firms, individuals and non-profit entities tend to use accounting information for decisions concerning the investment of their limited funds. An investor attempts to analyse the accounting information to determine which company best meets his investment goals. The utilisation of financial information in allocation of limited funds from the point of various segments of society may be explained as under:

(i) A supplier of goods will decide whether or not to sell goods on credit and will determine the total amount of credit that should be provided?

(ii) The grantors of loans such as banks or specialised financial institutions will decide whether or not loans should be advanced for the existing or future projects.

(iii) An owner will decide whether or not he should continue or increase his investments in the company.

(iv) Labour unions are assisted in negotiating working conditions and wage agreements.

(v) A prospective investor will make a decision between different investment opportunities.

Even the Governments use accounting information to decide whether the resources should be allocated to defence, construction of infrastructure, welfare programmes, space research, etc.

2. Accounting As The Basis of Decision-Making. Accounting is a service activity. It's purpose is to provide quantitative Information about economic entities. The information is primarily financial in nature and is intended to be useful in making economic decisions in making reasoned choices among alternative courses of actions. In fact the accounting information is used as an input to the decision-making process. Decision-making is a unique human capability. One of the main distinctions between the human being and other forms of animal life is the ability to make conscious decisions. If the entity for which the accounting information is provided is a business, the information is used by its management to make decisions some of which are listed below:

3. Identification of Economic Information. There is a wide variety of information which may be collected and used in the decision making process. Accounting, is one source of information for decisions. The ascertainment of information which is to be included in accounting relies on the criteria of relevance and quantifiability. This is the basic characteristic of the accounting information since if information is not relevant it is useless. To be relevant to a decision, the information must be available on a sufficiently timely basis to influence the decision. The accountant is faced with the problem of selecting from the mass of data those things which are most likely to meet the needs of different goals. For example, the information required by bankers or some security analysisists is not necessarily the same as required by small investors or internal managements. The accountant must analyse the needs of various users (known and unknown) and determine which information is common and relevant to all existing and potential decision-makers.

4. The Accounting Process. One of the most important tasks of modem accounting is, therefore, to assist different users in making decisions outlined above. In order to adequately serve this task accounting is concerned with the processes of:

(A) identifying;

(B) measuring; and

(C) communicating useful economic information to permit informed Judgments and decisions by users of the information.

The accounting processes of identification, measurement and communication involve financial transactions about business entities the primary motive of which is to earn profits. As noted earlier, resources are assumed to be limited; therefore choices must be made.

5. An Aid in Resource Management. To a man in the street, the accounting is a study of commercial or profit-making activities. Even an ordinary individual with some academic background relates the role of accountant to prepare the tax-returns or as an adviser on the financial to of business or investments. But these misconceptions about the role of accounting can be cleared to a great extent when we find in practice that individuals, both in private business and in public bodies, engage in transactions which may be recorded classified and summarised yet which may have no profit motive. The point is that the accountant may serve any social unit, large or small, private or public, profit seeking or not. He serves it by recording the resources at its disposal, who owns these resources and any change which occurs in the amounts held. The accountancy has constantly changed to meet the different requirements of society.

FINANCIAL ACCOUNTING PROCEDURE

Financial Accounting is the traditional form of accounting which is mainly concerned with the recording of business transactions. Under the system of accounting, business transactions are first recorded in the books of original entry then classified into ledger and finally summarized by preparing trial balance. From trial balance the profit and loss a/c is prepared to ascertain the periodic profit or loss. The profit and loss a/c or Income statement shows the operating results of the business done during the accounting period. The B/S is prepared which is, as a matter of fact, position, statement of the business. It shows the financial position of the business as at the end of the accounting period. This whole system of financial accounting is of historic nature. It is static in character. During the initial stages of business development, the financial accounting has served the business world very well but with the growing complex business organisations the limitations of financial accounting have become obvious. Though, nobody can deny with the utility of the two basic financial statements - income statement and position statement, but there are certain important limitations and deficiencies too in this system. In shdrt, financial statements of system of financial accounting suffers from the following deficiencies:

1. **Financial Accounts are of Historic Nature.** Financial accounts are of historic nature. They record the net effect of events which take place in the business, *i.e.* expenses are recorded when they have actually been spent. Such recording of past facts does not help the management in planning for future and decision-making. Profit and loss a/c shows the amount of profit or loss earned during the last accounting period but it cannot analyse the causes for low profits. It cannot suggest anything to increase the profits in future. This work is "done by management accounting. Management accounting analyses the past records and presents the relevant facts in a suitable manner before the management so he may take decision for the future.
2. **Incomplete Knowledge of Costs.** From the costing point of view also the financial accounts are incomplete. In trading and profit and loss a/c all expenses are debited to one account only. The existence of profits in a particular period is taken as an index of efficiency of business under financial system of accounting. But product wise or job wise cost of production can not be determined on their basis. Information regarding wastages and losses is very difficult to get from financial accounts. Prices cannot be fixed on the basis of information given by these accounts because they deal with total expenditure arid not with expenditure incurred on even product or unit of service. These accounts cannot indicate the exact remunerative price which may be quoted in periods of difficulties.

These all deficiencies of financial accounts have been over-come by management accounting as it makes intensive use of most accounting. Cost accounting records the costs product, process or job wise as necessary. It can throw a good deal of light on unnecessary losses and wastage. A good system of cost Accounting affects an independent and most reliable check on the accuracy of final accounts too.

3. **No help in Decision Making.** Financial accounts do not help in decision making also. Due to the historic nature of accounting data available from financial accounts is not of much help to the management. Management accounting presents this data in a suitable form and useful manner and helps the management in selecting a profitable alternative on the basis of that information. Management accounting is very dynamic and forward looking in this respect.

4. **Financial Accounting is a Technical Subject.** It is also a serious limitation of financial accounting that it is highly technical in nature. People possessing adequate knowledge of accounting concepts and principles, well conversant in the practice of accountancy can prepare and interpret the financial accounts. Management accounting is not technical. It presents the accounting information in a simple, easy, non-technical and intelligible manner. It does not follow any set format for the presentation of data. Various statements in management accounting are prepared according to the needs of the business and its management. Any educated man can understand them easily.

5. **Recording of Actual Cost.** In financial accounts assets and properties are shown at their cost acquisition. No effect of changes in their value is recorded in the books after their acquisitic data. Generally, assets are shown at going concern value which has nothing to do with the realisable value or replacement value of the assets. This limitation of financial accounts reduces their utility. This financial accounts report about the profitability of the assets as a whole.

6. **No Evaluation of Business Policies and Plans.** Financial accounts do not provide for evaluation of business policies and plans. They do not throw any light on the implementation of programmes and policies of the Management. They do not make any study of variances in the performance and possible reasons for it. On the other hand, Management Accounting does not help only in me formulation of the policies; it is intimately concerned with their implementation also. Budgetary control system is a unique device to carry on the programmes in the desired direction.

7. **Financial Accounts do not Provide for Cost Control.** Cost can not be controlled through financial accounting. Its main reasons are as follows:
   (i) Here expenses are recorded after when they have actually been spent. Hence they provided no change to take corrective action.
   (ii) Financial accounts do not have any technique to check the reasonableness of any expenditure.
   (iii) Financial accounts do not fix definite responsibility on any authority for wastage or excessive expenditure.

Management accounting makes intensive use of standard costing, marginal costing, cost-volume-profit analysis, etc. Responsibility accounting is also an important aspect of management accounting. The various tools and techniques of management accounting help the management in exercising effective control on the cost and revenues.

Thus, we see that Financial Accounting serves only general purpose. In spite of the accounting devices, improved techniques and elaborate subsidiary records, financial accounting is of limited use to the management due to the above said obvious limitations of them. The Management Accounting which has -grown out of traditional accounting, is the most dynamic aspect of accounting. The main purpose and function of management accounting is to help management in planning and controlling the operation of a business. It is a service function. It aids management in doing better management. But, however, Financial Accounting and Management Accounting are not conflicting. The both are complementary and co-operative in character. The advent of management accounting has added strength and vitality to thc main stream of accounting.

MEANING OF MANAGEMENT ACCOUNTING

Till recently accountant's role was as one of book-keepers and his duties ended with the, balancing of accounts for a given period. The growing complexities of the business and the awareness that the figures can unfold the behaviour of production and distribution have enhanced the demand for accountant's work. The characteristic feature of modem business is the tendency to large size. The gulf between management and ownership has widened, thus raising the problem of 'control'. Moreover, the stiff competition has necessitated the need to raise productivity and shorn off wastes. Such problems cannot be solved through the there procedural financial accounting. Truly speaking, the resultant effects of World War I, the great' depression of thirties and subsequent World War II attacked the thoughts of businessmen to devise the ways and means by which efficiency, that is, productivity, could be stepped up and control achieved with the aid of organisational methods. Management became conscious of the accountants contribution and the term Movement accounting began to acquire universal status.

Management accounting has been defined by the Anglo-American Council on Productivity as "the presentation of accounting information in such a way as to assist the management in the creation of policy and operation of day-to-day undertaking". It is, therefore, the provision, analysis, reporting and discussion of accounting information as a guidc to management in the day-to-day running and future planning of the business, as distinguished from the recording part of the accounting function for historical and statutory purposes. The accountant does not furnish only routine figures to the management but renders a well-designed service and advice and management can work on the principle of reporting by exception whereby only items calling for special attention are brought to the notice of senior management and not a multitude routine.

There is a general misconception that the management accounting is something new and complex and requires an expensive system capable of comprehension only by experts. This contention is not true. A reference to the accounting literature would reveal that even in the past, the accountant went beyond figure work and discussed with his management the implications of events and trends in broad financial terms and that is what the management accounting does. It is the role of the accountant as an adviser or helper, instead of the "accountant" who feels his task done when the results are ready. The accountant is a partner in the management team though this feeling has been realised now because the accountant is a **'Johny come lately'** to the team management accounting system works on simple lines in that management must be provided with the relevant figures in a 'well presented' manner. It is not always necessary to seek the assistance of expensive electronic data though the utility of the same cannot be discounted. Even if the amount spent is considerable the benefits derived in the long run would outweigh the costs.

In nutshell, management accounting serves the information requirement of the insiders-directors, managers and employees. When it issues reports, it need not adhere to specified accounting principles. The number, frequency and content of reports can be determined at the discretion of management.

FUNCTIONS OF MANAGEMENT ACCOUNTING

An efficient management strives to raise productivity by utilising the available resources. Management, therefore, has to make important decisions from time to time. Management accounting plays an important role in this connection. Accounting is opinion expressed in numbers and since decisions are based on opinions, accounting is one of the most useful tools for decision-making. With sound data to base its decisions, management can operate more efficiently, more economically and more profitably. Managerial function of planning, co-ordinating and control etc. are assisted by facts, figures and their interpretation provided by originating and control etc. are assisted by facts, figures and their interpretation provided by management accounting. The following is the description of managerial functions:

(A) Planning. Management has to plan the activities well in advance to cope with the prevailing dynamic conditions. Planning offsets uncertainty, focuses attention of objectives, obtains economical operations and facilitates control. Plans have to be based upon detailed information and must be flexible and for longer terms, if the business is to survive.

An important plank is the forecasting which is preliminary to business planning. The success in forecasting is achieved when the past events are related to the future and to this extent the alert management is guided by the accounting data from the historical reports and therefore the coming events can be accurately predicated.

Planning is the selection from among alternatives for the organisation as a whole and each part within it. In business, financial factors are involved. The accountant has the past data of the firm and relevant information of other enterprises as well from the published records. An analysis and interpretation of such information is of material help to management in choosing between alternatives.

The formal outcome of forecasting and plans are put in budget which as a plan is a statement of expected results expressed in numerical terms. The budget, in fact, is sheet-anchor of management accounting and it covers all phases of business ranging from the production function to the marketing of the products.

The accountant participates in the preparation of various types of budgets, by providing past data so as to work out the future changes. The accountant must organise the process of budgeting for optimum benefits. The sales budget is only one budget and the real problem, as a part of planning, is to find out the plan which provides for sales which give the lowest cost or production, the lowest employment of funds in working capital, and lower requirement for new capital investment. It is not 'merely putting the figures together; the management accountant will have to make intelligible conclusions and a firm commitment to the plans. The accountant, therefore, assists management planning as:

(a) By presenting and analysing the results of the enterprise in terms of income and expenses.

(b) By converting technical details in terms of money.

(c) By estimating the future figures of profits and the overall general financial position.

It is imperative to underline that the accountant can be a good partner in management planning function only if he is fully aware of the objectives of the Chief Executive and realises that he is a member of the planning team.

(B) Controlling. Control function is best studied in three parts: Motivating, Checking and Restraining.

Motivational aspect of the control function entails to induce people to work as they are able and trained to do. Inducement comes from pecuniary and non pecuniary benefits. Accountant is required to assist management in framing schemes regarding pecuniary benefits and report the cost of benefits like incentives, wage plans, fringe benefits (*i.e.* holidays with pay, premium plans and so on) etc.

The vital contribution to control function is found in the 'checking aspect.' As **Fayol** puts it: 'In an undertaking, control consists in verifying whether everything occurs in conformity with the plans adopted.' The accounting reports, made to different levels, are used to compare the actual performance with the scientifically laid standards, the details of which are contained in the reports. A clear revelation should be made in the reports regarding the success of the plan objectives; the reasons for difference, if any, must be clearly stated.

Leadership and persuasion are the necessary elements of the restraint aspect of control for desired results. What is required is the fixation of realistic standards and well established uniform procedures to be followed by inspection and review of results. The accounting reports should be drawn to make this review feasible.

Controlling is, therefore, related to the determination of success in planning and the best control corrects deviations from plans before they occur. It is rightly held that 'management control seeks to compel events to conform to plans'. Management must ensure that the existing devices of control are adequate and used by the individuals concerned. The activity of 'internal auditing' is an effective tool to provide this help. An internal audit is a review of operations and records and the internal auditor, an employee of the firm, assures the management of the effectiveness of the policies and procedures in carrying out the aims of management. Summing up the control function, the management is aided by budgeting, methods, procedures and internal audit-the facets of management accounting."

(C) Developing New Products and Capital Projects. The development of new products and the projects requires the estimates of the expenditure and the returns thereof. It is the balancing of these two factors which is necessary for decision making. Management accounting does the job by taking help from such disciplines as cost accounting. In a talk delivered under the auspices of the Forum of Free Enterprise, Bombay, Shri P.L. Tandon, the then Chairman of Hindustan Lever Limited pointed out, "Our accounts department offers much services in the field of development of new packs, new products and new projects. Whenever our management thinks of something new, they turn to the accountants to study the financial implications. This, in short, is where the accountants and our general management together look ahead to make sure that a change or new development will produce healthy results. It should be underlined that it is not the accountants who dictate the managers' policy. Managers must make their own decisions, based upon the information they receive. And they may decide for other perfectly valid reasons to go ahead with the project which has a longer pay-back period and lower yield: it may have broader economic or social objectives; but management must know where they stand and what they base their decisions on. This is where the accountant can help them."

(D) Co-oridinating. Co-ordination, the essence of the management functions, aims at achieving harmony of individual effort towards the accomplishment of the enterprise goals. The best co-ordination occurs when individuals see how their jobs contribute to the dominant goals of the enterprise, that is, achieving maximum benefits with minimum of expenses. The accountant can bring about complete co-ordination in the organisational structure by spelling in details the responsibilities of each function and its relationship with other positions. Accounting records must be drawn in terms of the costs and accomplishment. It may be emphasised here that the accountant must be conversant with 'the organisation hierarchy' and be alert to the changes if he is to prove his abilities in co-ordinating business activities.

SCOPE OF MANAGEMENT ACCOUNTING

Management accounting has a very wide scope. It embraces within its ambit not only financial accounting and cost accounting but tax accounting, auditing, reporting and office services also. The following are the different fields which are covered under management accounting:

(1) Financial accounting provides the basic information for analysis for managerial use. The historical data, records and accounting details help management to plan for the future. Management accounting is futuristic but future trends and tendencies are always based on the past; hence the need for financial accounting first.

(2) Management accounting techniques are primarily cost accounting techniques. The techniques of marginal costing, budgetary control and standard costing which are techniques of cost control are important tools of control in the hands of management. The costs of different cost centres and cost units are calculated under cost accounting which are relevant for decision-making by the management. The concepts of controllable and uncontrollable costs, relevant and irrelevant costs, opportunity costs, differential costs-all are used in management accounting.

(3) Auditing, of course, internal, is another field which has been plunged into the arena of management accounting of late. Internal audit has become so important these days that management relies heavily on it for fixing responsibilities

and taking action against individuals. The system is used as a basis for performance appraisal.

(4) For planning business affairs, forecasting and budgeting both are very significant. Forecasts provide the basis for budgets. Predetermined targets help people in business to perform tasks accordingly and if there are deviations, corrective steps can be taken by management.

(5) Financial analysis is a part of management accounting. Through analysis of financial statements, interpretations can be made about the profit-ability, solvency and liquidity positions of an enterprise. Financial appraisal can be made and after assessing the short-term and long-term financial position by applying various techniques of financial analysis, decisions can be taken regarding several issues to improve the financial position and to increase the profitability of the business.

(6) Management accounting lays out its hands on different control procedures and methods. As a matter of fact, the basic objective is to use various resources available the most economical, effective and efficient manner and this can be fulfilled when different techniques of control are adopted and implemented successfully.

(7) Reporting is another significant aspect of management accounting. Prompt and timely reporting is essential for quick and timely action. Reports are prepared at lower managerial levels and submitted to middle-level management and by middle-level management to top management. Both routine and special reports are prepared. The reports may take the shape of statements, graphs, charts, diagrams, tables, accounts, narratives etc.

(8) Tax has become an important part of business life. How can such a crucial burden on the funds of the enterprise be left ignored by management accounting. Large amount of liabilities is required to be paid by business and it has

necessitated tax planning by every management. Proper tax planning and tax management save business from the clutches of this monster to a very great extent.

LIMITATIONS OF MANAGEMENT ACCOUNTING

Despite the fact that the development of an effective discipline in managerial accounting is one of the most significant steps to improve managerial performance, the new discipline has to face conditions which limit the effectiveness of management through accounting. Such conditions are:

1. Though the main contribution of management accounting has been the elimination of intuitive management, there is always a temptation to take an easy course of arriving at decisions by intuition rather than taking the tortuous path of scientific decision-making.
2. Adoption of a system of management accounting brings about a radical change in the established pattern of the activity of management personnel. It calls for a rearrangement of personnel as well as their activities. This is bound to encounter opposition from some quarter or the other.
3. As the emergence of management accounting has been the result of fusion of a number of subjects like statistics, accounting, management theory, economics, engineering, etc. an inadequate grounding on the part of management in anyone or more of these subjects is bound to have an unfavourable effect on the consideration and solution of problems relating to management performance.
4. The installation of a system of management accounting requires a very elaborate organization and a very large number of rules and regulations with the consequence that the entire proposition becomes quite costly and can, there-fore, be adopted only by very big concerns.
5. Comparatively, management accounting is a new discipline and is still very much in a state of evolution. Therefore, it

comes across the same impediments as a relatively new discipline has to face - sharpening of analytical tools, improvements of techniques and fluidity of concepts creating uncertainty about their applications.

6. The ambitious nature of the objective, which management accounting seeks to serve, and the extremely wide scope of the subject-matter dealt with by it create many difficulties. Thus, it is one thing to record, interpret and evaluate an objective historical event convened into money figures while it is something quite different to perform the same function in respect of past possibilities, future opportunities and unquantifiable situation.

SIGNIFICANCE OF MANAGEMENT ACCOUNTING

The Management Accountant's services are invaluable management in all their functions. Indeed, the Management Accountant may be said to act as the eyes and ears of management. All the necessary information and data are provided by him to the management. He also gives his suggestions and recommendations as to where and when management should exercise vigilance and control and what course of action should be pursued in any given situation. It is through the timely submission of accounting reports by the management accountant that the attention of operational managers and supervisors is drawn to adverse trends and thus precautions and correctives can be applied in time.

Management accounting is the blending of all processes connected with financial and cost accounting and is also concerned with the establishment and operation of internal controls. The shaping, timing and circulation of resulting information constitute, so to speak, the premise on which management functions are carried out. But for the informational materials supplied by the management accountant, planning, control and operating activities would have been lacking in objectivity and teeth.

The significance of management accounting has increased very rapidly in recent times due to the improvement in analytical and problem-solving techniques and the availability of more efficient data processing equipment. With the help of these techniques and apparatus, the management accountant is able to process data and satisfy the management's informational needs for assessing the causes and effects of cost and revenue changes, the cost implications of making and buying a component, whether it would be profitable to process a by-product beyond the split off or to sell it without further, processing, whether output should be expanded beyond the existing level, and similar other matters.

Management accounting involves a process of selective and discriminating reporting of data. It emphasises and highlights the relevant facts, out of the mass of data-facts which would be useful in the solution of problems at hand. Thus it aids and facilitates prompt decision-making by the management.

In the large, complex organisations of today, it is hardly possible for managers particularly at higher levels to maintain adequate contact with all operations on a continuous basis. It is thorough systematic meaningful reports that efficient management of operation can be secured in the modern enterprises. Moreover, the management accountant consolidates all relevant information about which activities are clearly related to the principal objectives.

OBJECTIVE OF MANAGEMENT ACCOUNTING

Decision making in any business concern is the primary function of management Technological developments and data processing by computers have left traditional accounting far behind in its ability to serve the decisional needs of management. Traditional accounting very well served the purpose under simple conditions of business but the tremendous expansion of the scale of production has brought out its inadequacy in grappling with the new business conditions. The two key elements in the success of an undertaking are accounting control and management capacity. These two are fully met by management Accounting through the harnessing of accounting for the purpose of management.

The evolution of management accounting has given a new dimension to the function of accounting. The basic objective of management accounting is to help the management in their functions of formulating policies, making decisions, planning activities and controlling business operations. The manner in which management accounting satisfies the diverse needs of management for arriving at proper business decisions are the modification of accounting data and the analysis and interpretation of this data. It does not restrict itself only to financial data but also draws upon sources, other than accounting, for such information as is not capable of being convertible into monetary terms. Management accounting processes accounting data in a way that yields concise information covering the entire field of business activities as to serve the top management.

The main objective of Management Accounting can be summarised as follows:

(1) Business success very much depends upon proper planning which is the primary function of management. It includes analysing properly the available data and forecast on the basis of available information. When the data is put in a proper prospective it helps the management in effective planning. The financial accountant presents the relative figures of the past and estimates of the future. These assist the management in determining courses of action and deciding on the programme of activities to be undertaken by the concern. Management accounting provides costing and statistical data to be utilised in setting goals and framing policies. Management accounting assists in planning for a specific purpose as well as over all planning for the organisation.

(2) Accounting is the language for communicating the financial facts about the organisation and its activities to those who have an interest in making their proper use by interpreting them. It improves the efficiency of the concern and assist the management in its task of maximising profits or minimising losses. Management accounting provides a means of communicating management plans through the

organisation. It is an important part of the company's management information system.

(3) Assistance in the interpretation of financial information. Management accounting is concerned with the analysis and the interpretation of such data which has opened up new directions. It is concerned with records of past achievements, maintenance of values, fixation of responsibilities and basis for assisting the future development. The financial accountant maintains detailed record of transactions affecting assets of the organisation, creditor's claims, owner's equity, revenues and costs etc. The management may not find time to go through all this information provided in the law form. Management accounting presents accounting information in an intelligible form that will enable business executives, investors and creditors in analysing and interpreting the various financial statements.

(4) Decision making is primarily a function of management. Management accounting helps the management in making sound decisions. These decisions may relate to expansion of the business or contraction or diversification of an existing business or it may be in question of starting a new line, the management accounting helps in solving all such questions. Management accounting uses the available accounting figures in solution of the various management problems. Its function is to provide necessary data and not decisions. It only informs the management and leaves the task of decision making with them. It provides and presents the alternative plans in a comparative manner and gives an insight into the implication on the future of the organisation. With the help of the available information placed by management accounting, it is up to the management to choose the best course of action. Its useful techniques regarding marginal costing, cost volume profit analysis, standard costing and capital budgeting assist the management

in arriving at rational and sound decisions. Anthony has described Management Accounting as "the use of accounting figures in recognition or solution of management problems.

(5) Marketing management emphasises on budgetary control, marginal costing, standard costing, funds flow analysis, internal financial control etc. All this requires an intensive study Of the organisational structure of the organisation.

It helps in rationalising the organisational structure of the business concern more efficiently.

(6) Management accounting facilitates management in controlling the destiny of the organisation. Standards for performance are maintained and any deviation from them is measured and estimated. Measuring actual performance against approved operating plans, standards and budgets are interpreted and reported to the heads of the departments at higher levels. All these help the management in controlling the overall performance of the organisation. Cost control techniques and functional control enables the management to delegate the authority easily and successfully.

(7) The setting of goals, proper planning, employment of economical course of action, measuring the performance go a long way in improving and increasing the effectiveness of the organisation. Thus management accounting helps the management in motivating their employees.

(8) Management accounting is concerned with the efficiency of the various phases of management. It helps in overall control and proper coordination of business operations. Budgets serve as the best means of coordination. The various plans are based on budget which is a statement of plans in financial terms. Planning is followed by directing the planed operations coordinating the activities of different departments and units and controlling the operations so as to achieve the desired goals.

TOOLS AND TECHNIQUES USED IN MANAGEMENT ACCOUNTING

The presentation of accounting information in such a way as to assist management in the creation of policy and in the day-to-day operation of an undertaking In order to discharge its duty of helping the management sincerely and faithfully in the various managerial functions planning, co-ordination, control and appraisal of activities management accounting uses the following tools and techniques:

(1) **Historical Costing Accounting.** Cost accounting is an integral part of the accounting process which provides management with cost data relating to products, processes, jobs and operations. The statement of actual costs after they have been actually incurred is called historical cost accounting. These are based on recorded costs and can be easily verified with the help of evidences regarding are transactions involved. These costs are accumulated continuously over time and summarised at the end of each accounting period so that a comparison can be made with the standard costs.

(2) **Funds Flow Statements.** Preparation of funds flow statements is also an important tool of management accounting. A Funds Statement is technical device designed to analyse the changes in the financial condition of a business enterprise between two dates. In other words, it describes the sources from which additional funds were derived and the uses to which these funds were put. Funds-flow statements help a lot in financial analysis and control, future guidance and comparative studies.

(3) **Marginal Costing.** Marginal costing is also known as opportunity costing or costing for alternatives. It is an important tool of managerial decision-making. Marginal cost is the increase or decrease in total cost which results from producing or selling certain additional or fewer units of a product or from a change in the method of production or distribution Marginal costing includes the discussion of

cost-volume-profit analysis and break-even analysis also. An integrated application of these techniques help the management in taking sound production and distribution decisions.

(4) **Analysis of Financial Statement.** Analysis of financial statements is the second important tool of management accounting. In the words of Kennedy and MC Multer, "The analysis and interpretation of financial statements are an attempt to determine the significance and meaning of the financial statement data so that a forecast may be made of the prospects for future earnings, ability to pay interest and debt maturates and probability of a sound dividend policy." The preparation of comparative financial statements, trend analysis, funds-flow techniques and ratio analysis are some important techniques of financial analysis. The analysis and interpretation of financial statements results in the presentation of information that will aid to business executives, investors and creditors.

(5) **Budgetary Control.** One of the essential features of modern management is planning and control. There are a number of devices which help in controlling. The most widely used device for managerial control is 'budget'. A 'budget' is a quantitative expression of plan of action. It is an estimate of future needs arranged according to an orderly basis, covering some or all of the activities of an enterprise for definite period of time. 'Budgeting' is the process of preparing budgets and budgetary control is the technique of managerial control through budgets. It is an important technique of directing business operations in a desired direction, *i.e.*, a satisfaction return on investment.

(6) **Financial Planning.**Planning is always concerned with the future course of action. Financial planning is the act of deciding in advance the financial activities that are necessary if the firm is to achieve its primary goal. It involves three fundamental steps: *(a)* determining both long-term and short-term financial objectives of the firm; *(b)* formulating

financial policies and *(c)* developing the financial procedures to achieve the objectives. A business firm's ultimate objective is to make the optimum use of all factors of production in order to maximise the return of' investors. Financial policies act as a guide to the firm achieving this goal. The determination of the following financial policies is important in this connection:

(i) Policies that determine the optimum level of investment in various current and fixed assets.

(ii) Policies that govern the determination and distribution of income.

(iii) Policies that act as a guide in the use of debt and equity capital.

(iv) Policies that determine the amount of capital required for the firm, and policies that determine the sources of funds.

(7) Standard Costing. Standard costs are pre-determined costs, *i.e.* estimates of what costs should be under best possible conditions. They provide a yardstick for measuring actual performance. Standard costing is the preparation and use of standard costs, their comparison with actual costs and the analysis of variances to their causes and points of incidence. Thus standard costing is an important tool of cost control which is one of the main objectives of management accounting.

(8) Decision Accounting. Decision making is the primary function of top management. It is a process of selecting the one best alternative for doing a work. The increasing complexity of organisational problems requires that improved methods of decision.

(9) Others

(a) Reporting

(b) Statistical & Graphical Techniques

(c) Revaluation Accounting.

MANAGEMENT ACCOUNTING PRINCIPLES

Besides the basic accounting principles, which are accepted generally throughout the accounting profession, the following are the additional conventions/principles which are now generally regarded as essential part of management accounting.

(1) A profit cannot be said to be earned unless capital is maintained intact in real terms.

This convention recognises that the monetary unit is not stable attempts to overcome the effects of changes in the value of money have been made via revaluation accounting, but as yet there is no general acceptance of the theory. However, there is strong evidence that more and more accountants are modifying their views to meet the dynamic state of business and the economy.

(2) Costs are best controlled at the points at which they are incurred "Control-at-source accounting".

Recognition of this convention is acknowledged through the preparation of departmental operating statements and the design of costing system which control individual workers, material issues, and the usage of services. The inculcation of cost consciousness is also an essential part of this convention.

(3) The "principle of management by exception" is followed when presenting information to management.

This assumes that plans are predetermined and then actual results are compared with expected results. If there are no deviations there is no necessity to report. When there are variations from predetermined place management is informed precisely of what is going wrong. In this way, the information presented to management is kept to the minimum, yet at the same time all important fads are being revealed. What is more, management has less to read and study and, therefore, should have more time to take action.

(4) Accounting information, records, reports, statements, and other evidence of past, present, or future results should be designed and compiled to meet the needs of the particular business and/or specific problem.

This implies a certain flexibility of system. When a particular problem is to be solved the system should be capable of producing the relevant data. If necessary, there must be departure from double-entry principles. Accounting and operational-research principles should be linked together. Information should be accumulated and then presented to solve problems. The accounting information should be modified and adapted to meet each need whenever possible. However, it is important to remember that if this principle is carried too far, the cost of the management accountancy system may become excessive. It is partly for this reason that a systematic, rather than an ad hoc method, is used for accumulating costing data.

(5) Management accountancy should endeavour to show whether or not the resources of the business are being utilised in the most effective manner.

(6) Personal contact with departmental managers, foremen, and others cannot be replaced entirely by reports and statements.

(7) There should be integration of all management information so that fullest use is made of the facts available and at the same time, the accounting service should be provided at minimum cost.

(8) Management accounting systems and related forms should be used only as long as they serve a useful purpose.

This normally implies that mechanisation should be adopted as much as possible. It does not mean that every business should employee a computer. The machines selected should be of a size and, type that can economically be employed by the particular concern to deal with its own problems. If there is insufficient work for a computer, then clearly this should not be required.

(9) Return on capital employed is used as the criterion for measuring the efficiency of the business. For this purpose the capital employed should be calculated by reference to current replacement values.

(10) The most appropriate means of accumulating, recording and presenting the accountancy information should be selected.

(11) Management accountancy should seek to anticipate problems and prevent them. There should be a forward looking approach and actual costs should be employed only as measures of achievements realised. This principle recognises the importance of budgetary control and standard costing.

(12) Overhead cost should be apportioned to cost centres and absorbed to products on the basis of benefits received for fixed costs or responsibilities incurred for variable costs. The method or methods selected should bring about the desired results of recovering the overheads in the most equitable manner. However, this is subject to what is stated on this matter in the chapter on Marginal Costing.

(13) When tracing responsibility a clear distinction should be made between those costs which are controllable and those which are uncontrollable by the management of the business or department concerned.

The above list of conventions is fairly long. However it is not exhaustive on account of the subject of management according to being a growing one. It may be possible that in the times to come many more suitable convention may be developed by the management accountants all over the world which may take the form of universally acceptable management accounting principles.

ESSENTIALS FOR SUCCESS OF MANAGEMENT ACCOUNTING

1. Reporting to management in time is necessary so that management can take timely action. The management should observe the 'principle of exception' for control purposes.
2. Proper systems of performance evaluation should be in operation. Actual performances should regularly be compared with those budgeted and pre-determined on the basis of standards. Quick and constant comparisons will help management to remain alert about off-standard performances.
3. Looking 'ahead' is a must for the management. The management must be competent enough to look into the future so that effective planning may be possible through forecasting and budgeting.
4. Human factor must be recognised by the management. Proper incentives, both pecuniary and non-pecuniary should be provided to people in the concern.
5. Sound financial and cost accounting systems must exist.
6. It is essential that the people with whom management accountant has to work have faith in management accounting.
7. The objectives and basic policies of the business should be made clear to everyone in the organisation.
8. There must be a team spirit among all members of the organisation. Management must objectively criticise the functioning of a department and the departmental heads should also take it sportingly. They should work in the interest of the concern as a whole rather than of their own department alone.

MANAGEMENT ACCOUNTING IN THE INDIAN CONTEXT

With the increasing tempo of industrial growth and product development which started with the second five year plan, there has been a phenomenal change in the business methods and systems in India. Management of large and medium scale industries has become increasingly more complex and difficult partly due to the adoption of modem technology and partly due to the necessity of tackling multifarious problems in the operational and financial fields. Under these conditions, the professional manager's need for information and data which have been discreetly selected, organised and interpreted has become all the more greater.

On the other hand, the scope of using quantitative techniques and analytical tools has been increasing rapidly with greater opportunities of management education and training. The usefulness of management accounting techniques like standard costing, budgetary control, marginal costing, cash flow and funds flow analysis, inventory control techniques, probability estimates, operations research and others have been recognised more consistently in the process. Indeed, the Management Accountant is now regarded as an important member of top management in many companies.

A special feature of Indian economic development since independence is the rapid growth of the public sector as a direct consequence of the objective of working towards the realisation of a socialist pattern of society. The significance of management accounting in public enterprises can hardly be overemphasised. The necessity of successful management of large undertakings has posed a new challenge to the public sector. Advance planning and control have as much importance in public enterprises as in the private sector. Planning is a pre-condition of success as it provides the basis for organisation, assembling resources, direction and control. It has been observed by the Planning Commission that the preparation of advance costs, operation and capital budgets greatly reduces the need for making references to the administrative Ministry and straining then the autonomy and flexibility of the enterprises. Besides, advance planning provides an opportunity for seeing that each part fits in with the other and is directed towards the overall purpose. Setting up of specific goals and subgoals is an inseparable part of the whole planning process. A wide variety of operating standards and 'norms' need also to be set up to express the anticipated results of the detailed plans. Comparable data from other similar plants in the country and outside are often found to be of great value in this connection for administrative control. Continuous appraisal of results is equally vital. Availability of necessary information and data for planning, decision-making and control is thus of prime importance. The role of management accounting in that context can make or mar the success of the whole enterprise.

When public enterprises run efficiently and follow proper price policy for their goods and services, the results of their operations must be reflected in larger earnings and surpluses. In a developing economy, these constitute a ready and increasingly important source for financing investment it is therefore incumbent on public enterprises to produce efficiently and to accumulate surpluses which should be earmarked for further development. As an aid to management providing meaningfully arranged data with objective analysis and interpretation, management accounting can go a long way in making public enterprises efficient and productive.

The role of the Financial Adviser who performs the role of Management Accountant as well in the public undertaking has often caused serious misgivings. However, the Planning Commission it made the position clear as early as 1961. The Financial Adviser is expected to function subject to the authority of the General Manager. In case of difference of opinion, it should be quite open to the General manager to overrule the advice of the Financial Adviser, but there should be a convention that such cases should be brought to the notice of the Board by the General manager at the next Board meeting. According to the Planning Commission, the Financial Adviser of any public undertaking should concern himself with problems of financial management rather than devote exclusive attention to the control of expenditure.

ACCOUNTING AND BOOK-KEEPING

There is some confusion over the distinction between accounting and book-keeping and some people took upon them as one and the same. Although the two are clossly related and there is no universally accepted line of separation. Yet, book-keeping is only a part of accounting *i.e.* the record making part and the book-keeper is one who records the transactions. Much of the work of the book-keeper is clerical in nature and is increasingly being accomplished through the use of mechanical and electronic equipment.

Accounting is primarily concerned with the design of the system by which business transactions are to be recorded by a book-keeper. An accountant may supervise the work of the book-keeper; he may prepare reports based on the recorded data and interpret the reports. Although the work of the book-keeper is more routine, it is difficult to draw a line where the book-keeper's work ends and the accountant's begins. The work of the accountants at the beginning levels may possibly include some book-keeping. "In any event the accountant must possess a much higher level of knowledge conceptual understanding and analytical skill than is required of the book-keeper". Simply stated the confusion over the difference between the book-keeping and accounting therefore is understandable because of following reasons:

(A) Even in education, the inclusion of accounting as a subject in the courses of studies at the stage of secondary education is of recent origin; the major thrust earlier was on book-keeping.

(B) Record keeping as a trade is ancient, that is many centuries old; accounting is yet to make its impact felt.

(C) It is very common to find some financial records almost in every type of business. Only few are aware of the problems of analysis and interpretation involved in dealing with large mass of financial data in commercial transactions.

(D) The first part of the definition-recording, classifying and summarising is the major source of confusion between book-keeping and accounting, the former is only one aspect of the latter.

General Considerations

It is relevant to mention that in its book-keeping aspect the accounting proceeds on the following general considerations:

(i) Only Cost is The Basis of Record. The assets are recorded in the books only at their cost, that is, the actual price paid or incurred for them. To this price we may add the incidental charges incurred-on their acquisition.

(ii) Money-As A Unit of Measurement. It means that for the purpose of recording transactions, only the items capable of being expressed in money values are considered. No attempt is made to record the general efficiency or health of the executive or employees of the organisation. For instance, business records are concerned only with the payment of salary in terms of money to the purchase manager and not his efficiency in effecting the economy in purchases which would be recorded in terms of total amount spent for the same.

(iii) Historical Facts. Only those transactions which have really taken place are recorded. There is no scope to record that will happen in future. Thus the buildings would be recorded as an asset only when they are actually purchased and similar treatment would be given to the sale of different items when they are actually sold. There is no such thing as the possibility or likelihood of sale or purchase of any item in the accounting records.

(iv) Cost Accounting & Management Accounting. Cost Accounting is the process of accounting for costs. It embraces the accounting procedures relating to recording of all income and expenditure and the preparation of periodical statements and reports with the object of ascertaining and controlling costs. It is, thus, the formal mechanism by means of which the costs of products or services are ascertained and controlled. On the other hand, management accounting involves collecting, analysing, interpreting and presenting all accounting information which is useful to the management. It is by associated with management control which comprises planning, execut measuring and evaluating the performance of an organisation. Thus, management accounting draws heavily on cost data and other information derived from cost accounting. Today cost accounting is generally indistinguishable from the so called management accounting of internal accounting use it serves multiple purposes.

However, management accounting can be distinguished from cost accounting in one important respect. Management accounting has a underscope compared to cost accounting. Cost accounting deals primarily with cost data while management accounting involves the considerations of both cost and revenue. Management accounting is an all inclusive accounting information item which covers financial accounting cost accounting and all aspects of financial management. But it is not a substitute for other accounting functions involves a continuous process of reporting cost, financial and other relevant to in an analytical and informative way to management.

We should not be very much concerned with the boundaries of cost counting and management accounting since they are complementary in nature. In the absence of a suitable system of cost accounting management will it be in a position to have detailed cost information and their function is bound to lose significance. On the other hand, the management cannot effectively use cost data unless it has been reported to them in a meaningful and informative form.

❑

8

Methods of Costing

TECHNIQUES OF COSTING

Costing techniques refer the ways in which cost data is proccesed and related to cost centres and cost units. It relates the principles and rules governing ascertainment of cost of procedure and services. These techniques offer a guide as to which types of costs are charged to cost units or cost centres *e.g.* whether all costs are to be charged or only variable costs or the differential cost. The choice of costing techniques depends on the objectives of costing. Following are the techniques or types of costing:

(1) Absorption Costing or Full Costing. Absorption costing is also known as orthodox or conventional costing because this is the oldest costing technique and is followed even today. It is also called full costing or total costing because all chargeable costs whether fixed or variable, are charged to cost centres and cost units.

Under absorption costing both fixed and variable costs are treated as product cost, *i.e.*, both these costs are distributed over the output during the accounting period in which these costs have been incurred. Both cost of sales as well as unsold stocks are valued at variable cost plus proportionate fixed costs. Absorption costing is, thus, the process of charging all costs, both variable and fixed, to products, services, operations, jobs or processes. Technique of absorption costing is widely used for purposes of reporting.

(2) Marginal Costing or Variable Costing. Under marginal costing variable costs are treated as product cost but fixed costs are treated as period cost. Only variable costs, *i.e.*, direct material, direct labour, direct factory expenses and variable overheads, are charged to products, operations and processes. Fixed costs are wholly charged to the accounting period in which such costs are incurred, irrespective of quantity and value of goods produced and sold. Cost of sales as well as unsold stocks are valued at variable cost only.

According to C.I.M.A., marginal costing refers to "the accounting system in which variable costs are charged to cost units and fixed costs of the period are written off in full against the aggregate contribution. Its special value is in decision-making." Marginal costing is basically used for managerial decision-making and internal reporting. It helps in dumping decisions, make or buy, shut-down and product-mix decisions. It is more precise and offers a better yardstick for performance appraisal.

Direct costs are those which are conveniently and wholly identified with cost units. Therefore, it is said that under direct costing a unit is assigned only the direct cost. Indirect costs, including variable overheads, are disregarded for valuation of cost of sales and unsold stocks. It is said that marginal costing is based on variability of costs while direct costing is based on traceability of cost to cost units. Direct costs may include part of fixed costs which exclusively related to a particular product, and exclude variable overheads. The former are excluded under marginal costing and the latter are included.

However, in practice, the term marginal costing, variable costing and direct costing are used interchangeably, and they have been used as such in this text also.

(3) Uniform Costing. It is not a distinct form of costing. When a number of undertakings follow the same costing principles practices and procedures, it may be called uniform costing. According to C.I.M.A. Terminology it is "the use by several undertakings of the same costing system, *i.e.*, the same basic costing methods, principles and techniques." This involves standardisation of costing principles, methods and techniques by a number of undertakings, generally related in some way-being member of the same trade or industry association governed by the same regulatory agency. Standardisation may extend to defining costs and cost classifications, accounting, coding, depreciation methods, creation of cost centres, and methods of allocation and apportionment of cost.

Trade and industry associations, regulatory bodies or some such agencies may direct uniform costing to the undertakings under its control for purposes of cost comparision, common controls, establishment of common pricing policies, comparative performance evaluation, fixation of quotas, and collecting revenues in the form of duties, cess, etc.

(4) Differential Costing. As per C.I.M.A. Terminology, differential cost is "the difference in total cost between alternatives calculated to assist decision-making" Differential costing is the technique of comparing cost of two alternative for the purpose of deciding which alternative is the best.

The technqiues distinguishes between fixed and variable costs and also considers semi-variable costs. For example, if a producer is producing 10,000 units and he gets on order for 8,000 units more, he has to calculate cost of additional 8,000 units for comparing it with the price offered. The difference between the total cost of 18,000 unit and 10,000 units is the differential cost of 8,000 units and may involve semi-variable and fixed cost also, in addition to variable costs. It is a suitable technique for both short-run and long-run decision-making. Differential costing is a valuable technique for accept-reject decisions and for choice of alternatives.

DIFFERENT METHODS OF COSTING

The choice of a method of costing depends upon the nature of product, service and industry. Costs may be accumulated for a group of identical products, specific jobs, individual processes. Accordingly an appropriate method of costs collection is used.

Basic Methods

According to C.I.M.A. (Chartered Institute of Management Accountants) Terminology there are basically two methods of costing:

(i) Specific Order Costing. It includes job costing, batch costing and contract costing. Costing methods are applied to separate jobs, batches and contracts authorised by specific order. Each job, contract, etc. differs from the other and hence needs to be costed separately.

(ii) Operation Costing. It consists of costing methods applicable to standardised goods and services involving respective and continuous operations or processes. All costs are first charged to each individual operation or process. Cost of a product is ascertained by accumulating cost of its each process. Process costing and operating costing are examples of operation costing.

Many costing methods may not neatly fall into the category of either job costing or process costing. They may use some features of both the main costing systems. Such methods which combine the features of the basic costing methods may be called hybrid costing methods. Various variants of basic costing methods are discussed below?

(a) ***Job Costing.*** Under job costing costs are collected and accumulated for each job, project or work order separately. Each job is a separate cost unit. Each job is distinct, it is different from the other : and therefore, is to be separately costed.

Job costing is applicable to cases where the work is done according to customer's specification. In such cases a simple averaging of costs incurred during a period for different jobs does not give a meaningful value because costs vary markedly from job order to job order. Job costing is applicable to printing work, machine repair, machine installations, foundries, vehicle repair and servicing, engineering works, machine tools, etc.

(b) ***Contract Costing.*** A contract is a big job—big in terms of cost required and the time involved in completing a contract. Like jobs, each contract is different from the other. A contract is a cost unit. Costs are collected for each contract

separately. Large number of costs can be casily identified with specific contract because contracts are physically separate. Contract work is generally site-based. A separate account is maintained for each individual contract. A contract account is akin to mini Profit and Loss Account. It gives costs and profitability of each contract. This method is used in house building, engineering works, plant installations, ship-building, etc.

Job costing and contract costing are also known as 'Terminal Costing'

(c) ***Single, Unit or Output Costing.*** This method is applicable where an undertaking is producing standardised products in large number. Manufacture is continuous and the units produced are identical. The objective is to ascertain cost per unit of each product as well as the detailed components of costs. The cost per unit is determined by dividing the total cost incurred by the total number of units produced. Cost accountant periodically prepares cost sheet for each product giving full details regarding its cost.

Unit costing methods is applicable in industries like mining, oil drilling, cement works, brick works, breweries, steel production, etc. In all these cases there is a natural or standard unit of cost. The whole production cycle is costed as a single process.

(d) ***Process Costing.*** This method of costing is suitable for industries where manufacturing is carried on by distinct and well defined process. For example, in textile industry the three distinct processes are spinning, weaving and printing. Output of one processs becomes input for the next process, *e.g.*, output of spinning process is spun yarn which is input of weaving process, and output of weaving process is plane cloth which is input for printing process. Each procees produces identical units. Final output is obtained at the end of final process. There may be losses

and wastage at different processes. Some of the products may be produced jointly.

In process industries, make or buy decisions are involved before and after each process. Such decisons can be taken only if cost at each process is ascertained separately. Moreover, considerations of ascertaining efficiency at each process also require collection of cost at each process. This is done by preparing Process Account for each process. Total cost incurred at a process divided by total number units produced at the process gives cost per unit at the process. Due to this averaging, the method is called average costing. As the products are manufactured in continuous processes, particularly during modern times of mechanisation and automation, this is also called Continuous Costing. Process costing is suitable for textiles, chemicals, cement, breweries, paper, sugar industry, etc.

Conditions for use of process costing are:

(a) Continuous mass production;

(b) Production in distinct stages or processes;

(c) Output of one stage is input for the next stage;

(d) Units produced at each process are identical;

(e) Each stage or process produces saleable product; and

(f) Complete standardisation of products and processes.

(e) ***Operation Costing.*** Application of this method requires that production process of a product is separated in different operations. For example, production of a steel almirah is divided in operations, such as, cutting a steel sheet, welding the body, welding compartments, fixing the door and the handle, and polishing. Each operation is costed separately. The system is used when large quantities of standardised units are produced under repetitive conditions. Operation costing involves simultaneous production of different part of a product through use of different operations. Cost unit

may be a component or operation involved in production. Sum total of cost of all component or of all operations involved in obtaining the final product gives cost of the product.

Use of operation costing is very beneficial for cost control and achievement of high degree of efficiency where each production activity and process is divided into minute operations and a minute analysis of costs is done operation-wise. The system of operation costing is used where a repetitive production is carried out, production can be divided into distinct operations, or where components are to be stocked in semi-finished conditions for execution of special orders. The method is suitable for industries like leather products, toy-making, engineering, repair shops, etc.

(f) ***Composite or Multiple Costing.*** This method of costing is used where cost of a product cannot be ascertained by using any one of the above methods. It requires application of two or more of the methods of costing because the production is complex involving production of large number of parts of different types and sizes. The method is used in industries where a large number of components are produced separately and ten assembled into a final product. Cost of final product is obtained by adding cost of all components. Computation of cost of different components may be made by using different methods of costing due to varying nature of these components. Assembly of these components into final product may require use of still different method of costing. this type of costing is used in industries such as, automobiles, refrigerators, televisions and other electronics, computers, aeroplane, etc.

(g). ***Operating Costing.*** The method of operating costing is used for undertakings rendering service rather than producing tangile products. It is also used for service

departments of an undertaking. Examples of such services are passenger and freight transport, power generation, education, hospital, hotel, water works, gas supply, etc. An appropriate cost unit is to be selected to suit the nature of service. Operating costing, which is also called service costing, generally uses composite unit. The cost unit may be passenger-kilometre, ton-mile, kilowatt-hour, per lecture, per bed or per guest per day, etc.

(h) ***Cost-plus Costing.*** In case the payment of cost of work done to the contractor includes sum total of direct and indirect cost and also profit calculated as per agreed formula, the system is called cost-plus costing. The practice is prevalent in contracting business.

(i) ***Alternative-use Costing or Opportunity Costing.*** This is not strictly a method of cost ascertainment. It deals with the problem of demonstrating the most profitable course of action out of several available alternatives. The method involves comparison between not only costs and benefits from any particular project, but also from all available alternative. It is, therefore, more concerned with comparative rather than actual costs.

(j) ***Activity Based Costing (ABC).*** ABC is a new practice of assigning costs of jobs and process. As per ABC the cost are collected according to activities in business, such as, material ordering, material handling, quality testing, machine setups, soldering, insertion of parts, field demonstrations, after sale services, etc. Cost of each activity is ascertained separately. Jobs and processes for which cost is being determined are loaded with the cost of these activities depending on which job or process has made use of which activity to what extent. According to C.I.M.A. Terminology activity based costing refers to "cost attribution to cost units on the basis of benefits received from indirect activities, *i.e.*, ordering, setting-up, assuring quality, etc." ABC is also called 'activity accounting'.

ABC attempts to ascertain cost of units on the basis of cause and effect relationship. It emphasises inter-relationship between individual activities and the demand they make on the organisational resources. It also establishes a link between the activities required for producing products or services and their cost. ABC thus gives a clearer picture of revenues generated by products, brands, territories, clientage groups, facilities and distribution channels, and the resources consumed by them. ABC regards activity as a cost object and highlights inter-relationship between activities in different departments.

Under ABC overheads are not viewed merely as a burden which need to be minimised. Due importance is attached to overhead functions because a number of these functions, *e.g.*, production design, quality control, production planning and scheduling, attending to customer orders, after sale services etc., are as important as physical production process. All these overhead functions are separately costed under ABC.

ABC recognises that products, jobs and processes, etc. do not directly consume resources, but consume activities, which consume resources. The focus is on efficient management of activities-break them into parts, or combine them, or even do away with them if they are redundant or too expensive. Costs are brought down by managing the each activity well, *i.e.*, performing them most efficiently and economically. If the cost of activities is kept low, the cost of final product or service will also remain low.

ABC approach recognises a business as collection of activities—research and development, product design, product development, product introduction and promotion, and customer support activities. The business activities convert input from suppliers into output for consumers. The emphasis is on value addition and customer services.

(k) ***Life Cycle Costing.*** Product life cycle starts from the time of initial research and development till the time sale to the customers is completed. *i.e.*, after sale support is wihtdrawn. Various stages in the product life cycle are : research and development, product design manufacturing, marketing, distribution, and customer service including all after sale services.

Life cycle costing traces all types of capital costs and revenue costs to different stages in the product life cycle starting from initial research and development till the last stage of after sale customer services. It accumulates cost for all activities occurring over the entire life cycle of a product from its inception till it is finally abandoned.

Life cycle costing considers total cost—both capital cost and revenue cost, over the entire life of the product including all types of production office and administration, and marketing overheads. Since this costing considers the entire life span of the product it is also called 'cradle to grave' and 'womb to tomb' costing. As per C.I.M.A. Terminology life cycle costing is "the practice of obtaining over their life-times, the best use of physical assets at the lowest cost to the entity". The system is of great value for long-term decision-making and is especially usefull in capital budgeting.

VALUE CHAIN ANALYSIS

Value Chiain analysis is useful for the firms which manufacture any product and sell it or sender services. The concept of value chain was first of all sugested by Michael Porter in 1985. Porter described the value chain as "the internal processes or activities a company performs to design, produce, market, deliver and support its product. The further stated that a firms value chain and the way it performs individual activities are a reflection of its history, its strategy, its approach of implementing its strategy, and the underlying economies of the activities themselves." Porter has classified the business activities under two titles *e.g.* primary activities and secondary activities. Primary activities are concerned with converting the inputs directly into outports and delivery of products and after sale devices. In other words they include the following items:

(1) Movement and storage of materials

(2) Converting the inputs in to the end products.

(3) Getting orders and making their supply.

(4) Communication pricing and sales medium management.

(5) Establishment, repair and restoration of parts.

Secondary activities are those which are helpful for primary activities. These include the following items :

(1) ***Getting Materials.*** Supply of materials and purchase of consumable materials and assets.

(2) ***Technical Development.*** Technical know-how, processes and knowledge of technical input necessary for value chain activity.

(3) ***Human Resource Management.*** Recruitment, promotion, work place, evaluation, reward, management development and labour/employee relation.

(4) ***Basic Infrastructure.*** General management, planning, finance, accounting, legal, official work and quality management.

John Shank and V. Govindarajan have described the value chain in a comprehensive sense. According to them, "The value chain for any firm is the value-creating activitis all the way from basic raw material sources from components suppliers through to the ultimate end use product delivered into the final consumers hands." This statement shows the firm is a part of whole chain of the processes creating value of the firm.

The firms utilise the cost of internal processes and value chain concept in identifying the sources of profitability. Value chain analysis is not a proper science nor it is easier to understand. It is more an art in spite of being proper accounting report. There are a number of limitations in applying and interpreting the value chain analysis. It is, therefore not very practical.

ACTIVITY BASED COSTING

Activity based activity is a new search in the field of cost accounting in which overheads are absorbed in the cost of products on more practical basis. It is often argued by the supporters of this technique that a number of costs are located unnecessarily as common costs and they are absorbed on hypothetical basis. Number of firms have now adopted developed product technique resulting in overheads and labour cost hs now become a small part of the total cost. It is not relevant to absorb the overheads on the basis of direct labour in such an environment. The main basis of the activity based costing is that costs should be classified on the basis of their operation or reasons, then the cost drivers are utilised is a basis of absorption.

Coplan and Kooper of Harbard Business School who evolved this new concept for identifying the product cost in costing process. Stated that costs are to be classified into long term variable costs and short term variable costs. Traditionally short term variable costs are changing costs and long term variable costs are called fixed costs. Short term variable costs are related to product quantity and varies in proportion to the changes in product quantity. Long term variable costs varies in long run and not with production.

Coplan and Kooper further claims that this concept links the overhead costs with the forces inherent behind them commonly known as 'cost drivers'. Cost drivers may be defined as the activities or practices which are important cost determiner. In the method of activity based costing, product cost is identified keeping in new the better understanding of cost practices and the resources consumed through each product. Cost driver is an activity which creates cost. Activity based costing is dependent on this belong that activities create cost and therefore a relation between activities and products must be established.

Activity based costing follows this concept that all the activities of a company are in fact performed for the assistance and support to the product and delivery of materials and services. That is why they are to be treated as product cost. Almost all costs are separate as per factory and office overheads. They may be marked as individual products and product families as well. This is the concept of activity based costing under which costs may be controlled more effectively by managing the forces causing such activities. We can understand the reasons of overhead costs with help of the report of cost consumed through major activities of the firm and their cost drivers. Thus the activity based costing provides more useful and suitable information for product mix decisions and controlling the performance activities.

Activity based costing is an accounting technique which emphasizes the cost of activities against the product and services. Due to this process the consumers of the product and services have to bear the burden of resources and overhead costs.

Step in Activity Based Costing

The following steps are needed for activity based costing :

(1) The major activities performed in firms are identified as product, collection etc.

(2) Identify the components effecting the cost of each activity cost drivers.

(3) Collect the correct datas regarding direct materials, direct labour and overhead costs.

(4) Determine the cost drivers for each activity relating the product with overhead costs.

(5) The subsidiary activities should be based on major activities.

(6) The cost of activities should be based on product as per the demand of product activities. For this the activity cost driver rate will be identified in the same way as overhead absorption rate in traditional system is identified:

$$\text{Activity Cost Driver Rate} = \frac{\text{Total Cost of Activity}}{\text{Activity Driver}}$$

Activity driving rate may be utilised for identifying the cost of product but it may also be used for identifying the cost of customer services and that of distribution means.

The whole process of activity based costing may easily be understood with the following:

Illustration.

A company produces three products A, B and C for which the standard costs and quantities per unit are as follows :

Products	*A*	*B*	*C*
Quntity produced	10,000	20,000	30,000
Direct materials/p.u. (Rs.)	50	40	30
Direct labour/p.u. (Rs.)	30	40	50
Labour hours/p.u.	3	4	5
Machine hours/p.u.	4	4	7
No. of Purchase requisitions	1,200	1,800	2,000
No. of set-ups	240	260	300

Production overhead split by departments

—Department 1 = Rs. 11,00,000

—Department 2 = Rs. 15,00,000

Department 1 is labour intensive and Department 2 is machine intensive

Total labour hours in Department 1 = 1,83,333

Total machine hours in Department 2 = 5,00,000

Production overhead split by activity

—Receiving/inspecting	Rs. 14,00,000
—Production scheduling/machine set-up	Rs. 12,00,000
	Rs. 26,00,000

Number of batches received/inspected = 5,000

Number of batches for scheduling and set-up = 800

You are required to :

(i) Prepare Product Cost Statement under traditional absorption costing and Activity Based Costing method.

(ii) Compare the results under two methods.

Solution.

Traditional Absorption Costing :

Absorption r ates :

$$\text{Department 1} = \frac{\text{Rs. } 11,00,000}{1,83,333 \text{ labour hours}} = \text{Rs. 6 per labour hour}$$

$$\text{Department 2} = \frac{\text{Rs. } 15,00,000}{5,00,000 \text{ machine hours}} = \text{Rs. 3 per machine hour}$$

Product Cost Statement :

Products	*A*	*B*	*C*
	Rs.	Rs.	Rs.
Direct materials	50	40	30
Direct labour	30	40	50
Overhead :			
Department 1	18 (3 hrs. × Rs. 6)	24 (4 hrs. × Rs. 6)	30 (5 hrs. × Rs. 6)
Department 2	12 (4 hrs. × Rs. 3)	12 (4 hrs. × Rs. 3)	21 (4 hrs. × Rs. 7)
	110	116	131

Activity Based Costing

Cost driver rates :

$$\text{Receiving/inspecting} = \frac{\text{Rs. } 14,00,000}{5,000 \text{ (No. of batches received / inspected)}}$$

$$= \text{Rs. 280 per requisition}$$

Production scheduling/Machine set-ups

$$= \frac{\text{Rs. } 12,00,000}{800 \text{ (No. of batches for scheduling)}}$$

= Rs. 1,500 per requisition

Product Cost Statement (per unit)

Products	*A*	*B*	*C*
	Rs.	Rs.	Rs.
Direct materials (Rs.)	50	40	30
Direct labour (Rs.)	30	40	50
Overhead :			
Receiving	34*	25	19
Production scheduling	36*	20	15
Total cost per unit	150	125	114

(Rs. 280 × 1,200) ÷ 10,000 units = Rs. 34*; similarly Rs. 25 and Rs. 19)

(Rs. 1,500 × 240) ÷ 10,000 units = Rs. 36**; similarly Rs. 20 and Rs. 15

The two absorption methods produce different results. Product C apears to be much more expensive using the traditional method than it does with ABC, while product A is the opposite. If it is assumed that ABC is more accuate, which it may or may not be, then product C would be overpriced on the traditional method and sales would presumably be poor as a consequence—assuming competitors supply more cheaply. Product A would be the opposite: sales would be high and it is possible that the company would unknowingly make a loss per unit on product A.

MATERIAL CONTROL

Material or inventory control involves systematic control and regulation of procurement, storage and usage of materials so as to maintain a smooth flow of production with optimum investment in inventories. Thus, basically material control is to be exercised at three stages:

(a) Control on policies, systems and procedures connected with the procurement of materials:

(b) Control of storage of materials; and

(c) Control on issue and usage of materials.

These controls primarily aims at ensuring that:

(i) Prodcution process is not hampered due to non-availability of materials at right time and of right quality; and

(ii) Investment in materials is kept at optimum level so that cost of materials per unit of output is kept at minimum.

Importance of Material Control

Material cost is a major element in total cost of production. Materials constitute more than 60 per cent of total cost in large variety of manufacture, such as, cotton yarn, cotton textile, earth moving equipment, small tools, sugar, woollen textile, jute products, bread and other confectionary items. In a modern competitive world, a small percentage of wastage in material handling and material use may push an organisation into losses.

There could be losses at the time of purchase of materials in a large number of ways:

(i) purchase of too large quantities resulting in larger storage costs;

(ii) purchases in too small lots resulting in larger ordering costs;

(iii) purchases at higher price either due to inefficient buying or invol ving manipulations;

(iv) delayed purchases;

(v) purchases of inappropriate quality, etc.

Lack of control on materials or loose control results in higher consumption of materials per units of output, wastage, spoilage, higher scrap and pilferage. All these result in higher cost of output.

In many cases overheads are also related to material cost. An economy in material consumpton also results in reduction in overhead cost per units of output.

Inefficiencies and frauds relating to materials have an impact on overall culture and environment in the organisation. These inefficiencies and frauds tend to penetrate deeper and spread wider. They tend to result in total collapse of the undertaking unless a costly surgery is undertaken at some stage.

Quantitative and Financial Controls

Material control involves control at two levels:

(i) Control on total quantity of materials purchased, stored and used, called quantity controls: and

(ii) Control on total monetary investment in materials, called financial controls.

There is no conflict between the two. In fact the two are complementary. A control on physical units of materials at the time of purchasing, storage and use in production will automatically result in lower investment in inventories.

CONFLICT IN DEPARTMENTAL OBJECTIVES

Purchase department is interested in reducing its work load and simultaneously demonstrating that purchases are made at lowest prices and at lowest overhead costs relating to purchasing function. Consequently they are interested in bulk purchases. This will mean larger investment in inventories. Production manager is cautious that production must never stop or slow down due to inadequate supplies of materials. He is also interested in longer production runs to minimise production cost. As a result he always wants abundant supplies of materials to take care of all production related contingencies. These considerations lead to larger investment in inventories.

Finance manager aims at pruning all unnecessary investment in inventories. His objective is to facilitate smooth production with minimum necessary investment in materials.

Material control reconciles these conflicts through encouraging efficiency in material procurement, efficieny in storage and efficiency in issue and usage of materials, the last largely falling within the domain of production function.

Aspects of Material Control

There are two aspects of material control: (a) Accounting and procedural aspect, and (b) Operational aspect:

(a) ***Accounting and Procedural Aspect.*** This is concerned with laying down detailed procedures for requisitioning, ordering, receiving, stocking, issuing, and paying for materials, This includes maintaining documentary evidence from the stage requirement of materials is initiated till the time materials are used in production.

(b) ***Operational Aspect.*** This deals with maintaining adeqaute supplies of all types of materials for smooth production operations; and also keeping investment in materials at lowest levels.

Objectives of Material Control

Two basic objectives of material control are; Continuous supply of materials for smooth production, and meeting material requirement at least cost. These can be further elaborated into the following objectives of material control:

1. **Continuous Availability of Materials.** Materials of all types should always be available for production. Situation of production stoppages due to materials running out of stocks, should be avoided. Such production stoppages are very costly in terms of loss of overheads and denial of sale. Panicky purchases should also be avoided.
2. **Optimum Investment in Materials.** Excessive investment in materials resulting from over stocking reduces profitability of the business. An important objective of material control is to ensure that the requirements of materials are met with minimum investment in materials.

Over stocking of materials locks up capital unproductively and increases storage cost. It is as bad as under stocking.

3. **Economy Purchasing.** Materials should be purchased at the lowest possible price without sacrificing quality, regularity and dependability of supplies.

4. **Regular and Dependable Information about Materials.** There should be up-to-date records of each type of material—the stock position, the minimum and the maximum level, special problems regarding certain types of materials and the list of dependable suppliers. This helps placing order of right size, at the right time and to the right supplier.

5. **Strict Quality Control.** There should be a strict system of quality control. The order for supplies of right quality of materials should be authorised. Materials should be tested at the time of their receipts and the person who has tested them should initial his work so that responsibility can be fixed if the quality has been compromised.

6. **Minimum Handling Cost and Time.** Materials should be stored at such a place and in such a manner that:

    (i) materials can be located at ease,

    (ii) there is minimum effort involved in making materials available to the user departments, and

    (iii) time consumed in tracing the materials and making them reach the user department should be least.

IMPORTANCE OF FIXED AND VARIABLE COST FOR DECISION-MAKING

Both fixed and variable costs are important for decision-making. However, their comparative importance differs at project stage and at operations stage.

Project stage or planning stage is one when the firm is in the process of deciding. What to produce? Which technology to deploy? How much capacity to create? And where to locate?

When the above basic decisions have been taken and implemented, and the firm is actually producing and selling, then it is said to be at the operations stage or operating stage.

At project stage both fixed and variable costs are relevant to decision-making process. The choice of product, technology, capacity size and location, and all governed by both these costs. The firm will not install a plant unless it hopes to recover both fixed variable costs fully and earn an adequate profit. It will choose that technology and location which result in least total of fixed and variable cost at the anticipated level of activity.

However, at project stage fixed cost acquires greater importance due to its various characteristics already mentioned. Decision regarding fixed costs involve large sum of money, are of irrevocable character, and affect operations of a firm for a long period of time. Hence these decisions attract greater attention.

At operations stage most of the fixed costs are sunk costs. They have been incurred and we can do nothing about them. Only way to recover them is to utilise them. The golden rule is let bygones be bygones. Let the dead remain buried in the grave. This approach holds true in all spheres in life. If we understand the rules of life deeply, the rules in spiriutal life and materialistic life are not so much different as they apparently appear. Whatever has happened, has happened. Our current decisions should be based on current costs. Therefore most decisions at operations stage are guided by variable costs.

Fixed costs become irrelevant for a number of decisions at operations stage. There is no point crying over costs which have already been incurred and we can do nothing in respect of them. Let our present decisions be not distorted by past costs. Certain fixed costs, such as, cash fixed costs, avoidable fixed and discretionary fixed costs have a role to play in certain decisions at operations state. Understanding the distinction between fixed and variable costs and their role in different types of decisions at different stages, is the crux of decision-making-budgeting, cost analysis, cost control, price fixation, make or buy, shut down, acceptance or rejection of a proposal, profit planning, etc.

CONTRACT COSTING PROCEDURE

The basic procedure for recording costs of contracts is as follows:

Contract Number. Each contract is assigned a distinct contract number for the purpose of identifying contracts and costs associated with contracts.

Contract Ledger. A Contract ledger is maintained in which a separate ledger account is opened for each contract for recording complete details of costs incurred, work-in-progress, revenues and profits or losses from each contract. Specimen of contract ledger is as follows:

Contract Ledger

Contract Account

Contract No........................	Contract Price.....................
Site Location.......................	Terms of Payment...............
Date of Commencement......	Work Certified....................
Date of Completion............	Date...............Rs..............
Remarks.............................	Date...............Rs..............

Dr. Cr.

Date	Particulars	Materials	Wages	Direct Expenses	Overheads	Sub-Contract Costs	Other exp	Total	Date	Particulars	Materials	Wages	Direct Expenses	Overheads	Sub-Contract Costs	Other exp.	Total
Total																	

COST OF PRODUCTION

Sum total of prime cost, production overheads and office and administration overheads is known as 'cost of production'.

Selling and Distribution Overheads

All cost incurred in making the finished product reach upto the customer are grouped as 'selling and distribution overheads'. These costs can be categorised as: *(i)* selling costs, *(ii)* publicity costs, and *(iii)* distribution costs.

(i) Selling costs refer to all those incurred on maintaining the sales office and sales staff *e.g.*, sales office rent, expenses relating to sales office-telephohe, stationery, light, etc., sales salaries, sales commision, marketing research, etc.

(ii) Publicity costs include expenditure incurred on advertisments and sales promotion, such as, publicity through television, radio, sign boards, neon signs, posters, hand bills, etc.

(iii) Distribution expenses include all expenses incurred in transporting the product from producer's premises to the customer's place, *e.g.*, carriage outward, expenses relating to delivery van, etc.

Cost of Sales

Total of prime cost, production overheads, office and administration overheads and selling and distribution overheads is known as 'cost of sales'.

Cost Sheet or Cost Statement

Cost sheet is prepared periodically to present details of cost incurred during a particular period on producing a particular cost unit. It gives details regarding total cost as well as different components of the total cost and cost per unit. Following are the components of cost:

1. Prime Cost = Direct Maerials + Direct Labour + Direct Factory Expenses.

2. Production Cost or Works Cost = Prime Cost + Factory Overheads.
3. Cost of Production = Production Cost + Office and Administration Overheads
4. Cost of Sales = Cost of Production + Selling and Distribution Overheads.
5. Sales = Cost of Sales ± Profit/Loss.

The build-up of cost and the details of cost components are given in the form of a chart also.

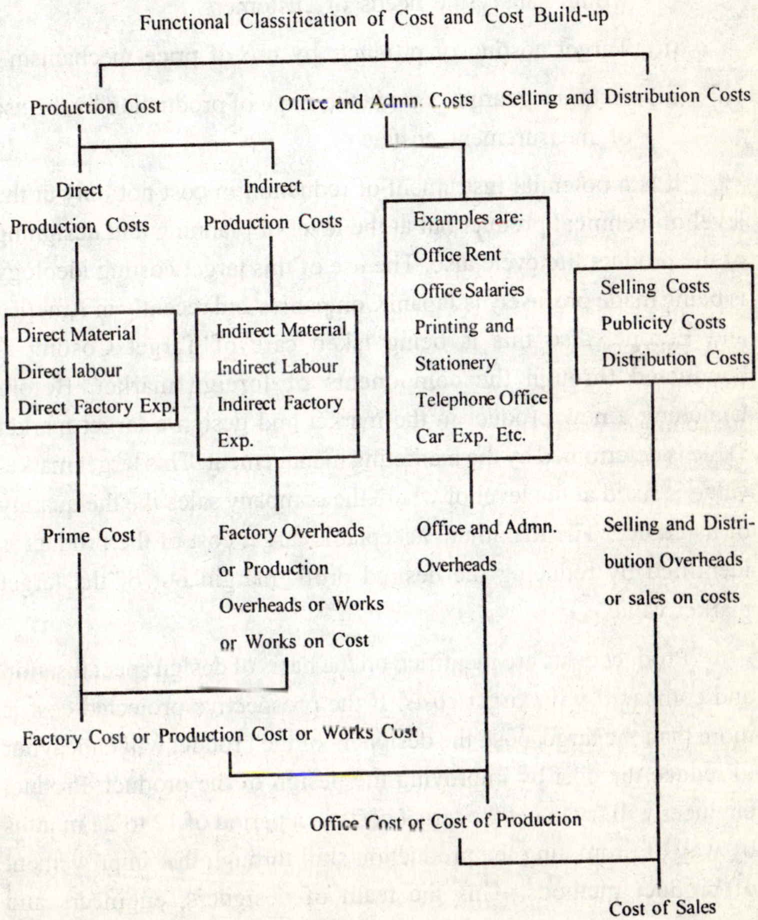

TARGET COSTING

Target costing was evolved in 1970's in Japan. Target costing may be defined as an instrument of cost management utilised in reduction of the total cost of product with the help of production, engineering, research and development etc. in its life cycle. Target cost is the projected cost of a product that enables a company to persist and compete in the market for a long time.

Shakugai has stated the process of target costing as under:

(i) Designing and planning of products of high quality which would satisfy the needs of customers.

(ii) Target costing of products by use of price mechanism.

(iii) Acquiring target costs in the stage of production by the use of measurement costs.

It is a potential instrument of reduction in cost not only at the level of technical product but at the level of planning and designing of the product life cycle also. The use of this target costing ideology is being made profusely is Japani Companies and recently in America and Europe, also this is being taken care of Target Costing is conducted through the components of foreign market. Before launching a new product in the market and design a target market value is determined by the marketing management. This target market value is fixed at the level of where the company sales the the quanity of its choice. The maximum acceptable target cost of the product is identified by reducing the desired profit margin out of the target market value.

Product costs are identified on the basis of design specialisation and compared with target costs. If the prospective projected cost is more than the target cost, the designers of the product will endeavour to reduce the cost by improving the design of the product. Product engineer will try to get the target costs in a period of 12 to 24 months by way of promoting the production skill through the improvement of product methods. This the team of designers, engineers and market managers will concentrate on the necessity of getting the target cost in the production along with cost accountant.

This concept is also used for reduction in the existing product cost. Where the target costing concept is used, the cost of the product is determined by market value and cost pricing is not utilised for the purpose. The cost of a new product may be more than the target cost yet the target cost is the only base of the product decisions. It is expected to equalise the product target cost at a particular demand level with product management like target competetive price. Ultimately it becomes the target of the company.

Steps in the Target Costing Process

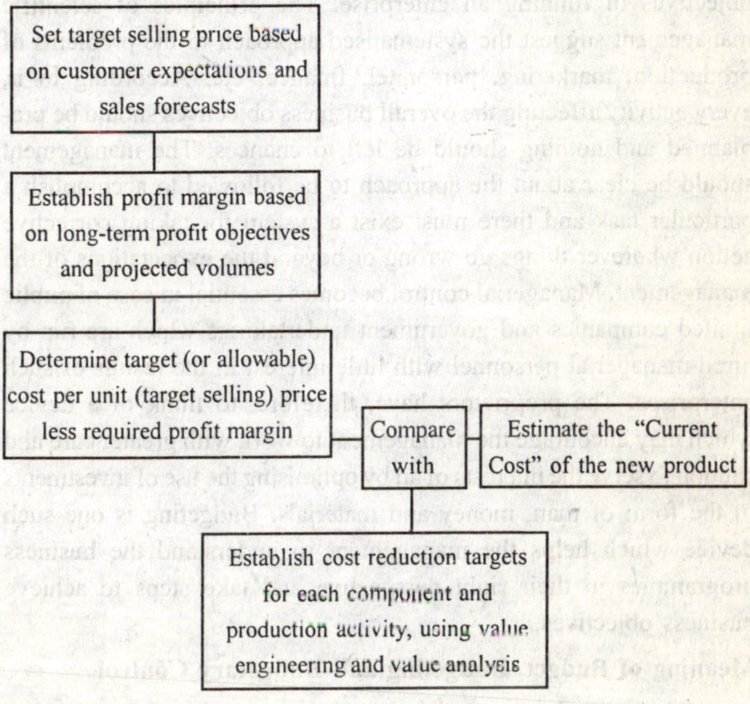

9

Budgets and Budgetary Control

The management of business activities on scientific basis is essential for optimising the use of resources with a view to achieving ultimate objectives of running an enterprise. The principles of scientific management suggest the systematised approach to the problems of production, marketing, personnel, finance, etc. According to it, every activity affecting the overall business objectives should be pre-planned and nothing should be left to chances. The management should be clear about the approach to be followed to accomplish a particular task and there must exist a system for taking corrective action wherever things go wrong or beyond the expectations of the management. Managerial control becomes essential in case of public limited companies and government undertakings which are run by hired managerial personnel with little interest in the results of such enterprises. The proprietors have, therefore, to think of a device which may encourage the management to work with greater care and caution to serve the interests of an by optimising the use of investments in the form of man, money and materials. Budgeting is one such device which helps the management to understand the business programmes in their right perspective and take steps to achieve business objectives.

Meaning of Budget, Budgeting and Budgetary Control

We know about central and state governments budgets which are presented in the parliament and state assemblies every year. These deals with the expected revenues and expenditure for a years time. In the field of commerce, business firms prepare different types of budgets such as sales budget, production budget, cash budget, etc. A budget is a formal business plan for some future period. According to J.J. Hampton "A budget is a formal plan expressed in dollars." Charles T. Horngren states, "A budget is a formal quantitative expression of management plan." Brown Howard are of the view that "a budget is a pre-determined statement of management policy during a given period which provides a standard for comparison with the results actually achieved." According to the Institute of Cost and Works Accountant, England a budget is "a financial or quantitative statement prior to a defined period of time, of a policy to be persued for that period to attain a given objective." From these definitions, the salient features of a budget may be noted as under:

1. A budget is a document in writing.
2. It pertains to a policy which is to be executed during budget period.
3. It relate to a defined period in future.
4. A budget is expressed in terms of physical quantities, money values or both.
5. Some specific objectives are to be achieved through the establishment of budgets.
6. Budgets provide a basis or standard for comparison with actual performance for control purposes.

Budgeting means planning for future. It involves the preparation of departmental budgets, budgetory control and related issues. The budgetory control is concerned with the management of business activities with the help of budgets. In this way, budgets serve as a control device. The Institute of Cost and Works Accountants, England, has defined budgetory control as the establishment of departmental budgets relating to the responsibilities of executives to the requirements of a policy, and the continuous comparison of actual with budgeted results, either to secure by individual action the objectives of that policy or to provide a firm basis for its revision." J. Batty defines budgetory control as "a system which uses budgets as a means of planning and controlling all aspects of producing and/ or selling commodities and services." In the opinion of Brown and Howard, "Budgetory control is a system of controlling costs which includes the preparation of budgets, coordinating the departments and establishing responsibilities, comparing actual performance with the budgeted and acting upon results to achieve maximum efficiency."

A close study of the above definitions of budgetary control clearly brings out the important features of the system as under:

1. Budgetary control involves the establishment and preparation of departmental budgets *i.e.*, budgets for different types of activities like sales, purchases, production, capital equipment, cash, etc.
2. It specifies the responsibilities of the departmental heads who are required to achieve the targets set out in the budgets for the realisation of business objectives.
3. It calls for continuous comparison of actual results with the budgeted specifications for the purpose of controlling activities concerning production and sales.
4. Budgetory control is aimed at enhancing over-all efficiency and profitability of an organisation through proper planning, coordination and control of activities for which budgets are prepared.
5. Budgets may be revised, if found necessary.

From the above it will be realized that budgets and budgetory control are not the two separate subjects to be studied separately. In fact, they are inter-linked as the budgetary control is not possible without budgets and budgets are meant for controlling business activities.

OBJECTS OF BUDGETARY CONTROL

The management of an organisation is primarily concerned with the realization of organisational objectives. In its efforts to achieve these objectives, it has to manage the enterprise efficiently by optimising the use of resources and eliminating or minimising the wastes, if any. Budgetory control is one of the important techniques which help the management in controlling business activities in a desired direction.

It serves the following objectives in an enterprise:

1. Formalise Business Objectives. The business objectives are formalised in the form of different types of budgets which sets targets in physical and/or monetary values.

2. Coordination and Balanced Efforts. Budgeting seeks to achieve coordination between departments. Budgets for different departments are prepared only after taking into account their interdependence. For example, production budget is influenced by the sales budget and the available production facilities. The coordination which is an essential element in management becomes effective when budgets are rightly drawn and implemented.

3. Communication. Budgeting fills the communication gap between management and employees through departmental budgets which are used as a vehicle to communicate the targets in explicit terms to various levels of management. Since budgeting accomplish the task of communicating goals and targets, the top management is not required to tell and guide the departmental heads about their areas of responsibilities.

4. Control. Controlling of various types of activities is the prime objective of budgeting. Budgets serve as an index of effeciency expected of the employees. The comparison of actual performance with the budget specifications sharply tells the difference. Management action is needed in case the actual performance is less than the desired performance. Thus budgeting fulfills the objective of control which is always desirable for smooth functioning of an enterprise.

5. Delegation of Authority. Budgeting aims at effective delegation of authority and decentralization of responsibility. This objective is achieved by communicating the functional budgets to different levels of management.

ADVANTAGES OF BUDGETARY CONTROL

Budgetary control has assumed a special significance in almost every organisation. There is hardly any enterprise and government department in which budgeting is not done. The budgetary control system enables the management to enhance over-all efficiency for the achievements of organisational objectives. It contributes in the development of an undertaking in the following manner:

1. Budgetary control provides an action plan which is prepared after a great deal of exercise on various issues which might affect the execution of the plan. With the adoption of formal budgets, everybody in the organisation knows and understands his responsibilities which prevents all sorts of confusions as regards authority and responsibility.

2. With a prior knowledge of work to be done the management can develop an appropriate strategy for the achievements of the targets set out in the budgets.

3. Budgeting develops a sense of responsibility among the employees who are required to do a particular work in a given period of time. The powers can be delegated without much fear of its being misused.

4. Budgeting helps in the coordination of business activities without which an enterprise cannot run in perfect harmony. For example, production budget is drawn in accordance with the expected sales as set out in Sales budget. Similarly, purchase budget is prepared according to quantity production as shown in production budget.

5. Budgetary control provides for the preparation of variance report which contains a comparatives study of actual and budgeted figures with variances. An adverse variance, *i.e.,* actual performance falling short of budgeted performance, is brought to the knowledge of top management which finally takes corrective action to avoid such a situation in the next budget period. In this manner control becomes more effective.

6. Delays in the implementation of the business programmes is avoided by the preparation and implementation of budgets well in time.

7. Budget serves as a medium of written communication. It ensures better understanding and harmoneous relation between top management, managers and workers.

8. Budgets, if properly drawn economise the use of resources. For example, if the budget for inventories is rightly drawn up, it will reduce the requirements of the money to be tied up in inventories.

9. Overheads budget sets limit to expenditure on various items. Any expenditure beyond the limit specified can be incurred only with the prior sanction of the competent authority. Thus there is opportunity to scrutinize the expenditure before it is actually incurred. Thus over-spending of overheads can be checked and scarce financial resources put to proper use.

10. Budgets suggest the arrangement the facilities well in advance for maintaining the operational efficiency of any enterprise. For instance, Cash budget clearly indicates the deficit/surplus cash position at different timings and accordingly additional working capital may be procured or surplus cash invested for effective working of the organisation.

11. Budgetary control provides a basis for rewarding the employees who perform better. It is generally not used as a punitive measure.

12. A sound budgetary control system can contribute in the set up the standard costing which can act a complementary to budgeting.

LIMITATIONS OF BUDGETARY CONTROL SYSTEM

Budgets and budgetary control system is, undoubtedly, very important for running an enterprise on scientific basis for optimising the use of available resources and achieving organisational objectives. However, the system suffers from certain limitations and the management should keep them in view while adopting and implementing the system. The main limitations are as under:

1. Budgets are Estimates. The figures contained in a budget. are simply an estimate about future. Budgets are prepared on the basis of certain assumptions about future. It is likely that the assumptions might not hold good. In that case, the whole budget will have to be recast. The revision of budgets in accordance with the changes in business conditions is a must for the success of budgeting.

2. Wrong Budgets may be Prepared. The success of budgetary control system largely depends upon the accuracy with which the budgets are prepared. If the forecasting is done on the basis of inadequate informations or subjective considerations of management, then the wrong budgets will be formulated. Wrong budgeting leads to wrong strategies which leads to wastage of resources and thus the very purpose of budgeting is forfeited.

3. Mismanagement. Budgetary control becomes effective only when the managers who are responsible for implementing the budgets are efficient and duty conscious. Budgeting itself is no guarantee for success in business if the management is inefficient or indifferent to the budgetary control system. There can be no substitute for better management.

4. Employees Resistance. Sometimes, the employees who are charged with the responsibility of operating the budgets and achieve the desired results oppose budgeting due to their inefficient character which is exposed when they fail to achieve the targets. Many a times, the resistance to budgeting is just psychological. The top management can lessen the workers' resistance to budgeting by the preparation of realistic budgets with the consent and cooperation of all those who are concerned with the implementation of budgeting in the organisation.

5. Rigidity. Generally, the management prepares the budgets for next year by making some changes here and there in the existing budgets. This method of budget preparation introduces an element of rigidity in budgeting which can be eliminated by introducing the system of zero base budgeting in which a fresh thought is given to the whole issue of budgeting.

6. Costly Affair. The system involves cost in terms of money, time and energy. Efforts should be made to reduce the cost by developing an appropriate and simple method of budgeting and control system.

Every system has its limitations, so is the case with budgets and budgetary control system. Most of the limitations can be avoided by intelligent management of the budgetary control system. Following points deserve special attention of top for being successful in budgeting:

1. **Defining Business Objectives.** The management should define business objectives both short-term and long-term in unambiguous terms so that everyone in the organisation understand them and budgets are prepared realistically.
2. **Defining Duties and Responsibilities.** The authority, duties and responsibilities of each level of executives should also be clearly defined. For this purpose, an organisation chart should be laid down.
3. **Fixation of Budget Period.** Budget period is a period of time for which a budget is prepared. It should be clearly fixed.
4. **Identification of Key Factors.** Key factors means the basic or fundamental factors which powerfully hinder the budgets operations. The availability of skilled labour, raw materials or machine capacity may be a limiting factory. The management should prepare budget keeping in view the availability of basic facilities.
5. **Cooperation of Employees.** Budgeting cannot be successful without the cooperation and involvement of all these who are directly or indirectly concerned with the preparation and implementation of budgets. The management should involve all departmental heads in the preparation of budgets and seek their valuable opinion, support and cooperation which are vital for the success in budgeting.
6. **Support of top Management.** Budgeting cannot succeed if the top management is indifferent and lack enthusiasm for successful implementation of budgetory control system. The whole-hearted support of management is essential for the achievement of business objectives through the device of budgets and budgetary control.
7. **Realistic Budgets.** Realistic budgets based on objective assessment of things are necessary for success in budgeting. Budgets prepared on the assumptions of idealistic conditions

will set the targets on higher side which will cause frustration among the executives.

8. **Revision of Budgets.** The management should revise the budgets if the circumstances so warrants. Budget revision becomes necessary if the factors influencing budgeting have drastically changed. It is also needed when some errors with the existing budgets are found at later date.

9. **Efficient Accounting System.** There must exist an efficient accounting system to provide necessary data to the system of budgetary control. The accounting department should be actively involved in the process of budgeting.

10. **Proper Communication System.** The management should develop effective means of communication between different levels of management. The system of communication should enable the flow of information from top to bottom and from bottom to top without any hinderence. Any communication gap will retard the smooth functioning of the budgetary control system.

11. **Appointment of Budget Committee and Budgetary Controller.** The task of preparation of budgets may be entrusted to a Budget Committee consisting of various departmental heads and a budgetary controller may be appointed to act as a coordinator or convener of Budget Committee.

12. **Introduction of Incentive Plan.** Since the budgeting tends to be mechanical over a period of time, the management should keep alive the interest of executives in budgeting by educating them about the need and importance of budgeting for the enterprise with which their fate is associated. The management may introduce an incentive. plan to reward all those who are able to achieve the performance expected of them.

Organisation for Budgetary Control System

An efficient organisation for budgetory control is highly important for achieving the objectives of budgeting. It provides the framework within which the managerial functions of preparation, execution and control of budgets take place for the successful performance of business programmes. The organisation for an effective budgetory control consist of a Budget Committee and appointment of a Budgetory Controller.

Budget Committee

Budgeting is a continuous process. It requires full attention of the management so that timely action is taken on issues concerning the preparation, maintenance and administration of budgets. Generally, the top management appoints a committee known as Budget Committee which works under the supervision of a budget officer. The Budget Committee consists of the executive heads of different departments in the undertaking. Following functions are usually performed by a Budget committee:

1. Defines management policies relating to budgeting.
2. Prescribes general guidelines for the preparation of budgets.
3. Collects and provides necessary informations to divisional managers for the preparation of budgets.
5. Coordinates departmental activities through budgets.
4. Scrutinizes, revises and approves the budgets as prepared by different divisional managers. In this process it reconciles the divergent views of the the departmental heads.
6. Receives budget performance reports to fix responsibilities and suggest corrective actions in case of less than expected performance of any department.
7. Prepares Master Budget which integrates the departmental budgets and also includes the estimated Profit and Loss Account and Balance Sheet.
8. Suggests revision of budgets, if necessary.

The Budget Committee works in an advisory capacity but its recommendations are generally accepted by the top management. Thus, the Budget Committee is a powerful committee which performs a very useful role for the success of budgetary control system in an enterprise.

Budgetary Controller

The top management appoints an officer to supervise and guide the Budget Committee in the discharge of its functions. This officer is variously designated as Budget Officer, Budget Director, Budget Coordinator cr Budgetary Controller in different organisations. He is generally a controller or chief accountant well versed in accounting and budgeting matters. The Budgetary controller is attached to the chief executive to whom he is accountable in matters of budgeting. He is expected to perform the following functions:

1. To call meetings of the departmental heads and educate them in the mechanism of budgeting.
2. To repare budget programme and budget schedules.
3. To develop necessary forms for the preparation of budgets and other reports.
4. To act as the secretary or coordinator of Budget Committee and guide its functioning.
5. To review and maintain budget manual.
6. To coordinate the efforts of departmental heads who are involved in budget preparation.
7. To prepare summary budgets for the consideration of the Budget Committee.
8. To get the budgets approved by the Board of Management before they are passed on to the departmental heads for execution.
9. To conduct special studies needed for the preparation and finalization of budgets.
10. To consider in the Budget Committee the proposals of the departments.

It should be noted that the functions of the Budget Committee and that of Budgetary Controller are not different. In fact, the functions of Budget Committee form part of the duties of Budgetary Controller who performs most of his functions through the Budget Committee. However, the budgetary controller is responsible and accountable to management for the smooth functioning of the budgetary control system. He seeks the opinion of the Board of Management on the critical issues and acts according to the instructions of the Board which formulates budget policies and set business objectives. A simple organisation chart for budgetary control system is presented below:

Board of Directors Budget
Committee—Budgetary Controller

Marketing Manager	*Production Manager*	*Purchase Manager*	*Financial Manager*
1. Sales Budget	1. Production Budget	1. Material Purchase Budget	1. Capital Expenditure Budget
2. Selling & Distribution Budget	2. Plant utilization Budget		2. Overheads cost Budget.
	3. Maintenance Budget		3. Cash Budget.
			4. Master Budget.

Personal Manager

I. Labour Cost Budget.

Types of Budgets

Budgeting in an undertaking may be done for a particular segment or it may cover all the activities depending upon the need and resources of the enterprise. The large scale business enterprises prepare different types of budgets covering almost all activities where control is desired. In order to understand the nature of budgets, it is desirable to know their classification which is usually done on time, functions and flexibility basis.

According to time, budgets can be of three types *viz., (i)* Long-term budgets, *(ii)* Short-term budgets, and (iii) Current budgets. Long-term budgets are concerned with planning activities for a long-period-a period of 5 to 10 or more years whereas short period budgets cover a period of 1 to 2 years. Current budgets relate to the current period within a short-period of 1 year. An yearly budget is generally broken on monthly, quarterly or balf-yearly basis for effective implementation of the same.

According to functional classification, a budget relates to a particular activity which can be a selling, production, purchasing or any other activity. The budgets prepared according to functions are known as functional budgets. The popular functional budgets prepared in a large scale enterprise are,

1. Sales budget
2. Production budget
3. Purchase budget
4. Capital expenditure budget
5. Overhead cost budgets
6. Cash budget
7. Research and development budget.

On the basis of flexibility, budgets are grouped into two categories, namely—*(i)* Fixed budgets, and *(ii)* Flexible or Variable budgets. A fixed budget is one which rigidly specifies the targets for a particular level of activity. The targets are not revised during the budget period irrespective of the fact that the actual level of activity attained in much different from the budgeted figure. Consequently the variances are violent and it becomes difficult to isolate the reasons for variances due to change in the level of activity. Fixed or static budgets can serve the purpose only if the budgets can be prepared with high degree of accuracy and budget-period is short because the forecast for short period can be made with reasonable degree of accuracy. On the other hand, a flexible budget is one which permits the change in accordance with the changes in the level of activity. According to flexible budgeting, budgets for different levels of activity are prepared and the management enjoys the benefit of adopting anyone of them according to changes in the attainment of the level of activity. Thus, the flexible budget has a series of fixed budgets for different levels of activity. It is always preferable to prepare flexible budget particularly when the economic conditions frequently change and it is difficult to forecast with any fair degree of accuracy.

PREPARATION OF BUDGETS

The preparation of realistic budgets is essential for success in budgeting. Budgets are prepared after having set the objectives, goals and strategies for the achievement of over-all business objectives. In this section, we will study as to how different types of functional budgets are prepared.

Sales Budget

A sales budget is a statement expressed in physical quantities or/and values of anticipated sales during a specified period of time. Sales forecasting is the basic step in the preparation of a sales budget. It is done by sales department under the charge of a sales manager in consultation and cooperation with the Budget Controller. The forecasting of sales is not an easy job. It requires a lot of skill and knowledge in the techniques of sales forecasting, collection of relevant facts and figure and an understanding of business environment in which the firm is placed. The techniques of sales forecasting for new products are different from those used for established products.

In case of established products, historical data relating to sales quantities and expenditure on selling compaign are available within the firm. The sales department also possesses good knowledge about its market share, nature of competition, availability of substitutes, consumers preferences etc. The sales data for the last few years are compiled in a form what is known as 'Time Series' which is statistically dealt to fit a trend line and extrapolate the sales figures for future. This technique is quite simple and widely used by business firms for the purpose of sales forecasting. However, it can be profitably used only if the Time Series do not show violent fluctuations and corrections are rightly made for seasonal and stochastic variations.

The amount of sales in any given period is much affected by the amount spent on advertisement and other sales promotion techniques. A study of correlation between expenditure on advertisement and amount of sales in different time periods will reveal the degree of impace of advertising cost on amount of sales. Thus sales should be predicted only after due consideration to the advertisement budget for the period for which sales budget is being prepared.

The sales force *i.e.* salesmen, selling agents and sales managers, being in actual field of selling activity, can contribute a lot in correct forecasting of sales by sending their assessment of sales to head office for the budget period. The management should accept the estimated figures as reported by sales personnel only after due allowance for subjectivity of field staff.

In case of new product, the question of availability of any data within the firm does not arise. Therefore, sales forecasting is done by conducting market research which consists of conducting market surveys for the collection of relevant data needed for sales budget. The market research tries to find out the consumers demand for company's products. It is carried out through a well-designed questionaire which is either sent to potential buyers for being filled and returned by them or get filled in through the personal investigation method. The data so collected are compiled and adjusted in the light of other factors which might affect consumers demand.

The consideration of prevailing and expected economic environment within and outside the industry is essential before any decision on budgeted sales is taken. The management should give proper valuation in their estimation for sales for factors such as the structure of national income, government fiscal and monetary policies, industrial policy, import-export policy, demographic structure, etc., insofar as they influence the demand for firm's products.

In a modern age of competition, sales is generally a limiting factor. In case of certain products, sales may not be a constraint and the estimated sales might be much higher than the production facilities available within the firm. Under such a situation, the possibilities of increasing production should be fount out and the production budget be prepared first.

The data of budgeted sales can be arranged in a number of ways. They can be grouped according to commodity, territory or salesmen-wise. Consider the following form of a sales budget according to commodity wise:

Sales Budget

for the 6-Months Ending on 30th June, 1987

Months	*Product A*		*Product B*		*Total*	
	Quantity	*Value*	*Quantity*	*Value*	*Quantity*	*Value*

Illustration—1

Priyadarshani Cement Ltd. manufactures two types of cement known as 'Black' and 'White'. The cement is sold in the three states of U.P., Haryana and Punjab through stock dealers. From the following data relating to budget period ended on 30th June, 1987 and the adjoining information, you are required to prepare a Sales Budget for 6-months period beginning from 1st July and ending on 31st Dec., 1987.

Commodity	**Territories**					
	Uttar Pradesh		*Punjab*		*Haryana*	
	Budgeted	*Actual*	*Budgeted*	*Actual*	*Budgeted*	*Actual*
Black Cement	25,000	24,000	20,000	18,000	10,000	10,000
White Cement	15,000	12,000	10,000	10,000	5,000	4,500
Total	40,000	36,000	30,000	28,000	15,000	14,500

Other Informations

1. The construction activity is expected to go up by 10% and accordingly the demand in all states except in Punjab, is likely to increase in the budget period. The Sales Department visualises a decrease in sales by 5% in Punjab.

2. The company has decided to appoint few more dealers in U.P. and it forecasts an additional sales of 5,000 bags of black cement through the new dealers.

3. With a vigorous advertisement campaign, the demand in Haryana for both black and white cement is likely to increase by 20% in addition to the 10% as pointed out above.

4. The company expects to make direct supplies to local bodies in the states of U.P. and Haryana. It hopes to sell 2,000 bags of black cement in each of these states.

5. Adequate production facilities exist and there is no limiting factor.

6. The selling price per bag is estimated at Rs. 60 and 100 for black and white cement respectively.

PRIYADARSHNI CEMENT LTD.

Sales Budget

For 6-Months (1st July to 31st December, 2004)

Territories	*For 1st Jan. to 30th June, 04*				*July-Dec., 04*			
	Black Cement (Bags)		*White Cement (bags)*		*Budget for 6-Months*			
	Budgeted	*Actuals*	*Budgeted*	*Actuals (Bags)*	*Black (Bags*	*White*	*(Rs.) Black*	*White (%)*
U.P.	25,000	24,000	15,000	12,000	33,400	13,200	20,04,000	13,20,000
Punjab	20,000	18,000	10,000	10,000	17,100	9,500	10,26,000	9,50,000
Haryana	10,000	10,000	5,000	4,500	15,000	5,850	9,00,000	5,85,000
Total	55,000	52,000	30,000	26,500	65,500	28,550	39,30,000	28,55,000

Statement of Sales Forecast (Bags)

	U.P.		*Punjab*		*Haryana*	
	Black	*White*	*Black*	*White*	*Black*	*White*
Present Sale	24,000	12,000	18,000	10,000	10,000	4,500
Increase due to construction activity (10% of existing)	+ 2,400	+ 1,200	—	—	+1,000	+450
Estimated decrease for Punjab (5%)	—	—	–900	–500	—	—
Additional sales by new dealers	+ 5,000	—	—	—	—	—
Increase due to massive advertising compaign (20% of existing)	—	—	—	—	+ 2,000	+900
Direct Supplies	+2,000	—	—	—	+ 2,000	
Total	33,400	13,200	17,100	9,50	15,000	5,850

Selling and Distribution Cost Budget

The selling budget is followed by a selling and distribution cost budget which provides an estimated expenditure on selling and distribution of the goods as shown in the sales budget. The sales overhead costs consist of expenditure on items such as salaries to salesmen and their commission, advertising, warehouse charges, delivery van's fuel and repairs charges, sales office expenditure, etc. All such and similar other expenditure of sales ar rclassified commodity-wise or territory-wise and shown in the selling cost budget in an orderly manner. The principles involved in the classification and presentation of selling and distribution cost in the budget are similar to that of sales budget.

Illustration-2

New Hosiery Products Ltd operates in North and West regions of India. From the following selling and distribution cost budget with actual expenditure for the 6-months period which expired on 30th June, 1987 and the adjoining information, you are required to prepare a Selling and Distribution Cost Budget of the company for the next budget period which will end on 31st December, 2004.

Selling and Distribution Cost Budget

for the Half Year Ended on 30th June, 2004

Elements of selling cost	*North* Budgeted	*North* Actuals	*West* Budgeted	*West* Actuals
(1)	*(2)*	*(3)*	*(4)*	*(5)*
1. Fixed selling overheads:				
Salesmen's salaries	9,500	9,500	6,000	6,000
Sales office salaries	6,000	6,000	2,500	2,500
Travelling allowances	2,000	2,500	1,000	1,250
Sales office rent	1,000	1,000	500	500
Show room charges	500	500	400	400
Advertising	2,000	2,500	1,500	2,000
Total (A)	22,000	23,000	12,500	13,250

Contd.

(1)	*(2)*	*(3)*	*(4)*	*(5)*
2. Variable selling overheads:				
Salesmen's commission	10 , 000	8,000	6,000	5,000
Packing charges	2,500	2,000	1,500	1,250
Carriage outward	5,000	4,000	3,000	2,500
Delivery Van's fuel and maintenance	4,000	3,200	2,000	1,600
Total (8)	21,500	17,200	12,500	10,350
Total (A) + (B)	43,500	40,200	25,000	23,600

Other Informations

The management has decided to incorporate the following decisions in the selling and distribution cost budget for the next budget period:

1. Existing salesmen's salary is to be increased by 15% and salaries of office personnel be enhanced by 10%.
2. One additional salesman in each region be appointed at a consolidated salary of Rs, 1,000 p.m.
3. Travelling allowances be increased by 10% of the actual incurred in current period.
4. Advertisement budget be enhanced by 50%.
5. The salesmen are entitled to a commission of 2%. Sales in next six months are expected to go up by 30% in each region.
6. Fuel consumption will increase in proportion to increase in sales.

Production Budget

The production budget deals with the amount of goods to be produced during the budget period. Sales budget is the forerunner of production budget. It suggests the quantities which should be produced in order to maintain sales and delivery schedules. Other considerations in the preparation of a production budget are:

New Hosiery Products Ltd.
Selling and Distribution Cost Budget
for Six Months (1st July to 31st December, 2004)

(Rs.)

Cost Constituents	*Budget for current period*			*Actuals for current period*			*Budget for Next Period*		
	North	*West*	*Total*	*North*	*West*	*Total*	*North*	*West*	*Total*
(1)	*(2)*	*(3)*	*(4)*	*(5)*	*(6)*	*(7)*	*(8)*	*(9)*	*(10)*
Fixed/Semi-variable cost									
Salesmen's salary	19,500	16,000	35,000	19,500	16,000	35,500	28,425	24,400	52,825
Sales office-salary	6,000	2,500	8,500	6,000	2,500	8,500	6,600	2,750	9,350
Travelling Allowances	2,000	1,000	3,000	2,5000	1,250	3,750	2,750	1,375	4,125
Sales office rent	1,000	500	1,500	1,000	500	1,500	1,000	500	1,500
Show room rent	500	400	900	500	400	900	500	400	900
Warehouse Rent	1,000	600	1,600	1,000	600	1,600	1,000	600	1,600
Advertising	2,000	1,500	3,500	2,500	2,000	4,500	3,000	2,250	5,250
Total	32,000	22,500	54,500	33,000	23,250	43,275	32,275	75,750	

Contd.

(1)	(2)	(3)	(4)	(5)	(6)	(7)	(8)	(9)	(10)
Variable cost:									
Salesmen's commission	10,000	6,000	16,000	8,000	5,000	13,000	10,400	6,500	16,900
Packing charges	2,500	1,500	4,000	2,00	1,250	3,250	2,600	1,625	4,225
Carriage outward	5,000	3,000	8,000	4,000	2,500	6,500	5,200	3,250	8,450
Delivery Van's- fuel and maintenance	4,000	2,000	6,000	3,200	1,600	4,800	4,160	2,080	6,240
Total	21,500	12,500	34,000	17,200	10,350	27,550	22,360	13,455	35,815
Total Overheads	43,500	25,000	68,500	40,200	23,600	63,800	75,635	45.730	1,11365

__________ Checked by   __________ Prepared by

1. The opening and desired closing inventories.
2. Installed plant capacity and existing utilization.
3. Availability of necessary production inputs.
4. Production cycle.
5. Production policy of management.

An analysis of the above factors will suggest the amount of goods that can be produced within the factory. If the calculated production is less than the budgeted sales, then the firm will not be in a position to maintain the sales budget and earn sufficient profits for which potential exists. In such a situation, the firm,should explore the following possibilities before taking a final decision on production budget:

1. Can the inventory level be reduced?
2. Can the plant utilization capacity be increased or additional plant installed to fill the gap?
3. Is there any possibility of additional work to be done outside through the system of sub-contracting.
4. Is it possible and desirable to introduce over-time or additional shift working to increase production?

Statement of Changes

	North	*West*
(1)	*(2)*	*(3)*
Existing Salesmen's salary	19,500	16,000
Add 15%	2,925	2,400
	22,425	18,400
Additional Salesman's salary	6,000	6,000
Sales office salary	6,600	2,750
Travelling allowances	2,500	1,250
Add 10% increase	250	125

(1)	*(2)*	*(3)*
Sales office rent	1,000	500
Show room rent	500	400
Warehouse rent	1,000	600
Advertising	2,000	1,500
Add increase	1,000	750
	43,275	32,275
Salesmen's commission	8,000	5,000
Add 30% increase	2,400	1,500
Packing	2,000	1,250
Add 30% increase	600	375
Carriage outward	4,000	2,500
Add 30%	1,200	750
Delivery Yan's—fuel and maintenance	3,200	1,600
Add 30%	960	480
Total	22,360	13,455

In case sales is a limiting factor and adequate production facilities exist, the final shape to the production budget should be given only after the consideration of the issues such as,

1. Possibility of increasing sale through massive advertising campaign.
2. Creation of additional demand by price reduction and other sales promotion techniques.
3. Utilization of surplus plant capacity for production of other goods or sub-letting the same to other producers.

A detailed enquiry into the above issues will lead the production manager to set up a realistic production budget which can be presented commodity-wise, department-wise or period-wise.

Illustration-3

Priyadarshani Cement Ltd. has budgeted sales as under:

Months	*Black Cement*	*White Cement*
July 1987	5,000	2,000
August	10,000	4,000
Sember	12,000	5,000
October	15,000	6,000
November	13,500	5,000
December	10,000	6,550
January 2005	12,000	5,000
	77,500	33,500

The company maintains inventory equal to half of the sales for next month and there is no work-in-progress at the end of any month.

Prepare the Production Budget for the half year ending on 31st December, 2004.

PRIYADARSHANI CMENT LTD.
Production Budget for Half-Year Ending on 31st Dec., 2005

Product y	*Months*					
	July	*Aug.*	*Sep.*	*Oct.*	*Nov.*	*Dec.*
(1)	*(2)*	*(3)*	*(4)*	*(5)*	*(6)*	*(7)*
Black Cement						
Budgeted Sales	5,000	10,000	12,000	15,000	13,500	10,000
Add closing inventories (50% of next month)	5,000	6,000	7,500	6,750	5,000	6,000
	10,000	16,000	19,500	21,750	18,500	16,000
Less opening inventories	2,500	5,000	6,000	7,500	6,750	5,000
Budgeted Production	7,500	11,000	13,500	14,250	11,750	11,000

(1)	(2)	(3)	(4)	(5)	(6)	(7)
White Cement						
Budgeted Sales	2,000	4,000	5,000	6,000	5,000	6,550
Add closing inventory	1,000	2,500	3,000	2,500	3,275	2,500
	3,000	6,500	8,000	8,500	8,275	9,050
Less opening inventory	1,000	1,000	2,500	3,000	2,500	3,275
Budgeted production	2,000	5,500	5,500	5,000	5,775	5,775

Production Cost Budget

The production cost budget is prepared to know the estimated expenditure on the budgeted production as set out in production budget. The production cost consists of the cost of raw materials, labour and production overhead costs. Therefore, the Production Cost Budget includes the cost of each of these components on the budgeted production. Separate budgets for raw materials, labour and overheads can also be prepared for better understanding and control of each of the element of cost.

Raw Materials Budget

The raw material budget deals with the quantities of raw materials and components required to produce the budgeted production. The production department determines the quantity of raw materials and the Purchase Department furnishes the rates at which the raw materials can be purchased. Total cost of each type of raw material required is arrived at by multiplying the quantity and rate of raw material.

Illustration—4

Priyadarshani Cement Ltd., has budgeted the production of Black and White Cement as 69,900 bags and 24,550 bags respectively for the 6-months period which will end on 31st December, 2004. The production engineer has reported the consumption of different types of raw materials in the production of one bag of 50 kgs. as under:

Material No.	*Black Cement*	*Material*	*White Cement*
MO 1	20 kgs.	MO 5	25 kgs.
MO 2	15 kgs.	MO 6	10 kgs.
MO 3	10 kgs.	MO 7	10 kgs.
MO 1	5 kgs.	MO 8	5 kgs.

The purchase department estimates the cost of raw materials as under:

Raw Materials	*Rate per bag (Rs.)*
MO 1	30.00
MO 2	35.00
MO 3	20.00
MO 4	40.00
MO 5	50.00
MO 6	70.00
MO 7	80.00
MO 8	60.00

You are required to prepare the Materials Budget for the half-year ended on 31st December, 2004. There is no wastage in production.

Material Budget for the Half Year ended on 31st December, 2004

Code Number of raw materials	*Quantity*	*Rate per Bag*	*Value (Rs.)*
(1)	*(2)*	*(3)*	*(4)*
MO 1	13,80,000 kgs. (27,600 Bags)	30/-	8,28,000
MO 2	10,35,000 (20,700 Bags)	35/-	7,24,500
MO 3	6,90,000 (13,800 Bags)	20/-	2,76,000
MO 4	3,45,000 (6,900 Bags)	40/-	2,76,000
	69,000 Bags		21,04,500

(1)	*(2)*	*(3)*	*(4)*
MO 5	6,13,750 kgs. (12,275 Bags)	50/-	6,13,750
MO 6	2,45,500 (4,910 Bags)	70/-	3,43,700
MO 7	2,45,500 (4,910 Bags)	80/-	3,92,800
MO 8	1,22,750 (2,45 Bags)	60/-	1,47,300
	24,550 Bags		14,97,550
Total	93,550 Bags		36,02,050

Raw Materials Purchase Budget

The raw materials purchase budget represents the physical quantities of different types of raw materials and other components which must be purchased during a given time period for the maintenance of production schedules. It also shows the money values required to purchase the budgeted raw materials. The quantities which must be purchased are arrived at only after the consideration of the opening and closing inventories of raw materials. The purchases to be made are also governed by the storage capacity and availability of necessary finances.

Illustration—5

Priyadarshani Cement Ltd. furnishes the following details regarding consumption and inventory levels of raw materials:

Materials	*Budgeted consumption for 6 months*	*Opening-Stock 1-7-2003*	*Closing stock 31-12-2003*	*Rate of purchase*
MO 1	27,600	3,000	5,000	30
MO 2	20,700	2,500	3,500	35
MO 3	13,800	2,000	4,000	20
MO 4	6,900	1,000	1,000	40

You are required to prepare the Raw Materials Purchase Budget.

PRIYADARSHANI CEMENT LTD.

Materials Purchase Budget for Half Year (July to December)

(Bags)

Particulars	*MO 1*	*MO 2*	*MO 3*	*MO 4*
Budgeted consumption	27,600	20,700	13,800	6,900
Add desired closing stock	5,000	3,500	4,000	1,000
	32,600	24,200	17,800	7,900
Less opening stock	3,000	2,500	2,000	1,000
Quantity to be purchased	29,600	21,700	15,800	6,900
Rate of purchase	30/-	35/-	20/-	40/-
Value of Purchases (Rs.)	8,88,000	7,59,500	3,16,000	2,76,000

Labour Cost Budget

Labour cost budget represents the total amount of money which will be needed for payment to workers, direct as well as indirect, during the production budget period. It can be prepared only if the total number of labour hours to produce the budgeted quantity and the rate per hour are known. The nature of production suggests the kind oflabour required and the work study tells the total labour hours required to achieve budgeted production. Labour rates can be collected from the personnel department. That should, however, be modified in the light of the likely changes in wage-rates. Total labour cost is arrived at by multiplying together the labour hours and the wage rate. A comparison of the existing labour force in terms of hours and the budgeted labour hours will disclose whether additional labour will be required or some existing labour will be rendered surplus.

Illustration—6

M/s. Ram Nath & Sons produces a chemical—'ST' which requires the employment of skilled and semi-skilled workers. From the following details prepare labour cost budget:

	July	*August*	*September*
Budgeted production (Tons)	1,500	2,000	2,500
Number of workers required :			
Skilled	5	5	6
Semi-skilled	3	3	4
Hourly wage-rate: Skilled	15.00	15.50	16.00
Unskilled	8.00	8.50	8.50

The production unit works on the basis of a single shift of 8 hours daily and there are only 25 effective working days in a month.

Solution

Labour Cost Budget
(July to September, 2003)

y	*July*	*August*	*September*
Budgeted production (Tons)	1,500	2,000	2,500
Number of hours required:			
Skilled	1,000	1,000	1,200
Semi-skilled	600	600	800
Hourly wage-rate:			
Skilled	15.00	15.50	16.00
Semi-skilled	80/-	8.50	8.50
Total Labour Cost:			
Skilled	15,000.00	15,500.00	19,200.00
Semi-skilled	4,800.00	5,100.00	6,800.0.00
Total Labour Cost	19,800.00	20,600.00	26,000.00

Production Overheads Budget

This budget presents a forecast of indirect expenses which are linked with production. All expenses of production office such as salaries of office personnel including works manager's salary, factory rent, depreciation, insurance, light and fuel, stationery, etc., are included in this budget. The total production expenses are classified into fixed and variable components. They can further be grouped into controllable and un-controllable categories with a view to exercise better control over them. The budget officer finalises the budget in consultation with the production manager. Following Production Overheads Budget prepared with imaginary figures gives sufficient idea about its format and presentation:

Production Overheads Budget

(for Three Months—July to September 2003)

Elements of cost	*July*	*August*	*September*
Production office salaries	9,600	9,600	9,600
Provision for A.D.A.	—	900	900
Works manager's salary	3,200	3,500	3,500
Stationery	500	500	500
Rent	1,800	1,800	1,800
Depreciation	1,250	1,250	1,250
Light and Fuel	600	600	600
Labour welfare charges	1,000	1,000	1,500
Proportionate Power			
House charges	800	800	800
Total	18,950	20,150	20,650

The production cost budget can be prepared by bring in it all the elements of cost of production, *i.e.* raw materials, labour and overheads. For a better understanding of cost structure, it is preferable to represent the cost of production data in the form of a cost sheet which shows the prime cost and other costs separately. The management can be better served if the budget for the preceeding period alongwith the actuals is also presented with the production cost budget for future.

Illustration—7

M/s. New Era manufacturers furnishes the following information relating to their production cost budget which ended on 30th June, 2003:

	Budgeted units (950 units)		*Actual production (1,050 units)*
Materials consumed (1,000 units)	15,000	1,100 units	18,150
Labour	12,000		13,200
Variable overheads:			
Power	1,900		2,100
Excise duty	3,800		42,00
Fixed Overheads:	5,000		5,000

The firm asks you to build up the production cost budget for the 6-months period commencing from 1st January 2004 on the basis of the following further informations:

1. The firm expects to produce 1,200 units during the next budget period.
2. The raw material units required will increase proportionately but the price per unit will remain unchanged.
3. Labour efficiency will be maintained but the wage rate will increase by 20% over the previous level.
4. Variable overhead rate will be maintained but fixed overheads will increase by 15%.

Solution

NEW ERA MANUFACTURING COMPANY

Production Cost Budget

(for 6-Months—lst Jan. to 30th June, 2004)

Particulars	*Budget Jan. to June 04 (950 units)*			*Actuals Jan. to June 04 (1,050 units)*			*Budget 1st Jan. to 30th June 2004 (1,200 units)*		
	Units	*Amount*		*Units*	*Amount*		*Units*	*Amount*	
(1)	*(2)*	*(3)*		*(4)*	*(4)*		*(5)*	*(6)*	
Variable cost:									
Raw material 1,000		15,000	15.79	1100	18,150	17.29	1,263	20,839	17.37
Labour		12,000	12.03		13,200	12.57		18,100	15.08

(1)	*(2)*	*(3)*	*(4)*	*(4)*	*(5)*	*(6)*
Power	1,900	2.00	2,100	2.00	2,400	2.00
Excise duty	3,800	4.00	4,200	4.00	4,800	4.00
Total Variable Cost	32,700	34.42	37,650	35.86	46.139	38.45
Fixed Cost	5,000	5.26	5,000	4.76	5,750	4.79
Cost of Production	37,700	39.68	42,650	40.62	51.889	43.24

Dated......................... ....

Prepared By......................... Management Accountant

Explanatory Notes:

1. Units of raw materials required for the proposed production:

$$\frac{1{,}000 \times 1{,}200}{950} = 1{,}263 \text{ units}$$

2. Price of raw materials per unit = 18,150 divided by 1,100 = 16.50

3. Cost of 1,263 units = 1,263 x 16.50 = 20,839

4. Labour cost per unit = 12.57

   Increase 20% = 2.514

   15.084

Total labour cost = 1,200 × 15.084 = 18,100

Research and Development Budget

Generally, large scale business enterprises set up research and development wing within their organisations to carry on research for developing new products and/or improving upon the existing ones with a view to minimising cost and earn maximum profits. Such enterprises prepare Research and Development Budget which depends upon the existing projects in hands and the new projects to be undertaken within the budget period. This budget has no direct linkage with sales, production or other operating budgets. The management decides the nature of research to be carried within the firm and also the expenditure to be incurred thereon. It also decides about the treatment to be given to the research and development expenditure *i.e.* what part of expenditure to be capitalised and what portion be treated as an ordinary business expenditure. The Research and Development Budget helps the management to carry on the research activities on a continuous basis for the benefit of the organisation.

Cash Budget

A cash budget deals with the expected cash inflows and cash outflows during a specified period of time for which the budget is prepared. The possible sources of cash inflows are: *(a)* cash sales, *(b)* realisation from debtors, *(c)* issue of shares and debentures, *(d)* raising loans, *(e)* sales of investments: *(f)* sale of any fixed asset. The cash-outflow results due to *(i)* purchase of raw materials, *(ii)* payment of wages, *(iii)* disbursement of overheads, *(iv)* purchases of fixed assets and investments, *(v)* redemption of debentures and loans, *(vi)* payment of dividend, *(vii)* discharge of tax obligations, etc. The budget officer forecasts the cash flows and cash requirements during budget period which must syncronize with the periods of other functional budgets as most of the informations for cash budget are derived from other budgets.

For a better cash planning and control, it is important that the budget period is divided into smaller periods. For example, a 6-monthly cash budget may be prepared on monthly basis with a view to knowing cash position at the end of every month. The cash budget enables the management to arrange the deficit cash balance well in time for maintaining operational efficiency of the enterprise. Similarly, surplus cash balance as shown in the budget at the end of any period can be invested in temporary investments. Thus cash planning in an enterprise is effective only when cash budget is in operation.

Preparation of Cash Budget

A cash budget may be prepared by using anyone of the following methods:

1. Receipt and Payment method
2. Adjust Profit and Loss method
3. Balance Sheet method.

1. Receipt and Payment Method

According to this method, Cash Budget includes all the cash receipts whether they are on revenue account or capital account. Similarly all expected capital and revenue expenditures are brought in a cash budget. The accruals *i.e.* income earned but not received and expenditure duc but not paid are excluded from the cash budget. Thus a cash budget is a sort of cash account which records cash receipts and cash payments and shows expected cash balance at the end of the budget period. The informations for cash budget are derived from other budgets. For example, the sales budget will provide the amount of sales and the the rceipts from sales and realization from debtors can be estimated by taking into account the terms of sales. The raw materials purchase budget, labour budget and overheads budget will provide information relating to payments for raw materials, wages and overhead charges. The management can forecast payments on account of capital expenditure, tax, dividend, etc. The difference of cash receipts and cash payments for a period is either positive or negative, which is carried to next period.

Illustration-8

From the following budget data prepare Cash Budget for 3-months July to September, 2005:

Months	*Sales*	*Purchases*	*Wages*	*Overheads*
June	85,000	48,000	10,000	12,500
July	90,000.	52,000	11,000	13,500
August	1,20,000	60,000	14,000	15,000
September	1,30,000	62,000	14,000	16,000

Other Informations

1 20% sales is for cash and the remaining amount is realised in the month following that of sales.
2. Suppliers supply raw materials at one months credit.
3. Wage-bill is paid in the first week of next month.
4. Overheads are paid in cash.
5. Monthly rent payment is Rs. 1,000.

6. Advance Income Tax of Rs. 15,000 is payable in September.
7. Bonus of Rs. 10,000 is payable to workers in July.
8. Plant costing Rs. 80,000 is due to be installed in July. The bill will be paid in August.
9. Interest on 12% 50,000 debentures is realised in July and January every year.
10. Cash balance on 1st July is Rs.5,000.

Solutions

Cash Budget for the 3 Months Period
(July to September, 2005)

	July	*August*	*September*
Receipts:			
Opening balance	5,000	11,500	-51,500
Cash sales	18,000	24,000	26,000
Collection from debtors (80% of 85,000)	68,000	72,000	96,000
Debenture Interest (6-months)	3,000	—	—
Total	94,000	1,07,500	70,500
Payments:			
Purchases	48,000	52,000	60,000
Wages	10,000	11,000	14,000
Overheads	13,500	15,000	16,000
Rent	1,000	1,000	1,000
Bonus	10,000	—	—
Income Tax	—	—	15,000
Plant	—	80,000	—
Total	82,500	1,59,000	1,06,000
Closing Balance	11,500	(-51,500)	(-35,500)

Adjusted Profit and Loss Method

Under this method the profit as shown in the Profit and Loss Account prepared in the conventional manner forms the basis for cash forecast. The profit is adjusted by adding back to it the non-cash items such as depreciation, outstanding expenses, other provisions etc. The other items which increase the total cash inflows are the increase in share capital, debenture and loans, current liabilities (creditors) and decrease in fixed assets, debtors and stock etc. Out of the total cash-inflows calculated as above, the items which results in cash outflow are substracted to arrive at the cash position at the end ofthe period. The items which reduce the cash position are accrued incomes, advance payments, dividend payment, redemption of debentures and loans, decrease in creditors, payment for fixed assets, increase in debtors and stock etc. This method of cash forecast may also be called as the Cash Flow Statement method as the net income as per the conventional income Statement is converted into a cash flow forecast. The main sources of information for cash forecast as per this method are the profit and loss account and balance sheet. This method suitable to prepare a long-period cash budget.

IIlustration—9

From the following Balance Sheet and Projected Profit and Loss Account, prepare the Cash Budget according to adjusted Profit and Loss Account method:

Balance Sheet
For the Year Ended on 31st Dec., 2003

Share Capital	1,50,000	Land and Buildings	1,25,000
General Reserve	50,000	Plant and Machinery	80,000
Profit and Loss A/c	25,000	Furniture and fixtures	15,000
Debentures	80,000	Sundry debtors	75,000
Creditors'	1,00,000	Stock	50,000
Bills Payable	20,000	Bills Receivable	10,000
Outstanding Salaries	3,000	Prepaid Rent	3,000
		Cash at bank and hand	70,000
	4,28,000		4,28,000

Projected Profit and Loss Account
for the Year Ended on 31st Dec., 2004

Particulars		Amount	Particulars	Amount
To Opening Stock		50,000	By Sales	3,00,000
To Purchases		2,25,000	By Cosing Stock	45,000
To Gross Profit C/d		70,000		
		3,45,000		3,45,000
To Salaries	10,000		By Gross profit b/d	70,000
Less last years outstanding	3,000			
	7,000			
Add outstanding	1,000	8,000		
To commission		1,500		
To Rent	9,000			
Add last years prepared	3,000			
		12,000		
To Interest		8,000		
To Establishment charges		2,500		
To Advertising expenses		2,000		
To Depreciation:				
Plant & Machinery	8,000			
Land & Building	6,000			
Furniture	1,500			
		15,500		
To Net Profit		20.500		
		70,000		70,000
To Dividend		30,000	By Next Profit (31-12-03)	25,000
To General Reserve		10,000	By Profit for 2003	20,500
To Balance carried		5,500		
		45,500		45,500

On 31st Dec. 2003, the position of some of the items was as under:

Share capital	2,00,000
Debentures	1,00,000
Creditors	80,000
Debtors	90,000
Bills Payable	25,000
Bills Receivable	8,000

Purchase of Plant and Machinery during 2004 28,000

Purchase of Furniture and Fixtures 21,500

Solution

Cash Budget (Adjusted Profit & Loss Method)
for the year ended on Ist December, 2004

Cash Balance (31.12.2003)			70.000
Add:			
Net Profit for 2003		20,500	
Depreciation:			
Plant and Machinery	8,000		
Land and Building	6,000		
Furniture	1,500		
		15,500	
Decrease in prepaid rent		3,000	
Decrease in stock		5,000	
Decrease in bills receivable	2,000		
Increase in bills payable	5,000		
Issue of share capital	50,000		
Issue of debentures	20,000		1,21,000
Less:			
Purchase of plant & machinery	28,000		
Purchase of furniture & fixtures	21,500		
Dividend	30,000		
Decrease in outstanding salaries	2,000		
Increase in debtors	15,000		
Decrease in creditors	20,000		1,16,500
Cash Balance its on 31st December, 2004			74,500

Balance Sheet Method

Under this method a projected Balance Sheet is prepared in which cash balance is not an estimated item but a difference between total projected assets and total estimated liabilities. In other words, the excess of projected assets over projected liabilities represents cash balance. If the liabilities are more than the assets, the balance shows the overdraft.

Illustration—10

Using the informations of illustration No. 9 prepare a projected Balance Sheet as on 31st December, 2004 to show the Cash position as on that date:

Solution

Projected Balance Sheet
as on 3tst December, 2004

Share capital	2,00,000	Land & Buildings	1,25,000	
Debentures	1,00,000	Less Depreciation	6,000	1,19,000
General Reserve	60 ,000	Plant & Machinery	80,000	
Profit & Loss A/c	5,500	Less depreciation	8,000	
Creditors	80,000		72,000	
		Add Purchases	28,000	
Bills Payable	25,000			1,00,000
Outstanding salaries	1,000	Furnitures & Fixtures	15,000	
		Less depreciation	1,500	
			13,500	
		Add Purchases	21,500	35,500
		Debtors		90,000
		Bill Receivable		8,000
		Stock		45,000
		Cash and Bank Balance (Balancing figure)		74,500
	4,71,500			4,71,500

Flexible Budgets

We have so far dealt with fixed budgets which are prepared for a specific level of activity. Such budgets are based on the assumption that the future can be forecast with certainty and there is no significant difference between actual performance and budgeted data. In actual practice, the assumption of accurate forecasting does not hold good, particularly when the future is distant and economic environment full of uncertainties. Consequently the actual level of activity attained is different from the budgeted one and the comparison between budgeted and actual data will be unrealistic as it will throw no light on the variations arising due to the change in the actual level of activity. In order to remove rigidity and introduce flexibility in budgeting flexible budgets are prepared. A flexible budget also known as variable or sliding scale budget is one which permits adaptability in accordance with the changes in the level of production. It is prepared for varying levels of production activity and thus provides a realistic basis for comparing performance of different departments/ products.

The preparation of a flexible budget is not difficult. Actually there is no difference between the preparation of a fixed budget and flexible budget except that in the later case costs and other data are estimated for varying levels of activity. In other words, a flexible budget consists of a series of fixed budgets. The element of fixed cost in the total cost make a lot of difference whenever the level of production is changed. The total fixed cost for all levels of production remains the same but the cost per unit of output decreases with an increase in the output and vice versa. Therefore, fixed cost should be segregated from the total cost and shown separately in a flexible budget.

Illustration-11

Modern Manufacturing Company Ltd. has budgeted the following expenses for the production of 1,000 Super-washing machines:

	Per unit (Rs.)
Direct Materials	700
Direct labour	500

Direct chargeable expenses	100
Variable overheads	50
Administration expenses	100
(Rs. 1,00,000 fixed for all levels of production)	
Selling and distribution Expenses	25
(60% fixed)	
Total cost per unit	1,475

You are required to prepare flexible budget for 8,000, 9,000 and 12,000 machines.

Solution

Flexible Budget

Particulars	*1000 units* Per unit	Total	*8000 units* Per unit	Total	*9000 units* Per unit	Total	*12000 units* Per unit	Total
Materials	700	7,00,000	700	56,00,000	700	63,00,000	700	84,00,000
Labour	500	5,00,000	500	40,00,000	500	45,00,000	500	60,00,000
Direct exp.	100	1,00,000	100	8,00,000	100	9,00,000	100	12,00,000
Prime cost	1,300	13,00,000	1,300	1,04,00,000	1,300	1,17,00,000	1,300	1,56,00,000
Variable overheads	50	50,000	50	4,00,000	50	4,50,000	50	6,00,000
Variable selling and distribution expenses	10	10,000	10	80,000	10	90,000	10	1,20,00
administration expenses	100	1,00,000	125	1,00,000	11.11	1,00,000	8.33	1,00,000
selling and distribution fixed cost	15	15,090	1.87	15,000	1.67	15,000	1.25	15,000
Total	1,475	14,75,000	1374.37	109,95,000	1372.78	1,23,55,000	1369.58	1,64,35,000

PERFORMANCE BUDGETING

We have seen different types of functional budgets which are prepared by a manufacturing organisation. These budgets highlights the targets in physical quantities alongwith their money values. A manufacturing concern is said to have adopted performance budgeting if its concentration is on physical targets and evaluation of the actuals with the budgeted figures with a view to exercise proper control over its activities for better performance. The budgeting adopted by private entrepreneurs is generally performance-oriented but if is not always true in case of government departments which set their targets in money values instead of physical quantities. Performance budgeting assumes special significance when government expenditure on developmental activities is desired to be evaluated in terms of physical targets. A government department may be satisfied if it is able to exhaust the funds allocated to it for a budget period without any regard to the amount of benefits derived from expenditure. It is so when the budgeted expenditure is not linked with the physical targets to be achieved for the achievement of some broader objective by the government. The modern governments have realized the disadvantages of the traditional budgeting and the performance budgeting is gaining popularity with them. The concept of performance budgeting developed when the Hoover Commission recommended in 1949 that the performance budgeting should be adopted for budgeting the Federal Government expenditure. The Estimate Committee and Administrative Reform Commission have also recommended the use of performance budgeting in government departments in India.

According to performance budgeting, the expenditure is presented programme and activity-wise and actual performance is recorded alongwith the targets for the consideration of decision-makers. In case of a manufacturing concern the target may be to achieve a certain rate of profit on capital employed (ROI) but the targets for non-profit making government organisations will depend upon the nature of work they carry out. For example, the over-all objective of expenditure on literacy programme may be fixed as increasing the literacy rate from 50 per cent to 60 per cent during the budget period. Similarly, the objective of expenditure may be set as an increase in the rat of employment, bringing additional land under cultivation of a particular crop, extension of areas under forests, etc. But the targets have to be interpreted in physical terms so that the effectiveness of expenditure is judged from the comparison of actuals with the budgeted figures. Effective performance budgeting needs careful consideration of the following:

1. Fixation of objective for which expenditure is to be incurred.
2. Establishment of responsibility centres.
3. Identification of programmes to be carried out by each responsibility centre.
4. Interpretation of programme in physical quantities or targets for each activity relating to a programme.
5. Forecasting the resources needed to implement the programme and also the expected income resulting therefrom.
6. Developing information and reporting system both in physical and monetary values for the purpose of control.
7. Evaluation of performance periodically and take corrective actions, wherever needed.

ZERO-BASE BUDGETING

Traditional method of budgeting known as incremented based budgeting is based on past year's prograrrames and performance which is generally regarded as satisfactory for developing future budgets. In this type of budgeting, the targets set in the past year are not questioned and some additions are made in the last year's budget itself to incorporate the necessary additional expenditure on on-going and new business activities to be carried out in the budget period. This is a very simple method which calls for few alterations and additions without going into the details of the whole budgeting process in the light of changed circumstances. The traditional method of budgeting is not workable where management is conscious of Innovative changes in the present business and administrative policies for achieving maximum over-all efficiency of the organisation.

Zero-base Budgeting pre-supposes the non-existence of any budget in the past and evaluates the budget activities in terms of benefits and costs in the light of prevailing business environment and likely changes in future. It is synonymous with budgeting from scratch from zero, requiring justification of everything irrespective of trends or past levels of expenditure. In other words, Zero-base budgeting implies co structing a budget without any reference to what has gone before. It is essentially an exercise of reappraisal of purposes, methods and resources. The budget so prepared is likely to be more realistic to serve the best interests of an organisation. Zero-base budgeting has been defined by Peter A. Phyrr as under:

> "A planning and budgeting process which requires each manager to justify his entire budget request in detail right-from the scratch (hence the term zero-base) and shifts the burden of proof to each manager to justify why he should spend any money at all. The approach in turn requires an indepth analysis of all the 'decision packages' to be evaluated on systematic and rational lines and also ranked in order of importance."

Zero-Base Budgeting (ZBB) as a system of budgeting was used by the U.S. Department of Agriculture for a year in 1964. It was developed in its present form by Peter A. Phyrr at the Taxes Instrument, U.S.A. It was given a boost subsequently by Jimmy Carter who as the governor implemented the system in the state of Georgia and later as the President in the Federal Government. Government of India proposed the adoption of Zero-base concept in the budget preparation for the year 1987-88 onward. The zero-base budgeting concept has been successfully implemented in a large number of U.S. Organisation including such giants as Taxas Instruments, Southern California, Edison, Xerox and New York Telephone Company.

INTEGRAL PARTS OF ZERO-BASE BUDGETING

Zero-base budgeting involves the following:

1. Identification of Decision Units. The decision units will be based on the level of responsibility. Different departments are generally, identified as Decision Units which are capable of carrying out different programmes or activities to achieve a single objective. The

Decision Units are the responsibility based budget centres under the charge of different senior officers of the organisation. For example, the Education Department could be a Decision Unit with the objective of increasing literacy and providing quality education. However, Adult Education, Child Education, Technical Education could be sub-functions or sub-units for which separate budgets will be prepared. Top management should specify the Decision Units in terms of resources required, capital projects, special projects or major expansion schemes.

2. Preparation of Decision-Packages. The Decision-Package is the building block of the zero-base budgeting process. A number of decision-packages make up one Decision Unit. A decision-package is a document that identifies and describes a specific activity in such a manner that management can evaluate it and rank it against other activities competing for limited resources and decide whether to approve or disapprove it. If, for example, Adult Education is the decision Unit, the objective of improving literacy among adults can be achieved through starting adult education centres in each district or through TV programme on adult education, etc. There activities are the Decision-Packages or independent activities, each capable of being measured in terms of cost, targets and objectives achieved.

It is important that Decision-Packages be developed in an effective manner. It involves examining alternative methods or activities of achieving the objectives and different levels of efforts of performing the operations. The Decision-Packages will contain the following informations:

— Goals of the Decision Unit

— Discription of the programme and activity

— Specific measure of performance

— Benefits expected from the performance

— Consequences of not approving the package

— Projected or expected costs.

— Costs and benefits for all alternatives studied including the recommended one.

It may, however, be pointed out that the preparation of decision packages is a gigantic task which requires technical knowledge, experience and resources. In order to economise resources and avoid, unnecessary controversy, some organisations may use less formal ways of presenting alternative ways of performing an activity, *i.e.* compromise solutions but this approach will be inconsistent with the very idea of zero-base budgeting.

3. Ranking of Decision-Packages. The ranking process is concerned with deciding about how met and "where" the limited resources are to be allocated. A Decision Unit with highest Benefit-cost Ratio is preferred and ranked as Number one. If the costs are incurred and the benefits obtained in the same year, the calculation of the Benefit-cost Rates is more straightforward. However, if the benefits are obtained over a long period, the BCR should be based on the Present Values of benefits and costs discounted at appropriate rates. In case of government expenditure, the more appropriate measure is social values, and the social benefit-cost Ratio will guide the ranking of Decision-Packages. It may, however, understood that the funds will be provided on the basis of financial cost. Thus the Decision-packages of individual Decision Units will be brought together and ranked in the order of importance on the basis of Benefit-Cost Ratios. The list will show the Decision-Packages of various Decision Units in discending order of Benefit-Cost Ratios. Decision-Packages will be choosen from the top one after another to make up the available quantum of funds.

There may be few persons in the government who may not like the test of evaluation and ranking in case of very high priority or committed or policy programme. The zero-base budgeting process in the above manner will suggest the policy-makers the likely cost or loss of carrying on or undertaking a new programme, and as such it will be in their own interest to adopt this new method of budgeting.

4. Preparation of Detailed Operating Budget. The ranking process provides a number of approved Decision Packages which constitute the budget for the organisation as a whole and for the individual budget centres. The decision-packages incorporate in themselves the discription of the activities and the performance level appropriate to the expenditure level contained in the decision-package. This will provide the basis for reporting of actuals against budgets and review of performance.

The Difference

A budget analyst cannot loose sight of a traditional budgets which contain a lots of informations about the programmes and activities which have been undertaken in the past. Budgeting from the scratch does not mean that there is always a search for new data and old data as contained in a traditional budget cannot be used. Basic difference between the traditional or incremental budgeting and the zero-base budgeting may be realized from the following:

1. A traditional budget is function-oriented but a zero-base budget is a programme or project-oriented.
2. Traditional budgeting views critically only the cost increases whereas the zero-base budgeting critically examines existing levels of expenditure, as the level of expenditure approved for the last budget is not necessarily acceptable for the current budget.
3. In case of traditional budgeting, the existing programmes or projects are self-perpetuating for which no rejustification is required. Justification is needed only for new progranunes or projects. Zero-base budgeting presenting that all programmes or projects whether on-going or new, must be justified on the ground that they all compete for the same scarce resources.
4. Traditional budgeting is input-oriented *i.e.*, resources required; zero-base budgeting is output-oriented *i.e.*, results achieved.

Benefits from ZBB

Following benefits accrue to an organisation which implement Zero Base Budgeting on the right basis:

1. Continuous reviewing of on-going schemes ensures effective utilization of limited funds in the best possible projects and manner.

2. The programmes or activities which have outlived their utility are pruned and thus the organisation can be saved from unproductive expenditure.
3. It facilitates the accommodation of high priority projects by reducing existing activities.
4. Ranking of projects and programmes on cost-benefit analysis basis secures an efficient allocation of funds.
5. ZBB helps in the management of projects, programmes and activities according to availability of funds. If the cuts in budgets become imperative due to shortage of funds, the BCR for different programmes will be a correct guide in such a decision-making. Instead of introducing *ad hoc* cuts in budgets, the activities making upto the quantum of funds available will be choosen.
6. It improves communication all round, particularly top management's awareness of what is contained in each budget centre's proposal.
7. It provides an in-built system for reviewing actual costs and performance against budget.
8. It promotes innovative ideas in terms of alternative ways of performing an activity and alternative levels of efforts.

Problems with ZBB

Like any other technique of planning, the Zero-base budgeting is not an unmixed blessing. Following problems may be encountered in the implementation of ZBB in any organisation or government department.

1. Zero-base budgeting is a costly affair as it involves too much energy, time and money in the collection and analysis of data regarding alternative projects, programmes and activities. It can freeze an organisation in a paper work blizzard for several months in a year.

2. The evaluation of legal necessity or technical feasibility of Decision Packages is itself a highly difficult and technical job which

might not be done rightly in the absence technically qualified personnel for the purpose. It cannot be said that a Zero-base budget is always realistic and in the best interest of the organisation.

3. There is every possibility that "Pet" projects might be ranked arbitrarily as there is no way of avoiding 'pet projects' being given a high ranking.

4. ZBB requires measurements on performance levels and cost effectiveness that might not be readily available.

5. It may complicate communication and administration of data as more and more people are involved in this exercise.

6. Zero-base budgeting provides more scope for manipulation as the officers incharge of different budget activities are, generally, in the habit of exaggerating the importance of activities of their respective departments.

7. Benefits of many programmes or decision units are not measurable in terms of physical quantities or money values. The success of ZBB depends upon the evaluation of benefits and ranking the decision units on that basis. ZBB fails to work as an effective tool of planning due to problem of measurement or inaccurate measurement of benefits.

8. Divergent activities are impossible to be compared with one another and ranked. Education, health and policy activities cannot be compared with each other. Therefore, ZBB cannot be taken to its logical end. There have to be adjustments and compromises.

Pre-requisites for Success

From the study of the problems associated with the Zero-base budgeting, it will be wrong to conclude that ZZB is an unreal concept and it cannot be translated to achieve maximum benefits out of the budget activities. ZBB can be made an effective tool of planning and control provided management properly appreciate the problems and provides a framework suitable for formulation of realistic and objective budgetary proposals with the cooperation of all concerned in the organisation. Prerequisites for the success of ZBB may be stated as under:

1. Top management's strong involvement is a must for the success of ZBB. Other officers associated with the formulation and implementation of the ZBB should also cooperate in the joint exercise to make the system a success.
2. Imaginative approach and a genuine commitment to change on the part of managers at all levels in the organisation are highly important for the success of ZBB.
3. In order to discourage 'pet projects, the decision-packages may be discussed in groups and prejudices should not be allowed to affect budgeting processes and the evaluation and ranking should be done as objectively as possible.
4. The area wherein ZBB could be applied should be choosen carefully and ZBB applied deliquently.

❐

10

Standard Costing and Variance Analysis

Standard costs are the scientifically pre-determined costs of manufacturing a single unit or a number of units of product or of rendering a service during a specified future period. According to the Terminology, it is "a pre-determined cost calculated in relation to a prescribed set of working conditions, correlating technical specifications and scientific measurements of materials and labour to the prices and wage rates expected to apply during the period to which the standard cost is intended to relate with an addition of an appropriate share of budgeted overhead. Its main purposes are to provide bases for control through variance accounting for the valuation of stocks and work-in-progress and in exceptional cases for fixing selling prices."

What is evident from the above definition is that standard costs are planned costs of a product under current, or anticipated operating conditions. The dictionary meaning of the word 'standard' is that it is a "thing serving as a basis for comparison", "thing recognised as model for imitation". But it should be noted that 'standard' is a relative term. Admittedly, what is standard for one may be sub-standard for another and vice versa. However, what is significant is that within an organisation, it serves as a desirable target.

The term 'standard cost' consists of two parts, *viz.*, 'standard' and 'cost'. Standards can be established in respect of qualities and quantities like materials and labour. Cost involves the expression of the standards so established in values:

Standard costs are highly detailed scientifically pre-determined costs of material, labour and overhead chargeable to a product or service. Standard costs represent excellent target costs that should be obtained. This Institute of Cost and Management Accountants defines standard cost as "a predetermined cost which is calculated from management's standards of efficient operation and the relevant necessary expenditure. It may be used as a basis for price fixing and for cost control through variance analysis". The Institute in its terminology defines standard costing as "the preparation and use of standard costs, their comparison with actual costs, and the analysis of variances of their causes and points of incidence, "Standard cost expresses what costs should be under attainable good performance, They are projections of what actual cost should be under an assumed set of conditions', The term "standard", has been called by different names in accounting *e.g.*" "a norm", "a model or example or comparison", "a measure of comparison", "a criterion, of excellence", "a yardstick", "a benchmark", "an index of waste or potential savings", "a sea-level from which to measure cost attitudes", "a gauge", A standard may be a norm or a measure of comparison in terms of specific items such as pounds or kilograms of materials, labour hours required, hours of plant capacity used.

The definition given by W.W. Bigs makes the concept of standard costing more clear. According to him, "Standard Costing discloses the costs of deviations from standard and classifies these as to their causes, so that management is immediately informed of the sphere of operations in which remedial action is necessary.

Thus, standard costing statistics are prepared to show:

(i) the standard cost.

(ii) the actual cost.

(iii) the difference between these costs which is termed as variance.

Standard costs are determined for each element of cost-direct materials, direct labour, overhead (fixed and variable)—separately and then variations from actual costs are in respect of each element distinctly so as to detect which part of the costs needs control and which department, process or operation, the responsibility may be placed. The standard costs are organised to uncover and report off-standard conditions. The management should strive for the attainment of standard costs because they are attainable ideal costs and are practical from the point of view of business.

OBJECTIVES OF STANDARD COSTING

The companies using standard costing reported to management at various levels the significant variances with written explanation. In some companies standard costing was a part of regular costing system, while in others it was used on an *ad hoc* basis. The following represented the broad objectives of the standard costing system:

(1) Exert effective control and an adequate check at various levels and in different areas of management.

(2) Determine future managerial policy in respect of marketing and production and.

(3) Ensure accuracy in costing.

The few companies having effective standard costing system used such system to attain the following specific objectives.

(A) Cost Control. Cost control was exercised by comparison of actual costs against the standard. Such comparison took place in respect of each element of expense, departmental or cost centre, costs and product costs. In many cases costs were broken down into controllable and non-controllable components with a view to focussing the management attention only on such costs which were control lable.

In respect of purchase activity standard costing system enabled the management to control purchase prices. With regard to production activity by use of standard costing, the management was able to control material usages and reduce waste. Some companies considered benefit of economy of usage by bulk issues to cost centres. These companies were also able to use labour with greater efficiency and derive optimum usage of power and coal by efficient running of the equipment.

(B) Pricing. Standard costs were used to set prices where companies offered products of jobs under terms of contracts. Prices were also determined on the basis of standard costs by companies which operated in a competitive industry, but where they had certain measure of control in fixing prices.

(C) Evaluating Performance. Standard costing system was used to evaluate the performance of executives operating at various levels of management. Far example, a foreman may be held responsible if he is not able to achieve certain output which is laid down as a standard. In one company standard costing system was effectively used to grant bonus to executives where performance was better than standard.

(D) Cost Reduction. Cost reduction was possible by implementation of industrial engineering specifications. Variance analysis could locate inefficiencies and could bring a level of innovation which could increase productivity and reduce costs. A few companies had well-established cost reduction programmes where special efforts were made to reduce costs in certain directions pointed out by variance analysis.

ADVANTAGES OF STANDARD COSTING

Standard costing is a system of cost accounting which facilitates the performance of the entire managerial process-planning, organisation, coordination and control. Among the many advantages generally attributed to standard costing, the most important may be listed as follows:

(1) Cost Control. Cost control and cost reduction are probably the most important aims of any costing system; and standard costing gives due recognition to this fact. Cost control has the objective of production of the required quality at the lowest cost attainable under existing conditions. Effective control requires detailed standards, to show how much of each material should be used, how much labour should be required for each operation, and what facilities and services will be needed. Standards enable management to make periodic comparison of actual costs with standard costs in order to measure performance and to take action to maintain control over costs. Standard costs help management in cost control through the principle of exception, *i.e.*, highlighting only those activities which fail to come up to standard or which exceed standard. The off-standard conditions can be investigated and proper action can be taken before they continue for a long time. Standards help develop cost conscious attitudes, because it makes cost variances clearly observable by management. Cost consciousness tends to reduce costs and encourage economies in all phases of the business and guides management towards improvement.

(2) Economical Means of Costing and Record-keeping: The use of standard costs can reduce clerical labour and expense by avoiding the detailed record keeping which is necessary when actual costs alone are used. The following benefits are derived which reduce the cost of record-keeping:

(a) By carrying inventory at standard cost, store ledgers can be kept in terms of quantities only. This eleminates much clerical time in pricing and balancing items on the stores ledger. Total standard cost of inventory can readily be obtained at any time by multiplying the quantity in stock by the standard unit cost.

(b) When standard costs are used, requisition or bills for materials to be put into production can be written and priced more rapidly than when the goods must be priced at actual cost. In fact, materials, requisitions, labour time tickets, and production cost cards can be prepared in advance of production.

(c) The time required to assemble cost data for budget preparation or special cost studies such as pricing is reduced because it is not necessary to devote so much time to the analysis and collection of past actual costs.

(d) The time which must be devoted by management to the study and analysis of cost reports is much reduced when standard costs are used. Standard costs tend to eliminate unnecessary details and focus on those aspects which require management attention and thus bring economies and effectiveness in management reporting.

(e) The time required to prepare reports which are used by management can be reduced. Since most reports are useful in proportion to their timelines, standard costing helps management to take remedial action promptly by providing useful and timely reports of variances.

(f) The standard cost of goods finished can be obtained immediately upon completion since it is necessary to multiply the quantity by the unit standard cost. Simple and economical costing methods can be used in place of elaborate costing methods.

(3) Managerial Planning. Planning is a process of using all resources in such a manner that maximises business profits. Management must plan for efficient and economic operations for standard costs to be effective. The standard costs, carefully determined, will disclose inefficiencies in operations, which can be thoroughly investigated and remedial action taken. Standard costs are more convenient than actual cost for budget preparation because the standard costs at different production levels and for different product mixes are readily built up into total costs as called for by the budget. On the other hand, using actual costs requires a great deal of analysis and adjustment when extensive changes in product volume or product-mixes take place. Furthermore, actual costs are influenced by many temporary or random influences which make it difficult to predict the future behaviour of unstandardised costs.

(4) Coordination. The establishment of standards coordinates all functions-manufacturing, marketing, engineering, research, and accounting towards the achievement of a common goal. Setting standards involves defining and communicating targets so that they can work towards the attainment of the goal.

(5) Standards as Incentives to Employees. If standards are reasonable and attainable they act as incentives to employees to improve their performances and to maintain the quality of the product. Each worker performs his job with advance knowledge of the standard set for the particular job; he knows that if his work is less than the standard, he is responsible for the variance.

Standards motivate workers, supervisors and foremen to work more efficiently in the accomplishment of their respective standards. Many incentives like cash bonus, individual and group bonus, prizes, vacation time, and promotions can be given for equalling or surpassing standards. Similarly, management can decide upon action to be taken for below standard performance.

(6) Formulating, Price and Production Policies. Standard costs as compared to actual costs can be used for estimating selling prices. When standard unit costs are available, expected costs and sales prices can be computed on the basis of standard costs. Standards already established can easily be modified to reflect current conditions and changes in material prices or labour rates and the price of the product can lie determined on a realistic basis. Also, the problem of absorption of fixed overhead is better tackled and simplified by using standard costs. Standard costs are predetermined costs which help management in the decision process by providing standard unit costs for various levels of activity. Standard costs are thus useful to management in determining price policies, preparing bids for prospective orders, planning production of new products and new methods, and furnishing cost estimates in all managerial decisions.

Actual costs, on the other hand, may reflect excessive usage of material, abnormal labour times or an inequitable charge for overhead. Actual overhead cost per unit at any given time may be so influenced by temporary fluctuations in production levels as to make actual cost entirely unusable for pricing. Standard costs on the contrary, are based upon carefully determined and planned usages of material, labour and overhead facilities and thus are free from accidental and temporary distortions caused by.

Necessary adjustments in standards to incorporate changing conditions can be done without any difficulty whenever required. Standard overhead rates are determined upon a normal production or activity level and therefore, provide an acceptable base for determining product prices which will recover full overhead costs in the long run.

LIMITATIONS OF STANDARD COSTING

There are certain disadvantages in the Standard Costing System which are noted below:

(1) **Sometimes Standards Create Adverse Psychological Effects.** If the standard is set at a high level, its non-achievement will lead to frustration and resistance. This acts as a discouragement rather than an incentive for better efficiency.

(2) **For Fixing Responsibility for an Adverse Variance.** The controllable and the non-controllable portions of the variances should be segregated. This may be quite a difficult task.

(3) Even if the initial standards are fixed up with a certain amount of accuracy the management should be alert to factors which would necessitate an alteration to these standards. Unless standards are current, they are useless as incorrect standards. Such out of date standards will do more harm than any benefit.

(4) **Establishment** of standards may be costly and may require high degree of technical skill. This may make a standard costing system beyond the reach of small business concerns.

(5) **It is Difficult to Fix up Reliable and Workable Standards.** Unless the standards are correctly fixed, the control and study of variances on which the whole system is built up will not be effective. The standards are merely approximate and may adversely affect the values of standards as tools of control.

STANDARD COSTING *Vs.* HISTORICAL COSTING *Vs.* ESTIMATED COSTING

Standard costing can be distinguished from historical costing and estimated costing. Under historical costing, the costs are the actual costs and, therefore, the question of exercising control does not arise at all. It is simply an analysis of costs after they have been incurred and, therefore, pertain to past data. Estimated costing, on the other hand, refers to that system of costing under which costs are estimated in advance-meaning thereby that the costs which are likely to be incurred during given period of time are conceived of well before their being incurred. This is done with reference to historical costs and the prevailing condition of business. It is, thus, an estimation of the actual costs or historical costs of a business in anticipation. As apart from it, standard costing refers to that system of costing whereunder the costs which ought to be there and should be attained are determined in advance. Standard costs strive to make the actual costs equal or approximate to the predicted costs, whereas in estimated costs, the estimated must come into line with the actual costs. Thus, the term standard costs under standard costing does not referred what the costs are or what the costs shall be but refers to what the costs should be or ought to be. Standard costs are, therefore, above the efficiency level of normal or expected costs so that management can make efforts to achieve the goal and bring down the costs to that level.

Estimated costs represent merely figures based on average of past experience or personal opinion; while standard costs are based on carefully and scientifically established figures in respect of a product. The estimated costing simply plans the affairs while standard costing besides planning acts as a dynamic instrument of measurement of performance, comparison and control.

There is a point of similarity between the estimated costs and standard cost that both are determined before the process of production commences, but they differ in regard to their purpose. The main points of difference are as under:

Historical cost systems are principally associated with recording of historical, or as they are commonly called, actual costs. Historical costing is the ascertainment of costs after they have been incurred. It indicates to management the results actual transactions that have taken place in an organisation during some previous period. The recording of historical costs is useful as it determines the cost of resources used towards achieving organisational, objectives. Historical costs, however, have the following limitations:

1. Historical costs are collected after they have been incurred and therefore are ineffective in cost control. The costs have been incurred, they can not be undone and no steps can be taken to correct inefficiencies.
2. Historical costs are not helpful in cost reduction since they contain no standards or goals towards which employees can work.
3. Historical costs do not provide reliable guides to management in the tasks of budgeting, planning, and decision-making. Historical costs reflect a situation in a previous period. But the company, in facts, may be working under conditions different from those prevailing during that previous period. Therefore, historical costs are not useful in budget making, performance evaluation, detecting above or below-standard performance.

The need of standard costing arises because the historical costing system which is usually adopted in every business concern has certain deficiencies. In case of historical costing costs are known only after the production takes place while the policies are to be determined before the production begins, and hence it may not be much useful. Thus operating efficiency cannot be measured with the help of historical costing. Moreover, the historical costs may be too expensive to compile.

STANDARD COSTS AND ESTIMATED COSTS

The term "standard costs" should not be confused with "estimated costs" Standards costs and estimated casts differ in the following respects:

A. Estimated costs are frequently less accurately determined. Estimated costs are developed from projections using averages of past data regarding performance. Standard costs are predetermined realistically and much more scientifically through the use of time and motion studies, engineering estimates and specifications, selected measures of plant capacity, cost behaviour patterns. Thus the fund mental difference between an estimated cost and a standard cost is depth of analysis, prediction techniques and amount of effort used to develop cost information.

B. Estimated costs are not helpful to management in accomplishing managerial functions as they are not scientifically predetermined costs. But standard costs involve more sophistication, operation analysis and evaluation and comprehensive review of internal and external factors. They become reliable measures for product costing, product pricing, planning, coordination and cost control purposes.

C. Estimated cost emphasises on actual cost with which it is compared at the end of the accounting period. If the estimated costs are found higher or lower than actual costs they are revised for use in the next accounting period. Revisions in estimated costs are made in accordance with changes in actual cost conditions which are expected to continue during the next accounting period. In standard costing, the emphasis is on standard costs, *i.e.*, what costs of material, labour and overhead should be incurred if the factory is to be operated as a highly efficient unit with each manager, foreman, worker, plant and machine functioning as an efficient part of the production process. Under standard costing, actual costs are ascertained on by to facilitate their comparison with standard costs.

STANDARD COSTING AND BUDGETARY CONTROL

Both standard costing and budgeting are control systems. But each has got its own special features.

The principle points of difference between standard costing and budgetary control lie in *(a)* their scope of coverage, and *(b)* the approach to planning.

The scope of budget is wide. It is an integrated plan of action a coordinated plan in respect of all functions of an enterprise.

(i) It is possible to introduce standard costing into the accounting routine itself (as well as comparing actuals from books with standards outside the books). In such a case, the variances are given out by the accounting system itself. In a budgetary control system, the targets are not introduced into the accounting system; the comparison is made outside the books of account and forms the subject of reports outside the accounting system.

(ii) Budgets require functional coordination, whereas standard costing does not require such coordination since it is possible to think even of one aspect of cost. Mostly it is costs alone which form the subject-matter of standard costing—while considering one function, other functions can be ignored and hence functional coordination is not essential.

(iii) In India, at present, the approach to budgeting is generally through forecasts an expression of how things are expected to be rather than how things should be. Standards, in order to serve any useful purpose, must necessarily be exact and determined scientifically. Of course, budgets, too should be similarly drawn upon the basis of most careful study of what can be achieved given the realities of the situation. Thus budgets relating to costs can be drawn up using the information provided by standard costing. As far as possible that should be ensured.

(iv) The scope of standard costing, however, is limited to the operating level. Here too it is further linked to the costs. As the name suggests, its average is limited to costs whereas budgets embrace revenues as well as costs and all functions and activities—sales, finance, capital expenditure, personnel, purchase, etc., in addition to production. Budgets are mast useful when they are well coordinated.

In both the systems actuals have to be compared against standards; actual information has to be obtained. For the standard costing system, actual information can be obtained only from a well-maintained costing system, whereas for a budgetary control system, information may be obtained from the financial accounting system, supplemented by costing data.

One must remember, however, that the two control systems are never treated as exclusive. Standard costing is a specified system in respect of costs, budgets are also concerned with costs among other things; therefore, it would add strength to a budgetary control system if it adopts standard costs in respect of cost data. The two are complementary to each other. The distinction between the two systems is mainly on account of the field or scope and technique of operation.

Budgeting	*Standard Costing*
1. Budget can be operated without standards.	1. Standard costing cannot exist without budgets.
2. Budgetary control can be adopted in part also.	2. It is not possible to operate this system in parts.
3. Budget is a projection of financial accounts.	3. Standard cost is the projection of cost accounts.
4. It does not necessarily involve. standardization of products.	4. It requires standardization of products.
5. Budgetary control is concerned with the operation of the business as a whole and hence it is more extensive.	5. Standard costing is related with the control of expenes hence, it is more intensive.

In spite of the above differences, there are some similarities between standard costing and budgeting. Both have in common the establishment of predetermined measures of performance and the comparison of actual and planned performance so as to disclose deviations which are used for the purpose of cost control. Both have the same objective of managerial control and are therefore inter-related and cannot function independently. Both help in the preparation of reports which compare actual costs and predetermined costs for management planning and control. Matz and Usry have observed that standards are almost indispensable to the work of establishing and operating a budget. A study made by the National Association of Accountants (U.S.A) concludes that standard costs are especially valuable in developing the cost side of the budget because they provide a reliable and convenient source of data for converting the budgeted production schedule into requirements for raw materials, labour and services.

Manufacturing Cost Standards *vs* Non-manufacturing Cost Standards. Standards can be laid down for the manufacturing sector and the non-manufacturing sector. The manufacturing sector, however, more readily subjects itself to the process of planning and controlling *via* standards and standard costing. This is because the activities in the manufacturing sector lend themselves to statistical measurement, industrial engineering studies and time and motion studies. For example, input-output ratios can be prescribed for the usage of materials, efficiency of labour or Overhead incidence in the manufacturing sector. Standards and Standard Costs can be prescribed for the elements of manufacturing cost *i.e.,* Direct Material, Direct Labour and Manufacturing overhead. However, in the non-manufacturing sector; the activities are associated mainly with the external economic environment. A salesman would not now whether he would attract customers before visiting them or making telephone calls. Input-output ratios cannot be easily prescribed for these activities. At least not as rigidly and as accurately as in the manufacturing segment. Further, the non-manufacturing activity has always been neglected mainly because cost accounting techniques gained currency initially in the manufacturing sector. While it is rightly believed that the non-manufacturing costs do not lend themselves to the standards continued complacency may endanger the prosperity of strong companies and the viability of weak ones. Therefore, attempts should be made to subject the non-manufacturing costs also to as close a control as possible. In fact, there should be no discrimination between manufacturing costs and non-manufacturing costs in this regard.

FACTORS FOR FRXING STANDARDS

Certain factors are to be borne in mind while fixing the standards:

Period of Use

The first important criterion for establishment of standard costs is the length of the operation, period for which standards are to be used. Long-term as well as short-term standards may be fixed ranging for different periods. For long-term planning and growth standards for a longer duration, say 3 to 5 years, may be justified while for planning and budgeting for the accounting period short term standards for a year or so are beneficial. For measuring the performance and exercising control over costs, short-term standards are most suited. The standards according to length of time may be categorised as:

(a) Basic Standards. These are not altered over a long period of time; revisions are not frequent and there is a stability and stagnancy in standards fixed. These 'basic' or 'bogey' standards remain constant for a very long time and, therefore are applied in industries where only a small range of products are manufactured and long-term planning is required. But since the conditions do not remain static in this dynamic world, the standards become obsolete and require overhauling and, therefore, the long-term basic standards are not realistic.

(b) Current Standards. Short-term standards are known as current standards. These are more suitable for business since they take into account the current conditions and are related to the budget period.

In business, it will be useful to set both—long term as well short term standards. This will help in finding out variations in respect of both these standard in advance of actual production.

Reasonable or Desirable Level of Attainment

This we have discussed at length already in the foregoing pages and it can be said that standards are to be set assuming efficient working conditions and reasonably good performance.

Activity Level

The level of activity or performance required must be decided upon before establishing any standards. The level or output of production which shall be attained over the forthcoming period for which the standards are to be computed, is to be assumed or judged with regard to the capacity of the plant and the marketability of the products. The sales potential and production capacity decide the quantum of output to be manufactured within a particular period. The idle capacity, unutilised capacity and other limiting factors should be taken into consideration before determining the attainable level of output.

After bearing the above factors in mind, we can proceed to set up the standards for the different elements of cost separately.

How to Determine Standard Costs

Cost in its totality can be compared to a triangle. The three elements which constitute the triangle are material cost, labour cost and overhead cost. As already stated, standard cost involves fixing standards in quantitative terms and converting them into values. It is a coordinated exercise, though at the operational level, unlike the coordination required at a higher level for budgeting. It is important to think for all the three elements or cost at the same times while setting up standards. There is obvious connection between labour and overheads since the question whether to use manual labour or machines will have to be decided. Further, the time required to accomplish a task will also depend on the conditions in which materials are bought. If some cutting or further treatment is required, not only will there be some wastage of materials but also more time will be needed. Buying materials absolutely ready for use may mean some extra cost of materials but may mean less wastage and lower labour cost. Thus standard for all three elements of cost must be considered together. Setting up of standard cost involves two processes, *viz....*

(i) Determination of quantitative standards consistent with quality, and

(ii) Converting such quantitative standards into monetary values.

To start with, the production engineering department considers, approves and circulates the drawings for a proposed job (if it is an engineering concern) to the various concerned sections/departments. The engineering department itself has experts specialising in studies of materials, labour and machine requirements, etc. The approved designs provoke the concerned department/sections to study the implications and set standards in respect of their area of specialisation. Material specialists, fix standards for materials consumption, time and motion study experts determine the exact process and sequence of operations and standard time; and the buying department fixes the material prices, and so on. Then all the above data go to the 'standard cost committee' (comprising representatives of all the departments/ sections concerned) where the standard cost is finalised.

The main departments involved (co-operating in building up the standards) are following:

Material cost	:	Production Engineering Department (Material specialists) and Buying Department.
Labour Cost	:	Production Engineering Department (Time and motion study experts) and Personnel Department.
Overhead Cost	:	Production Engineering Department and Production and Service Departments.

The cost accounting department acts as the coordinator.

Determination of standard material cost involves first the laying down of quality standards for the finished products; the quantity of materials required depends upon the desired quality of the output. The standard quantity of materials is often dependent if the material is of better quality and vice versa. The quantity required is converted into money values on the basis of prices expected to prevail (in current standards). An ideal price can be used if ideal standards are expected, but this is only hypothetical. Price standards should take into account freight costs, discounts, etc. Ideal purchase efficiency should be assumed.

Determination of standard labour cost involves determining the standard time to be taken for each operation or each job as a whole on the basis of motion study and time study. It is the production engineering department which has to prescribe the categories of labour required and the time to be taken by each category. The time to be taken for each unit of output can be known from 'standard hour'. The standard time is converted into money values with the assistance of the personnel department which would know the wage rates likely to prevail. Thus, a current standard for labour can be determined. Determination of overheads cost standard is a little involved. "Overheads" is the aggregate of indirect materials, indirect labour and indirect expenses. The term 'indirect' is used here with reference to the costing unit these items of cost, however, may be 'direct' as far as the cost centre (*i.e.*, "the department") is concerned. Hence, a simple way is to fix standards for materials cost, labour cost and expenses in respect of each department both production and service. To the departments these costs are direct and hence it is easier to fix the standards. Before fixing the standards, the level of activity of each department is to be determined. This process can be simplified by classifying the costs as "variable" and "fixed". Variable would very according to the level of activity budgeted and fixed would remain constant for the period.

As ultimately the standard overhead cost per unit has to be determined, it is necessary to link the standard overheads of the departments to the products. For this purpose, the standard overheads of service departments have to be redistributed to the production departments. This should be done on a standard basis. For instance, the power house standard cost for a period is Rs. 7,20,000 and the standard output is 24,00,000 Kwh, the standard rate per kwh amounts to 30 paise. Depending upon the standard consumption for actual output, the standard cost charged for actual production will differ. Assuming that the standard consumption of power for one unit of output is 200 Kwh and actual production is 10,000 units, the standard cost applied to actual production would be Rs.6,00,000 (*i.e.*, 30 Paise × 200 kwh × 10,000 units). If the actual expenditure on power amount to Rs.7,30,000 the variances in power cost would amount to Rs.10,000 adverse. The above is a simplified example of power cost which can be easily linked to the final product.

For the cost of other overheads which cannot be linked with the final product so conveniently, again the same principle applies. The service departments' standard costs should be predetermined. It should be assigned to the production departments on standard recovery basis. For instance, the standard cost (budget) of "time office" is Rs.80,000. The standard working time of the three production departments is 20,000, 20,000, 10,000 hours respectively. Accordingly the time office's 'standard cost to .be distributed is Rs.32,000, Rs.32,000 and Rs.16,000 respectively among the three production departments. The production department's overheads collected like this would be converted into standard recovery rates.

Recovery rate for each production department is fixed on the basis of standard house. The rate is arrived at by dividing the standard overheads by the standard hours budgeted to be worked. The standard hours budgeted means the budgeted production muliplied by the standard time per unit. Thus the recovery rate for a production department is standard (budgeted) overheads divided by standard hours. This rate is determined in advance. This rate will adopted to coarge overhead for each unit, The recovery will be at the standard rate for standard hours of actual production, That is, if one unit takes 6 hours whereas the standard time is 5 hours, the unit will be charged with 5 hours multiplied by recovery rate per hour. The actual cost of a unit would be actual direct cost applied plus the overhead charged on predetennined recovery rate for the standard hours of actual output. The overheads charged to the production will differ from the overheads actually spent due to more less spending as well as due to volume of production being more or less than what is budgeted, These would be reflected in variances.

Illustration.

Standard recovery rate	Rs. 5 per standard hour
Units produced	100 units
Standard time per unit	2 hours
Total actual time taken	250 hours

Actual overhead charged from Service
Department to Production Department Rs.500

Actual overhead incurred in the
production department Rs.600.

Calculate the overheads charged and incurred.

Solution.

Actual overhead charged to production department	Rs. 500
Actual overhead incurred in the production department	Rs. 600
Total	Rs. 1,100
Total overhead charged to the costing units at Rs. 5 per standard hour (Rs. 5 × 2 hours × 100 units)	Rs. 1,000

The above illustration shows that there is an under-recovery of overheads to the extent of Rs. 100 (Rs. 1,100-Rs.1,000). The overhead of production department is Rs. 1,100 which consists of Rs. 500 charged from service, department and Rs.600 incurred in the production department. The former sum itself is on the basis of predetermined rates of recovery from the service department. The actual overhead in the service department may itself be different. The amount charged from the the service department to various production departments (like the Rs. 600 charged) may differ from the actual cost of the service department. Thus there can be overhead variance for the service department as well. Hence overhead variance can arise in the production department as well as at the service department stage. The discussion about overhead variances in this book is mainly based on production department.

How a Standard is Fixed?

The preparation of standards calls for liaison between many departments. It is not a responsibility of the costing department only. The Productions Engineer and the Cost Accountant will have to collaborate in setting standards. The Cost Accountant must have a detailed study of the functions necessary for the manufacture of the product. It is the task of the costing department to reflect in units of thing and money values the budgets standards and standard costs that result from the decisions of the operating management. After being done so standards are generally fixed for:

Production

(i) Direct Material:	(a) quantity per unit of output;
	(b) price per unit of quantity;
	(c) wastage per unit of input; and
(ii) Direct Labour:	(a) number of men per machine;
	(b) grade of men employed
	(c) wage rate for each grade; and
	(d) machine/man hours required per unit of output.
(iii) Indirect Materials:	Cost per machine, production hour.
(iv) Indirect Labour:	Cost per machine/production hour, or percentage of direct labour.
(v) Fixed Expenses:	Total amount for the period of budgeted production hours.
(vi) Variable Expenses:	Cost per unit of output, or cost per product hour.

The setting of Standard Costs requires consideration of the following:

(1) Quantities	for each element of cost entering into a
(2) Prices or rates	product *i.e.* Material, Labour, Overhead.
(3) Quantities or grades	

The Cost Accountant will have to collaborate with the Production Engineer for the purpose of fixing the standards.

HOW TIGHT SHOULD STANDARD BE?

The establishment of standards or standard cost is decided by the use to be made of them. It can be rightly said that a single standard may not be suitable for all purposes. For the purposes of cost control, tight standards need to be established. The attainable performance standards are useful for purposes of inventory valuation, product costing and income determination. Realistic standards are needed for pricing decisions and capital expenditure decisions.

High Standards

A high standard helps in cost reduction and motivating employees to try to reach the targets established. High standards represent the best possible performance and, if achieved, raise the levels of performance and efficiency as compared to poor or loose standards. High standards being unattainable in practice may not be good for the employees. Employees may not seriously accept them because they know that they are unattainable and impossible excuse the failure to reach them. High standards are also not realistic and therefore cannot be used in product costing, inventory valuation, financial statement, planning, and capital investment decision.

Low (Loose) Standards

A standard which is low or loose can be attained by poor performance. However, it defeats the purpose of standard costing and fails to disclose in efficiencies. Similarly, standards set in terms of average past performance expect too little. Since jobs on which performance is poor are likely to be more numerous than are jobs on which performance is exceptionally good, average past performance standards are usually considerably looser. Such standards do not help management in cost control as they are not accurate measures to compare actual results.

In conclusion, it can be said that accountants generally seem to favour currently attainable standards which are most appropriate for performance appraisal, accounting purposes, cost control and decision making. Such standards produce good performance, promote employee motivation and include unavoidable elements, such as spoilage, lost time, capacity not utilised in setting standards. The National Association of Accountants argues:

Revision of Standards

Standard Costs may be fixed for a period of three, six or eleven months or for an indefinite period. There are no definite rules for the selection of a particular period and each case is to be decided after considering the conditions prevailing in that business and the type of standard required to be established. Normally a period of one year is more realistic, as it coincides with the normal accounting period. Frequent revision of standards is very expensive and besides this it will defeat the purpose for which they are fixed. Periods longer than a year have the advantage of savings in clerical costs and continuity and uniformity in standard costs which would show trends over a longer period. A high degree of flexibility in the procedure is, however, necessary so that the long-term standards may be adjusted to suit current conditions. Where the prices of materials and wage rates are not likely to fluctuate appreciably, standard costs may be established for indefinite periods.

The main purpose of establishing Standard Costing System is to control actual performance by comparing with the standards. After standards are set, conditions may change because of change in methods of production, change in price level (revision of materials prices, labour rates, charges of gas, water, electricity, rates and taxes etc.) changes in specifications or designs of products (requiring more or less materireal or labour or change in the product mix and grades of labour required), and technological advances. Under such circumstances the management will have to change the entire standard cost structure. Some of the changes might have been anticipated and adjustments for the same might have been made while fixing the standards, but some of them might not have been anticipated. If the changes are of a temporary or a minor nature, then it is not advisable to revise the standards. It has already been stated that frequent revision caused by each change in working conditions is neither practicable nor desirable because if it is done, it loses its importance as a "measuring tool".

Any variance of costs due to deviations of actual conditions for the standards may be shown separately in variance. Analysis Reports as Revision Variance, so that management can be informed of the extent of change in cost.

TYPES OF STANDARDS

(A) Performance Level Standards

Performance Level Standards mean the quality or productivity expected from the inputs employed in production and other activities, and can be classified into two *viz.*, Theoretical/Ideal/Perfection Standards and Currently Attainable Standards. Theoretical or Ideal or Perfection Standards represent and expectation of the best performance given certain resources and equipment. These standards usually include allowance for rest periods of personnel but do not make any allowance for wastage, spoilage or lost time. These standards are the ultimate objective which the enterprise expects to strive for. The chances of attainment of the theoretical standards in actual day-to-day operations is rather remote. It may not be incorrect to say that the accomplishment of the theoretical performance level is not really possible.

Currently Attainable Standards could be in terms of performance levels which are 'Attainable Performance':

Attainable Performance is defined as Theoretical Performance minus unavoidable losses due to material spoilage, labour rest periods and fatigue and machine set-up time. Unlike theoretical standards, attainable standards are attainable. However, a high efficiency in input management is required to achieve the attainable standards. Also the concept of attainable standards could be nebulous inasmuch as capturing all potential unavoidable losses in the input management process is difficult. Avarage Past Performance Standards are based on the historical data, which is taken as the reference level for building up standards for the future. However, if past performance has been bad then the standards tend to be loose and good performance in the earlier years would render the standard rather tight. The past periods chosen as a representative year has to be a normal year neither super-normal nor abnormal. But if the corporate policy is to employ tight standards then the representative year will be slanted in favour of yearls with extra-ordinary performance. And of the policy is to have loose standards, the years with poor performance will be the representative periods

Normal Performance standards is a performance level likely to prevail over future period of years-over the product market life or over the phase of the business cycle. In terms of performance level it will lie in between the levels prescribed by Attainable Performance Level and Average Past Performance. Also, the normal standards are expectations which will characterize the average over a future set of years.

(B) Volume of Output

Volume of output standards can be expressed in terms of Theoretical capacity, Practical capacity, Normal activity, Expected activity. These terms have already been defined in the previous Chapter.

(C) Price Level Standards

Price level standards can be thought of in terms of Ideal Standards, Basic Standards, Current Standards and Normal Standards.

Ideal standards are set on the presumption of the most favourable prices likely to prevail for the inputs required. In at inflationary era, the idea of ideal standards will tend to be obsolete even while the standards are being set. Also favourable prices assumed can build-in frustration at the end of the budget period because of the unavoidable unfavourable variances. Also favourable prices imply less provision of cash for meeting obligations on cash account which can allow situations of deficit to emerge and cause difficulties and embarrassment. Ideal standards are strict standards and the performance level tends to be tight. Basic standards refer to the price level prevailing in a particular year. The said years is usually understood to be the first year following the establishment of standards. The basic standards do not undergo change following changes in the price level norms. Thus the basic standards present the index number of prices of the inputs *viz.*, materials, labour and factory overhead. It is analogous to the index number of prices. Current Standards mean the prices likely to prevail in the ensuing fiscal period. Based on the experience of the current year and the conditions likely to prevail in the coming future period the standards undergo revision. Normal Standards are price levels expected to prevail over a future period of time, say the product market life for the business cycle. These standards have a pre-determined tenure and undergo change only after the lapse of the tenure period.

(D) Physical Standards versus Financial Standards

Physical Standards are norms or input-output ratios expressed in physical terms such as the number of kilograms required or labour hours demanded for a given unit of output. It could also refer to broad norms such as number of personnel required for a given repair and maintenance operation or promotion activity. Physical Standards express the yardstick of performance in physical terms.

Financial Standards are norms or input-output ratios expressed in monetary terms, such as the rupee value of the input (material, labour overheads) required for a given unit of output. In fact, financial standards are always the product of the physical standards and the concerned price factor. Thus if the physical standard of materials for unit of output is 5 kgs. and the standard price of one kilogram is Rs. 4, the material price factor for a unit of output is Rs. 20 or the price factor for a kilogram of raw material input is Rs. 4. Again, financial standards can also be expressed in terms of broad norms such as monetary inputs required for any manufacturing or marketing operation. One more point needs to be reiterated. Physical planning precedes finance planning or financial standards stem from some physical standard with the price factor as the conversion link.

(E) Manufacturing and Non-Manfacturing Standards

Manufacturing Standards and standard and standard costs refer to the scientifically predetermined input-output ratios prescribed for production activity. The manufacturing segment lends itself to statistical measurement and hence input-output ratios can be, relatively speaking, easily prescribed. The input-output ratios are laid down after a lot a rigorous exercise with respect to choice of materials (material standards), motion and time studies (labour standards) and technical and engineering studies of production and service department facilities (factory overhead standards). Once again the norms are expressed as standards to begin with and eventually converted into monetary terms *i.e.* standard costs.

Non-Manufacturing Standards refer to input-output ratios for the non-manufacturing activities *viz.*, marketing administration. However, in the non-manufacturing segment input-output ratios cannot be prescribed with the same precision as the manufacturing segment. The activities of the marketing department depend to a great extent on the external economic and social environment. Thus, it is difficult of not impossible to quantify the number of can is to be made by a salesman before he attracts a favourable response from, the customers. Also, customers response in numbers and value is not easy to gauge to provide a yardstick in terms of input-output or 'call-response' ratio. In the marketing segment except for deliveries and commission all other inputs are fixed expenses and hence defy precise measurement through input-output, ratios.

The reason for this differential in behaviour between the manufacturing and non-manufacturing segments is not far to seek. Cost accounting techniques gained initial currency in the manufacturing segment. However, with the advancement in management science it may be possible to improve the situation in the non-manufacturing segment. And in time to come to the discriminating features of the two segments may disappear.

APPLLCATION OF THE TECHNIQUE OF STANDARD COSTING

Standard costing is not a method of costing just as process or job or unit costing. It is a system or technique of cost accounting which can be used in conjunction with process, job or operating costing without any difficulty, whatsoever, Industries where standard costing is more suitable can be categorised as under:

1. Engineering and textile industries where large range of products are manufactured.
2. Process industries where the method of production and nature of output are the same. The examples of such industries are chemical industries, distillaries, paper-making and metal processing etc.

3. Industries where the methods of manufacturing are repetitive and products are more or less homogeneous, *e.g.*, agricultural and food products.
4. Service industries where operation costing is also applicable like transport, gas and water, electricity etc.
5. Extraction industries such as coal, oil and timber.

Where the work is not repetitive, *e.g.*. construction work, contract work, ship-building and erection work etc., it is difficult to set standard and, therefore, standard costing would not be suitable. But in certain cases, it can be applied partially though not fully, at least to some advantage of the concerns.

DETERMINATION OF STANDARD COSTS

Installation of standard costing system for accomplishing the desired objectives require existence of certain pre-requisites. These pre-requisites can be put as follows:

(1) Existence of Budgetary Control System. Existence of budgetary control system is a pre-requisite for the standard costing system. Budgets fix the targets which the executives have to achieve. They create a sense of discipline, financial or otherwise, among employees at different levels. Budgets are the projections for the future and therefore they are of great use to the effective functioning of the standard costing system.

(2) Competent Staff. The successful operation of standard costing system requires existence of well qualified and trained staff for fixing of the standards, measuring performance and reporting variances to different levels of managements. The reports submitted to the management help the management in applying the principles of "management by exception" meaning thereby that the management pays attention only to those cases where performance is below or above the standard.

(3) Acceptance of the System. The standard costing system can have the desired effects only when the system is acceptable both to the management as well as to the workers. The management should take sufficient interest in the system to make it effective,

Similarly the workers should also believe that in the long run, the system would be beneficial to all of them. This is possible by fixing the standards in a way that they are capable of being achieved by an average worker.

(4) Reasonable Size. The system of standard costing can be introduced with advantage in concerns which are of a reasonable size. The system may not be suitable for small concerns since in their case careful scheduling of production may not be possible. For example, in a small concern a worker may be handling different machines and at times he may be called to handle different jobs and therefore, it may not be possible to correctly fix the standard time for different jobs or different operations handled by him. Moreover the system of standard costing requires specialisation of jobs and processes which may not be possible in a small concern.

(5) Efficient Accounting System. An efficient accounting system is also an essential requisite for successful operation of the standard costing system. The accounting information supplied should not only be accuarate but also be complete and up-to-date. The system of coding may be used for speedy recording and analysing the accounting information. Appropriate cost centre should also be set up in the organisation.

It has already been stated that the technique of standard costing requires pre-determination of standard cost. It became therefore, essential for us to understand how the standards are set. But before that it will be proper to consider the true meaning of the term "standard cost". Does it mean "ideal cost" or simply "cost based on past performance, or normal cost?" We are discussing below the different meanings which may be attached to the term "standard cost". There are, therefore, different bases on which standard costs may possibly be determined.

THE CONCEPT OF STANDARD HOUR

A standard hour is the expression of the actual output in terms of standard time instead of units. This would facilitate expression of dissimilar output in terms of a common factor. According to the Institute of Cost and Management Accountants, London, standard hour means: "A hypothetical unit pre-established to represent the amount of work which should be performed in one hour under standard performance." When the term standard hour is used it is assumed that it represents the amount of work to be done in sixty minutes. For example, if a welder welds one piece in 20 minutes according to the standard, the standard output in one clock hour will be 3 units. If the number of units actually produced in one day (of 8 hours) is 30, then the output can be expressed as 10 standard hours, though he has actually worked for 8 hours only. The concept of standard hour enables measurement of activity of a factory for producing dissimilar units and expressing them as a single measure. Accordingly, comparison of levels of activity between two periods can be done by converting the different output into standard hours.

Illustration.

A firm can produce 3 products, A, B and C the standard hours being fixed as 20, 25 and 35 respectively, The firm's output in 1975 were as follows:

	1975	*/976*
	Unils	*Unils*
A	10,00	12,000
B	8,00	5,900
C	5,000	7,000

Express the change in the level of activity in 1976 as a percentage of 1975 activity.

Solution.

Standard hours of output of 1975 and 1976:

		1975		*1976*
A	10,000 × 20	2,00,000	12,000 × 20	2,40,000
B	8,000 × 25	2,00,000	5,900 × 25	1,47,500
C	5,000 × 35	1,75,000	7,000 × 35	2,45,000
		5,75,000		6,32,500

Precautions in Use of Standard Costing

Ordinarily, the various variances that are worked out in standard costing may be relied upon to indicate the state of affairs and remedial action may be taken. For example, materials usage variance, if adverse, will indicate inefficiency in the use of materials; therefore, steps may be taken to remedy the situation and to pull up the foreman concerned. However, a degree of caution is necessary in coming to a conclusion on the basis of variances. Sometimes, they do not reveal the real situation without further inquiry. The following precautions may, therefore, be necessary:

(A) The emphasis should be on removing causes that lead to wastage or loss; for this, it is necessary that worker and staff members should frankly state what has happened. If the emphasis is one punishment, frankness will be missing; if punishment is not the idea, the real causes will come to light arid then proper remedial action should be possible.

(B) Price variance should not always be dismissed as beyond one's control. Could not the purchase be made at different point of time? Could not a substitute material be purchased? Stocks kept for a long time involve extra expense in the form of interest. How is this to be treated? Such questions should not be ignored.

(C) The real cause of the situation should be ascertained; for example, it is quite possible that extra time is being because repairs and maintenance work is not up to the mark.

(D) If the factors that existed when standards were framed have changed, it would be better to revise the standards realistically and them only compare them with actual performance. Suppose materials of a better quality are now available, this will call for revision of the materials standard. If a process has undergone change, the labour standard will need revision.

Standard Costing in India—A Glimpse of the Practices in Leading Companies

A company stated that they used standards only for manufacturing operations. They called these standards as target costs. They had established physical as well as monetary targets. They relied on historical costs, although transition to standards based on engineering specifications were in progress.

Another leading company mentioned that they did not have standards as referred to in accounting text-books. They made use of physical as well as monetary standards for controlling different activities. For example, in respect of service departments a great degree of control is exercised by applying physical standards. Such control is aided by arranging constant visits to the factories by members of the company's management audit team. In respect of production departments, they also applied value standards. In other words, standards were specified for each item of expenditure. However, even in these instances, control exercised was broad and general in nature rather than specific and individualistic. Standards were established to compare and measure the actual input and output and the resulting costs. Usage variance was a regular feature. Consumption standards were based on marginal usage and allowable wastage. This company did not lay down price standards, as it thought such standards would not serve any useful purpose. There was no sense in making price variance analysis. Company faced emergency situations more as a rule than as an exception whereby they were compelled to procure adequate quantities of raw material at an uneconomic price rather than stick to rigid economies of purchase price and face the shortage. It was stated that the economy achieved was more a result of technical development rather than buying policy. For example, company imported raw material, company developed a substitute made form castoroil which was never used before as a useful raw material input. The choice was mainly influenced by the low price of castor oil prevailing in India, as compared to other oils. So essentially the standards kept on changing as did the inputs.

Rationale of Standard Costs

Standard costs aid in the managerial process of planning control, evaluation and motivation. The process of planning starts with the establishment of standards and standard costs which have to be adhered to, if certain performance levels are to be attained.

Then the process of monitoring the extent of conformance or otherwise of the actual events (historic costs) with the intended events (established norms) starts *i.e.* Control. 'Given the variation of the actual events from the intended events attempts are made to evaluate the performance (favourable variance/unfavourable variance) so as to enable initiation of response action. And the favourable/ unfavourable variances are also the basis for operating a reward/ penalty system—bonuses/incentives for favourable variance and penalties of whatever sort for unfavourable variances. Thus, Standard Costs motivate personnel to achieve them and with a hope of reward or the fear of penalty.

In fact the entire process of initiating, evolving and implementing of a standard cost system is a motivational tool to the top middle and junior management to actively participate in the *modus operandi* of the control system and contribute to the success of the enterprise. By its very nature, the standard cost system involves the management and the managed in a common venture which seeks to steer the enterprise towards the direction of the best possible result-resource ratio. Standards motivate individuals and groups at all levels of responsibility towards organisational objectives, that is to say, it encourages goal directed behaviour. Again since standards and standard costs imply the laying down of norms for individual/group tasks, the structure must be so designed as to facilitate providing authority and pinpointing responsibility centres are evolved. And last but not the least standards/standard cost provide an opportunity and identify the need for all functional areas production, marketing, purchase, personnel and finance to come together and focus their attention towards the common goals that lie at the heart of the enterprise "Economic Performance". In this togetherness of the human resources, the financial controller and staff provide an important link and media of communication

So, we see that the entire process of management gets initiated on account of the installation and operation of a standard cost system—planning, control evaluation, motivation, organisation and co-ordination. Standards and standard costs provide a fillip to the practice of scientific management. In addition to contributing to scientific management within an enterprise, standards/standard costs also aid in specific functions like:

(i) **Book-keeping Economy:** The anxiety of quick collection of historical data of current operations and the installation of an elaborate paraphernalia for the efficient data collection can be dispensed with. Informative financial statements can be prepared in advance and as and when actual data are ready comparisons can be made with the norms laid down. Data reporting is more efficient, in terms of time and money.

(ii) **Product Costing: (Income determination and inventory valuation)** Pre-determined cost help in building product information in advance and facilitate the timely preparation of financial statements.

(iii) **Formulation of Budgets:** Budgets, which represent a quantified expression of the intentions of management, are invariable guided by standards and standard costs. Thus, the budget process gets based on scientifically pre-determined input-output ratios.

(iv) **Pricing Decision:** Pre-determined costs provide timely inputs to aid pricing decisions particularly for filling in tenders.

(v) **Cost Reduction and Cost Consciousness:** Standards and standard costs discolse the gaps in actual performance *vis-a-vis* intended performance. Further investigation into the causes of the gap reveal the weak spots of the enterprise and pave the way for corrective action. And the very presence of standards and standard costs inculcate sense of commitment towards cost norms and zeal to attain the cost targets. Thus, standard cost initiates and promotes cost consicousness.

Thus Standard Costs have a dual role in the organisation. As a generic contribution they facilitate the managerial process of planning, controlling, evaluation, motivation, organisation and co-ordination. In terms of specific functions they aid in the product costing, pricing decisions, budget formulation, book-keeping economy, and cost reduction and cost consciousness.

VARIANCE ANALYSIS

Standard costs (SC) are an indication of what costs should be for a unit of production. The difference between actual cost (AC) and standard cost (SC) is called a variance. Variances can be analyzed to determine why they exist and this analysis can provide a basis for taking corrective action. If the actual cost is greater than the standard cost, the variance is unfavourable, if actual is less than the standard, the variance is favourable.

AC > SC = Unfavourable Variance

AC < SC = Favourable Variance

A system of variance analysis helps in identifying the difference in terms of costs between actual performance and desired performance and hence helps to pinpont efficient and inefficient operating areas. It helps in assigning responsibility to individuals and also helps to motivate individuals to achieve the performance targets.

The technique of variance analysis also helps to isolate the causes of differences between actual costs and standard costs. For proper control both favourable and unfavourable variance should be analyzed. The causes for the occurrence of variances alongwith the individuals responsible for variance can also be identified and analyzed.

Hence the system of variance analysis helps management to find answers to the following two questions:

1. Are the variance due to loose or tight standards?
2. Have the standards been set scientifically?

The technique of variance analysis also helps management to rely on the principle of management by exception. Management is usually not concerned with analyzing all the performance reports. Rather, the management may decide that performance within ± 3 per cent of budget or standards is acceptable when examining performance reports. The management only examines more cost areas where differences exceed these limit.

Variances can be divided into three main broad categories:

I. Material Variances.

II. Labour Variances.

III. Overhead Variances.

I. Material Variances

Material variances include two factors: *(1)* the quantity of materials that should have been used to produce one unit of output and *(2)* the prices that should have been paid in acquiring this quantity of materials. The total material cost variance may result from difference between standard and actual quantities of materials used or between standard and actual prices paid for materials, or from a combination of these two factors.

Material Cost Variance. Material Cost Variance (MCV) is calculated as the difference between the standard cost of direct materials and the actual cost of direct materials for actual output.

MCV = (SQ for Actual Output × SP – AQ × AP)

where SQ = Standard quantity

AQ = Actual quantity

SP = Standard price

AP = Actual price

Material cost variance can be divided into Direct Material Price Variance and Direct Material Quantity Variance. The Material

Price Variance is the difference between the standard price and the actual price multiplied by the actual quantity purchased. The Material Quantity Variance is the difference between the standard quantity used and the actual quantity multiplied by the standard price.

1. Material price variance (MPV) = Actual Quantity (Standard price Actual price)
   = AQ (SP - AP)
2. Material quantity variance (MQV) = Standard Price (Standard quantity – Actual quantity)
   = SP (SQ - AQ)

Example

From the material related information given below calculate the various material variances for the XYZ Company for the month of October:

Standard

	Quantity (kilos)	Unit Price	Total	Quantity (kilos)	Actual Unit Price	Total
Material X	5	3,00	15.00	4	3.00	12.00
Material Y	3	2.00	6.00	4	1.00	4.00

Solution MCV = MPV + MQV

MPV = Actual Quantity (Standard Price Actual Price)

X = 4 (3 - 3) = zero

Y = 4(2 -1) = 4 (Favourable)

Total = 4 (Favourable)

MQV = Standard Price (Standard quantity Actual quantity)

X = 3 (5 - 4) = 3 (Favourable)

Y = 2 (3 - 4) = 2 (Unfavourable)

Total = 1 Favourable

$$\text{DMCV} = \left(\text{Standard Price} \times \text{Standard Quantity for Actual output}\right) - \left(\text{Actual Price} \quad \text{Actual Quantity}\right)$$

x = (3 x 5) - (3 x 4) = 15 - 12 = 3 (Favourable)

Y = (2 x 3) - (1 x 4) = 6 - 4 = 2 (Favourable)

5 (Favourable)

Thus MCV = MPV + MQV

5(F) = 4(F) + 1(F) 5

5(F) = 5 (F)

Material quantity or usage variance can be futher subdivided into two more variances, *viz.*,

1. Material Mix Variance
2. Material Yield Variance.

1. Material Mix Variance is that portion of the material quantity variance which arises due to the difference between the standard mix and the actual mix of different materials used in production. Material mix variance can be calculated as

Material mix variance

$$= \text{Total actual quantity} \left(\text{Standard price of standard mix} - \text{Standard price of actual mix} \right)$$

Alternatively, material mix variance can also be calculated as:

Material mix variance

$$= \text{Standard price} \left(\text{Revised standard quantity} - \text{Actual quantity} \right)$$

where,

Revised standard quantity (RSQ)

$$\frac{\text{Standard qty. of each material}}{\text{Total standard quantity}} \times \text{Total actual quantity}$$

2. Material Yield Variance. Material yield variance arises due to the difference bewteen the standard yield (output) specified and the actual yield obtained. If the actual yield is greater than the standard yield, the variance is favourable and vice versa.

Material yield variance can be expressed as:

Material yield variance =

$$\begin{array}{c}\text{Standard}\\ \text{rate per}\\ \text{unit of yield}\end{array} \left(\begin{array}{ccc}\text{Actual} & & \text{Standard}\\ \text{yield} & - & \text{yield}\end{array}\right)$$

In the above example the Material Price Variance was favourable because the actual price of the materials purchased was less than the standard price. The quantity variance was also favourable since the actual quantity used was less than the standard prescribed. The responsibility for price variances generally lie with the purchasing department while the production department is responsible for quantity variances.

Labour Variances

The total labour cost variance is the difference between the actual labour costs incurred and the standard labour cost for the actual units produced. If the standard labour cost of actual output exceeds the actual labour cost, the variance is favourable and vice versa

Labour cost variance = [Standard hours for actual output × Standard rate – Actual hours × Actual rate]

Labour cost variance can be divided into labour rate variance and labour efficiency variance. Labour rate variance is the difference between the standard labour rate and actual labour rate multiplied by the actual labour hours worked. The labour efficiency variance is the difference between standard hours worked specified for actual output and the actual labour hours worked. It is calculated by multiplyirig the difference between standard and actual hours by the standard rate per hour.

1. Labour Rate = Actual Time (Standard rate- Actual rate) Variance
2. Labour Efficiency = Standard rate (Standard time variance – Actual time)

Labour Rate Variance

This variance arises when labour is paid at a rate different from the standard wage rate. A rate variance usually occurs when a person is paid at a rate higher or lower than expected. The causes for labour rate variance are:

* Payment at a rate higher or lower than the standard rate
* Change in the grades of employees
* Inclusion of new workmen
* Change in the method of compensation etc.

Labour Efficiency Variance

The time taken to do a job indicates the efficiency of workers. Hence the variance arises due to the difference between actual time worked and hours which should have been worked. This variance can usually be traced to departmental supervisions. An example would be when a highly paid worker performs a lower level task. The causes for labour efficiency variance are:

* Change in the skill-grade of the workers
* Extent of supervision
* Change in the method of production
* Change in tools
* Quality of materials
* Working conditions, etc.

Like Material Quantity Variance, Labour Efficiency Variance can also be divided into two types.

(1) Labour Mix Variance. That portion of direct labour efficiency variance which is due to the difference between standard and actual gang composition of the workers. It is calculated as:

$$\text{Standard rate} \times \left(\begin{matrix}\text{Revised}\\ \text{Standard}\\ \text{Time}\end{matrix} - \begin{matrix}\text{Actual}\\ \text{Time}\end{matrix}\right)$$

$$\text{Revised standard time} = \frac{\text{Total time of actual workers}}{\text{Total time of standard worker}} \times \text{Standard time}$$

(2) Labour Yield Variance. That portion of direct labour eff1ciency variance which is due to the difference between the standard yield specified and the actual yield obtained. It is calculated as:

Standard cost per unit	=	Standard output for actual unit units	×	Actual output

Example

The various Labour variances from the following labour related information for the XYZ Company for the month of October can be calculated as below:

Actual data

Hours worked = 6,000

Labour rate = Rs. 25/- per hour

Standard data

Hours worked = 4,000

Labour rate = Rs. 40/- per hour

Solution

Labour cost = (Standard hours for Actual output × Standard rate) – Actual hours × Actual rate)

Variance = (4,000 × Rs. 40) – (6,000 × Rs. 35)

= 1,60,000 – 1,50,000 = Rs. 10,000 (Favourable)

Labour rate = Actual Time (Standard rate – Actual rate)

Variance 6,000 (Rs.40–Rs.25) = Rs. 90,000 (Favourable)

Labour Efficiency = Standard rate (Standard time - Actual time)

Variance Rs. 40 (4,000 – 6,000) = Rs. 80,000 (A)

LCV = LRV + LEV or 10,000 (F)

= 90,000 (F) + 80,000 (A) = 10,000 (F)

Overhead Variances

Controlling overhead costs is more difficult and complex than controlling direct materials and direct labour costs because it is difficult to assign the responsibility for over head costs.

The total overhead cost variance can be sub-divided into a budget or spending variance and an efficiency variance. The budget or spending variance is the difference between the budget and the actual cost for the actual hours of operation. This variance can be compared to the price and quantity variance developed for direct material and direct labour.

The efficiency variance measures efficiency in the use of the factor, *e.g.*, machine hours employed in costing overheads to the products.

The formula for calculating the various overhead variances are as follows:

(a) Standard Rate per unit $= \dfrac{\text{Budgeted overheads}}{\text{Budgeted output}}$

(b) Standard Rate per unit $= \dfrac{\text{Budgeted overheads}}{\text{Budgeted hours}}$

(c) Standard hours for actual output

$$= \frac{\text{Budgeted output}}{\text{Budgeted hours}} \times \text{Actual Output}$$

(d) Standard output for actual output

$$= \frac{\text{Budgeted output}}{\text{Budgeted hours}} \times \text{Actual Output}$$

(e) Recovered or Absorbed Overheads = Standard rate × Actual Output

(f) Budgeted Overheads = Standard rate per unit × Budgeted output or Standard rate per hour × Budgeted hours

(g) Standard Overheads = Standard rate per unit × Standard output for actual time
or Standard rate per hours × Actual output

(h) Actual Overheads = Actual rate per unit × Actual output
or Actual rate per unit × Actual hours

The various overhead variances can now be put as follows:

Total overhead cost variance = Recovered overheads – Actual overheads

The total overhead cost variance may be segregated into.

(i) Variable overhead cost variance =
Recovered variable overheads – Actual variable overheads

(ii) Fixed overhead cost variance =
Recovered fixed overheads – Actual fixed overheads

Fixed overheads cost variance can be segregated into:

(i) Expenditure Variance =
Budgeted overheads – Actual overheads

(ii) Volume Variance = Recovered overheads – Budgeted overheads

Volume variance may be segregated into:

(i) Efficiency variance = Recovered overheads – Standard overheads

(ii) Capacity variance = Standard overheads – Budgeted overheads

The reasons for the overhead variance are:

Fixed Overhead Expenditure Variance	Spending more money than budgeted
Fixed Overhead Volume Variance	Change in demand; Interruption of stoppage of work due to defective planning, shortage of material, absence of or faulty instructions, etc.

Fixed overhead Efficiency Variance	Actual efficiency in operations not as expected
Capacity Variance	Change in utilization of capacity from Lack of demand Lack of power Lack of raw materials etc.

For the XYZ Company for the month of October, calculate the various overhead variances from the information given below:

Normal overhead rate	=	Rs.2/-
Actual hours operated	=	20,000
Allowed hours for actual Production	=	22,000
Allowed overheads for budgeted hours	=	Rs. 60,000
Actual overheads	=	Rs .62,000

Solution

Budgeted overhead = Rs. 60,000

Recovered overhead = Standard rate per hour × Standard hours for actual output.

= 2 x 22,000 = Rs. 44,000

Standard overhead = Standard rate per hour × Actual hours

= 2 x 20,000 = Rs. 40,000

Overhead cost Variance = Recovered overhead – Actual overhead

= 44,000 – 62,000

= 18,000 (Unfavourable)

The total overhead cost variance can be analyzed into a budget or spending variance and a volume variance.

Overhead Spending variance

= Budgeted overheads – Actual overheads

= 60,000 – 62,000

= 2,000 (Unfavourable)

Overhead Volume variance

= Recovered overheads – Budgeted overheads

= 44,000 – 60,000

= 16,000 (Unfavourable)

Exhibit I shows the total variances that have been discussed.

Interpreting through Variance Analysis

As noted earlier, a variance exists when standard costs differ from actual costs. The difference between standard cost and actual cost is called a cost variance. Cost variance for material labour and overhead result from a variety of different causes. Hence, in evaluating the efficiency of a manufacturing organization, these variances should be measured and analyzed. Every manager should try and answer two important questions regarding every variance:

1. Is the Variance Significant?

Management should accept variance as a rule rather than the exception. The probability that actual quantities and prices will exactly match the standard are very much remote. Also, management must decide when a particular variance has to be investigated or when variances should be ignored.

The basic criterion here is the magnitude of the variance, *i.e.*, is a variance large enough to require investigation. For example, some managements may decide that variances under 10 per cent of standard need not be investigated.

Another criterion relates to the consistency of occurrence. A once-in-a-while variance of Rs.1,000 may not be as significant as a Rs. 500 variation that recurs frequently.

A third criterion relates to the management's ability to control the variance. If the variances are beyond the control of the management, the management has no choice but to forget about the variances.

Hence variances should be analyzed when the expected saving through investigation appears to be greater than the expected cost of conducting the investigation.

Exhibit I

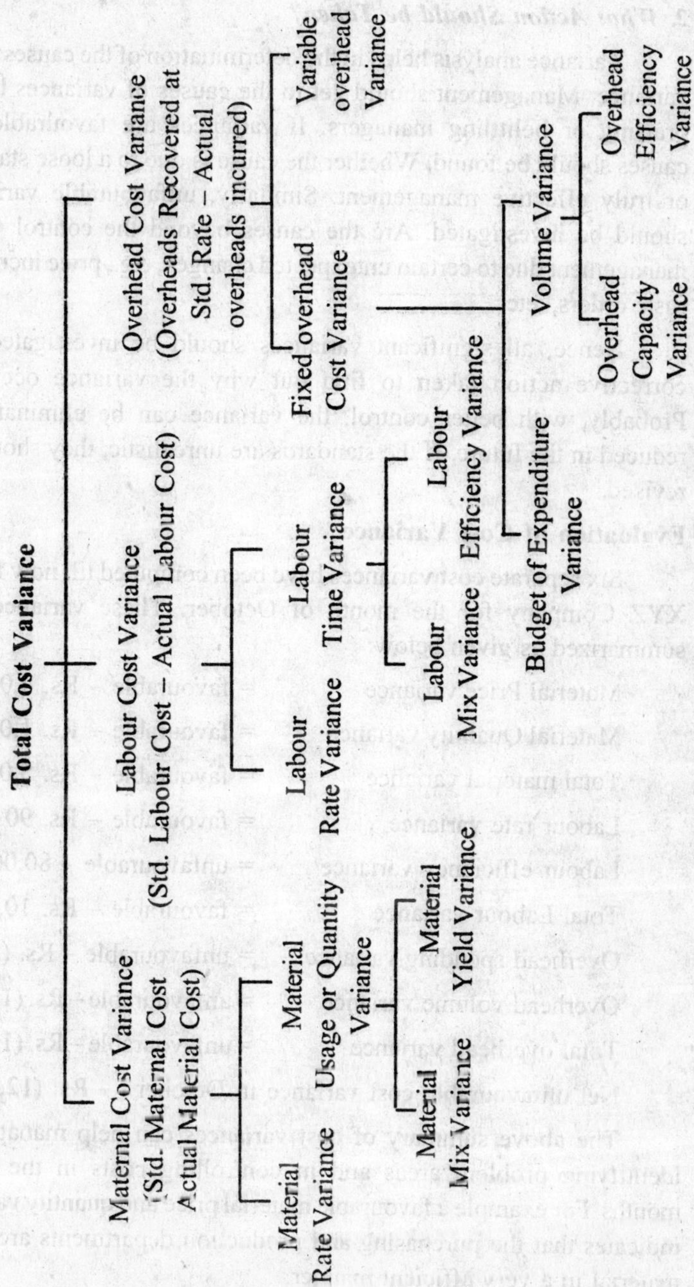
Total Cost Variance
Material Cost Variance (Std. Material Cost – Actual Material Cost)
Labour Cost Variance (Std. Labour Cost – Actual Labour Cost)
Overhead Cost Variance (Overheads Recovered at Std. Rate – Actual overheads incurred)
Material Rate Variance
Material Usage or Quantity Variance
Labour Rate Variance
Labour Time Variance
Fixed overhead Cost Variance
Variable overhead Variance
Material Mix Variance
Material Yield Variance
Labour Mix Variance
Labour Efficiency Variance
Budget of Expenditure Variance
Volume Variance
Overhead Capacity Variance
Overhead Efficiency Variance

2. What Action Should be Taken?

Variance analysis helps in the determination of the causes of the variance. Management should get to the causes of variances before praising or belittling managers. If variances are favourable, the causes should be found. Whether the cause is due to a loose standard or truly effective management. Similarly, unfavourable variances should be investigated. Are the causes beyond the control of the management due to certain untexpected changes, e.g., price increases, rush orders, etc.

Hence, all significant variances should be investigated and corrective action taken to find out why the variance occurred. Probably, with better control, the variance can be eliminated or reduced in the future. If the standards are unrealistic, they should be revised.

Evaluation of Cost Variance

Six separate cost variances have been computed till now for the XYZ Company for the month of October. These variances are summarized as given below:

Material Price variance	= favourable – Rs. 4,000
Material Quantity variance	= favourable – Rs. 1,000
Total material variance	= favourable – Rs. 5,000
Labour rate variance	= favourable – Rs. 90,000
Labour efficiency variance	= unfavourable – 80,000
Total Labour variance	= favourable – Rs. 10,000
Overhead spending variance	= unfavourable – Rs. (2,000)
Overhead volume variance	= unfavourable – Rs. (16,000)
Total overhead variance	= unfavourable – Rs. (18,000)

Net unfavourable cost variance in October — Rs. (12,900)

The above summary of cost variances can help managers in identifying problem areas and in controlling costs in the future months. For example a favourable material price and quantity variance indicates that the purchasing and production departments are using material in a very efficient manner.

However, the production manager has a serious problem regarding labour efficiency variance. The actual time being taken by the workers is much more than the standard time allowed to produce a given amount of product.

Unfavourable labour efficiency variances can be caused by a management decision to use poorly trained workers or poorly maintained machinery or by downtime resulting from because of low-quality materials. In some cases, generally bad working conditions and low employee morale may also adversely affect the efficiency of the workers. A favourable labour rate variance may signify that lower paid (or lower skilled) workers were used or that actual wage rates are below the standard labour rates.

An unfavourable overhead spending variance indicates excessive levels of expenditure. This could have resulted both from increasing prics of goods and services used and from excessive consumption of these goods and services. An unfavourable overhead volume variance indicates that the factors employed or the activity base used in costing overheads to the products has been used inefficiently.

Review Problem

1. Good Luck Ltd. has a manufacturing division which makes a product to which the following details relate:

Per unit

Materials	5 kg. at Rs. 3/- Rs. 15
Direct Labour	10 hours at Rs. 2/- Rs. 20
Variable overhead	10 hours at Rs. 2/- Rs. 10

Relevant fixed overheads are budgeted at Rs. 8,000 per month and planned output is 2,000 units per month. The selling price is Rs. 50/- per unit.

An incentive scheme is in operation in the division concerned whereby employees are paid a bonus of 10% of the standard cost of materials saved and 40% of direct labour time saved valued at standard direct labour hour rate. During a recent month when output was 1,700 units, the following actual results were recorded:

Direct materials used (8,000 kg)	24,800
Direct wages (18,000 hours @ Rs. 2.20 per hour)	39,600
Variable overhead	20,000
Fixed overhead	10,000

(a) Calculate the variance which occurred during the month.

(b) Calculate the total bonus payment to the employees.

Solution : Material Variances

MCV = MPV + MQV

Material Price Variance (MPV)

AQ (SR – AR)

AQ × SR – AQ × AR

(8,000 × 3) – (24,800)

24,000 – 24,800

800 (A)

Material Quantity Variance (MQV)

SR (SQ – AQ)

3 (8,500 – 8,000)

3 (500)

1500 (F)

Material Cost Variance (MCV)

(SR × SQ) – (AR × AQ)

25,500 – 24,800

= 700 (F)

Notes:

1. AQ = 1,700 × 5 = 8,500 kg

2. SQ × SR = 8,500 × 3 = Rs. 25,500

Labour Variances

LCV = LRV + LEV

Labour Rate Variance (LRV)

AH (SR – AR)

18,000 (2 – 2.20)

3600 A

Labour Efficiency Variance (LEV)

SR (SM – AH)

2 (17,000 – 18,000)

2,000 A

Labour Cost Variance (LCV)

(SR × SH) – (AR × AH)

(2 × 17,000) – (2.20 × 18,000)

(34,000) – (39,600)

5,600 A

Notes:

1. SR = 1,700 × 10 = 17,000 hours
2. SQ × SR = (1,700 × 10 = 17,000 hours at Rs. 2 = Rs. 34,000)

Variable overhead Variancies

VOHV = VOH Exp. V + VOH Eff. V

Expenditure or Spending Variance (VOH Exp. V)

= (Standard variable overheads – Actual variable overheads)

= (1800 × 10) – (20,000)

= 18,000 - 20,000

– 2,000 (A)

Efficiency Variance (VOH Eff. V)

= Standard Variable overhead rate per hour (AQ – SQ)

= 10 (1700 – 1800) = 1000 (A)

Variable Overhead Variance (VOHV) = Recovered variable overheads – Actual variable overheads

= 17,000 – 20,000

= 3,000 (A)

$$\frac{\text{Actual Hrs. worked}}{\text{Std. time per unit (hrs)}} = \frac{18{,}000\text{SQ}}{10} = 1800 \text{ units}$$

Fixed overhead Variances

Fixed overhead Expenditure Variance

= Budgeted Fixed overheds – Actual Fixed overheads

= 8,000 – 10,000

= 2,000 (A)

Fixed overhead Volume Variance

= SR (Actual output - Budgeted output)

= 4 (1700 - 2,000)

= 1200 (A)

Fixed overhead Cost Variance

= Recovered Fixed overheads – Actual Fixed Overheads

= 6,800 – 10,000

= 3,200 (A)

Recovered fixed overheads = 1700 × 4 = Rs. 6,800

Std, fixed overhead rate per unit

$$= \frac{\text{Budgeted Fixed overheads}}{\text{Budgeted output}}$$

Fixed Overhead Volume Variance can be divided into two types:

1. Fixed overhead Efficiency Variance = SR (AQ – SQ)
2. Fixed overhead Capacity Variance = SR (SQ – BQ)

= 4 (2000 – 1800)

= 800 (A)

Variable overhead Variance

Variable overhead cost Variance = Standard variable overhead cost – Actual variable overhead cost

= 1700 × 10 – 20,000

= 3,000 (A Variable overhead spending Variance = Actual Hours Std. Variable overhead rate - Actual variable overhead rate).

= 18000 × 1 – 20,000

= 2,000 (A)

Variable overhead Efficiency Variance = Standard Variable overhead rate (Std. Hours – Actual Hours)

= 1 (17000 – 18000)

= 1,000 (A)

Bonus

Material Quantity Variance = 1,500 (F)

Bonus 1500 × 10%= 150

Standard Cost of labour = 2,000 (A)

Since the labour efficiency Variance is negative, no bonus is paid to the workers.

Hence total Bonus payment to the employees = Rs. 150/

II. The following standards have been set to manufacture a product:

Direct materials (2 kg at Rs. 4/- per unit) Rs. 8/

Direct labour (10 hours at Rs. 8/- per hour) Rs.80/

In June, when 4,000 units were manufactured the following actual results were recorded:

Direct materials purchased (8,000 kg. at Rs. 4.20 per unit)

Material used 7,900 kg.

Direct Labour

(39,700 hrs at Rs. 8.10 per hour)

Calculate the variances which occurred during the month.

Solution:

Material Price Variance

AQ (SR – AR)

= 8,000 (4.00 – 4.20)

= Rs. 1,600 (A)

Material Quantity Variance

SR (SQ – AQ)

= 4.00 (8,000 – 7,900)

= Rs. 400 (F)

Labour rate Variance

AH (SR – AR)

= 39,700 (8.00 – 8.10)

= Rs. 3,970 (A)

Labour Efficiency Variance

SR (SH – AH)

= 8.00 (40,000 – 39,700)

= 2,400 (F)

Summary Statement of all the Variances

Material Price Variance	Rs. 1,600 (A)
Material Quantity Variance	400 (F)
Net Material Variance	Rs..1,200 (A)
Labour Rate Variance	Rs. 3,970 (A)
Labour Efficiency Variance	2,400 (F)
Net Labour Variance	Rs. 1,570 (A)

III. Shipco Manufacturing Company has a standard cost system and keeps all cost standards up-to-date. The standard variable costs for one unit of finished product are:

Direct Materials (3 kg. @ Rs. 12.50 per kg.)	Rs. 37.50
Direct Labour (1.2 hrs. @ Rs. 9.00 hrs.)	10.80

Variable overhead (1.2 hrs. @ Rs. 5.00)	6.00
Standard variable cost per unit	Rs. 54.30

Normal capacity is 15,000 direct labour hours, and budgeted fixed overhead costs for the year were Rs. 54,000. During the year, the company produced and sold 12,200 units. Related transactions and actual cost data for the year were as follows:

Direct materials consisted of 37,500 kg. purchased and used; unit purchase cost was Rs. 12.40 per kg. Direct labour consisted of 15,250 direct labour hours worked at an average labour rate of Rs. 9.20 per hour. Actual factory overhead costs incurred for the period consisted of variable overhead costs of Rs. 73,200 and fixed overhead costs of Rs. 55,000.

Using the data given, compute the following:

1. Standard hours allowed.
2. Standard fixed overhead rate.
3. Direct matrerials price variance.
4. Direct materials quantity variance.
5. Direct labour rate variance.
6. Direct labour efficiency variance.
7. Overhead spending variance.
8. Overhead efficiency variance.
9. Controllable overhead variance.
10. Overhead volume variance.

Solution

1. Standard hours allowed = good units produced x standard direct labour hours per unit.

   12,200 units × 1.2 direct labour hours/unit = 14,640 hours

2. Standard fixed overhead rate = budgeted fixed overhead cost normal capacity

   = Rs. 54,000

   15,000 direct labour hours

   = R 3.60 per direct labour hour

3. Direct materials price variance:

Price difference:	Actual price paid	Rs.12.40/kg.
	Less standard price	12.50/kg.
	Difference	Rs. .10 (F)

Direct materials price variance = (actual price – standard price) × actual quantity.

= Rs. .10 (F) x 37,500 per kg.

= Rs. 3,750 (F)

4. Direct materials quantity variance:

Quantity difference:	Actual quantity used	37,500 Kgs.
	Less standard quantity (12/200 units × 3 kgs.)	36,600 Kgs.
	Difference	900 (A)

Direct materials quantity variance = (actual quantity – standard quantity) × standard price

= 900 (A) × Rs. 12.50 / per kg.

= Rs. 11,250 (A)

5. Direct labour rate variance:

Rate difference:	Actual labour rate	Rs. 9.20/hr.
	Less standard labour rate	9.00/hr.
	Difference	Re. .20 (U)

Direct labour rate variance = (actual rate-standard rate) × actual hours

= Rs. .20 (A) × 15/250 hours

= Rs. 3,050 (A)

6. Direct labour efficiency variance:

Difference in hours:	Actual hours worked	15,250 hr.
	Less standard hours allowed 14,640 hr.*	
	Difference 610 (A)	

Direct labour efficiency variance = (actual hours – standard hours allowed) × standard rate

= 610 hr. (A) x Rs. 9.00/hr.

= Rs. 5,490 (A)

*12,200 units produced × 1.2 hr. per unit = 14,640 hr.

Difference		Re. .10 (F)

7. Overhead spending variance:

Overhead costs incurred		
Variable	Rs. 73,200	
Fixed	55,000	Rs. 128,200
Less flexible budget for effort expended		
Actual hours worked × variable overhead rate		
15,250 labour hours × Rs. 5/hour		
	Rs. 76,250	
Plus budgeted fixed costs	54,000	130,250
Overhead pending variance		Rs. 2,050 (F)

8. Overhead efficiency variance:

Flexible budget for effort expended (see computation in 7 above)		Rs. 130,250
Less flexible budget at level of achieved performance		
Standard hours allowed × variable overhead rate		
14,640 labour hours × Rs. 5/hour		
	Rs.73,200	
Plus budgeted fixed costs	54,000	127,200
Overhead efficiency variance		Rs. 3,050 (A)

9. Controllable overhead variance:

Actual overhead incurred		Rs. 128,200
Less budgeted factory overhead for 14,640 hours:		
Variable overhead cost		
(14,640 hr. × Rs. 5.00/ direct labour hours)	Rs. 73,200	

Budgeted fixed factory overhead	54,000	
Total budgeted factory overhead		127,200
Controllable overhead variance		Rs. 1,000 (A)

10. Overhead volume variance:

Total budgeted factory overhead	
(see calculation in 9)	Rs. 127,200
(see calculation in 9)	
Less factory overhead applied:	
Variable: 14,640 hr. × Rs. 5.00 /direct labour hour Rs. 73,200	
Fixed: 14,640 hr. × Rs. 3.60/direct labour hour	52,704
Total factory overhead applied	125,904
Overhead volume variance	Rs. 1,296 (A)

IV. A Company presents the following variance data for the month:

	Material A	Material B	Material C
Material Price Variance	Rs. 44,000 F	Rs. 20,000 F	Rs. 24,000 F
Material Quantity Variance	40,000 A	30,000 A	40,000 A
Net Material Variance	Rs. 4,000 F	Rs.10,000 A	Rs. 16,000 A
Units Produced requiring this material	50,000	90,000	160,000

Two kgs. of each kind of material are allowed for each unit of output requiring that kind of material. For material A, the average price paid was Re. 0.40 per kg. less than standard; for marterial B, Re. .10 less; for material C, Re. .06 greater. There are no opening or closing inventories of any kind of material (that is, materials are purchased and used in the same period).

For each of the three materials, calculate the following:

a. Number of kg. of material purchased.

b. Standard cost per kg. of material.

c. Total standard material cost.

Solution:

Material A:

a. Price variance = Re. .40 per kg.

Total price variance = Rs. 44,000 F.

Kg. purchased and used = Rs. 44,000

Re. .40

= 110,000

b. Standard kg. allowed for:

50,000 units = 100,000

Used over standard = 110,000-100,000 = 10,000

Quantity variance = 40,000 (A)

Standard unit price = Rs. 40,000 = Rs. 4.00

= 10,000

c. Total standard matrerial cost:

= 100,000 kg. × Rs. 4.00 per kg. = Rs. 400,000

Material B:

a. Kg. purchased and used

$\frac{\text{Rs. } 20{,}000}{\text{Rs. } 10}$ = Rs. 20,000

b. Standard unit price

= Rs. 30,000

(200,000 – 180,000)

$\frac{\text{Rs. } 30{,}000}{20{,}000}$ = Rs. 1.5

c. Total standard material cost:

= 180,000 kg. × Rs. 1.5 = Rs. 270,000

Material C:

a. Kg. purchased & used:

$\frac{\text{Rs. } 24{,}000}{\text{Re. } .06}$ = 400,000

b. Standard unit price = Rs. 40,000

(400,000 – 320,000)

$$\frac{\text{Rs. } 24,000}{80,000} = \text{Re. } 0.5$$

c. Total standard material cost:

= 320,000 × Re. 0.5 x Rs. 160,000

1. Overhead Variance:

V. AK Ltd. combined fixed and variable overhead costs are as follows:

Overhead Applied	Rs. 90,000
Flexible Budget Overhead	Rs. 95,000
Actual Overhead	Rs. 97,000

a. What is the amount of under or over applied overhead, assuming that full absorption costing was used?

b. What is the production volume variance?

Solution:

Actual Cost	Flexible Budget	Overhead Applied
Rs. 97,000	Rs. 95,000	Rs. 90,000
	Under applied overhead	
	Rs. 6,000 (A)	Production Volume Variance
		Rs. 5,000 (A)

VI. Overhead Variance:

Omega Company has record the following overhead in formations for the current year:

Budgeted fixed overhead Rs. 5,100

Actual overhead incurred Rs. 15,200 of which Rs. 5,500 is fixed.

Variable overhead rate per direct labour hour Rs. 2

Standard hours allowed for actual production 5,600

Actuala labour hours used 5,400 hours

Calculate:

a. the fixed overhead price variance.

b. variable overhead price or spending variance.

c. variable overhead efficiency variance.

Solution:

1. Fixed overhead price variance
   = [Actual rixed overheads-Budgeted fixed overhead]

   5,600-5,100 = Rs. 500 (A)

2. Variable overhead price or spending variance
   = Actual variable overhead – Actual hours at standard overhead rate

   [(Rs. 15,200 – 5,500) – (Rs. 2 × 5,600)]

   [Rs. 9,700 – Rs. 11,200] = 1500 (F)

Variable overhead efficiency variance:

(Actual hours × standard overhead rate) – (Standard overhead rate on actual production)

(2 × 5,400) – (2 × 5,600)

10,800 – 11,200

= 400F

VII. Following is the direct material cost for product X:

Standard price per materials unit	= Rs. 4.50
Actual quantity used	= Rs. 2,600
Standard quantity allowed for production	= Rs. 2,300
Materials price variance	= Rs. 390 F

Solution:

Materials Price Variance – Actual Quantity (Standard Price – Actual Price)

Rs. 390 = 2,600 [4.50 – Actual Price]

390 = 2,600 × 4.50 – 2,600 × AP

390 = 11,700 – 2,600 × AP

or Actual Price = Rs. 4.35

VIII. An Electronics Company's budget contains these standards for materials and direct labour for a unit of 10 boxes:

Material	2 kg.	@ Rs. 50	Re. 1.00
Direct Labour	1 hour	@ Rs. 4.40	Rs. 4.40

Although 100,000 units were budgeted for September, only 97,120 were produced. Two hundred thousand kg. of materials were purchased for Rs. 105,000. Direct labour costs were Rs. 380,000 for 95,000 hours.

a. Compute the materials price variance

b. Compute the materials efficiency variance.

c. Compute the labour price variance.

d. Compute the labour efficiency variance.

Solution:

a. Material Price Variance

= (Actual Material at Actual Prices) – (Actual Material at Standard Prices)

$$\frac{200,000(105,000 - \text{Rs.}50)}{200,000}$$

= 200,000 [.525 – .50] = 5,000 (A)

b. Material Quantity Variance = Actual Quantity at Standard Price Standard quantity at Standard Price

.50 [200,000 – 194,240]

= 2,880 (A)

c. Labour Rate Variance = Actual Hours at Actual rates Actual hours at standard rates

$$95{,}000 \; \frac{380{,}000 - 4.40}{95{,}000}$$

95,000 [4.00 – 4.40] = 38,000 F

d. Labour efficiency variance:

Actual hours at standard rates – Standard hours at standard rates

95,000 – 97,120 × 4.40

= 9,328 (F)

Presentation of Variance Analysis to Management

The benefits of any control system depend on how quickly and in what form the necessary data are presented to the management. There are no hard and fast rules for presentation of information. The following format may be considered suitable in many cases:

Comparative Statement of Cost

Production..... Month.......19

A. Summary

Element of cost		*Standard Rs.*	*Actual Rs.*	*Difference Rs.*
A 1	Direct material cost			
A 2	Direct Wages			
A 3	Variable Overheads			
A 4	Fixed Overheads			

B. Variance Analysis

No.	*Nature of Variance*	*Amount Favourable Adverse Rs.*	*Reasons Remaraks Rs.*
(1)	*(2)*	*(3)*	*(4)*
B 1	Material Price Variance		
B 2	Material usage and quantity variance		

(1)	*(2)*	*(3)*	*(4)*
B 3	Material mix variance		
B 4	Material yield variance		
B 5	Labour rate variance		
B 6	Labour efficiency variance		
B 7	Idle time variance		
B 8	Variable overhead variance		
B 9	Fixed overhead expenditure variance		
B 10	Fixed overhead volume variance		
B 11	Fixed overhead efficiency variance		
B 12	Capacity variance		

Date Cost Controller

Notes: A1 = Bl + B2 A2 = B5 + B6 + B7 A4 = B9 + B10

B2 = B3 + B4 A3 = B8 B10 = B11 + B12

11

Marginal and Absorption Costing

Marginal Costing is a system of ascertaining cost and not a method of costing like Single or Output Costing Contract Costing or Process Costing. It is a technique of determining cost and helping the management to know the effect on profits of changes in the volume or type of output. It has been defined by the Institute of Cost and Works Accountants, London, as, "the amount at any given volume of output by which aggregate costs are changed if the volume of output is increased or decreased by one unit". Marginal Costing necessitates the classification of costs into fixed and variable. These two types of costs behave differently with changes in the volume of output. Fixed costs tend to change with time rather than the level of output. They tend to remain constant for all volumes of production within the installed capacity of plant. For example, rent of office or factory manager's salary, insurance charges, telephone rent etc. shall remain the same even if the production goes up or comes down. They are related to period or time and not to volume of output hence are known as period costs. Variable costs, on the other hand, are known as product cost as these are related to the volume of output, *i.e.* it increases or decreases directly with the change in the volume of output.

Marginal costing is basically concerned with the ascertainment of product or variable cost of the product *i.e.,* direct materials, direct wages, direct expenses and variable overheads. Thus marginal cost is the aggregate of variable cost of a product. Marginal costing is also known as Variable Costing.

By analysing this definition, we find that with the increase in one unit of output, the total cost is increased and this increase in total cost from the existing level to the new level is known as marginal cost. For example, a company produces 1,000 exhaust fans per annum. Total Fixed cost is Rs. 50,000 per annum. Variable cost per exhaust fan is Rs. 400. Total cost of 1,000 exhaust fans will he as follows:

	Rs.
Variable (Marginal) cost (1,000 × 400)	4,00,000
Fixed Costs	50,000
Total cost	4,50,000

If output is increased by one exhaust fan, the cost will appear as follows:

Variable cost (1,001 × 400)	4,00,400
Fixed Cost	50,000
Total cost	4,50,400

Marginal cost per unit is, therefore Rs. 400

From the above, it will be clear that in marginal costing, costs are separated into fixed and variable. Only variable costs are regarded as the costs of the products being manufactured. The fixed costs are treated as period costs which will be incurred during the period regardless of the volume of output and are charged directly to the Profit and Loss Account.

The advocates of Marginal Costing plead that the cost of production should constitute the variable expenses incurred in production, as they are direct expenses incurred in production. The fixed costs are time costs and are incurred irrespective of the fact whether the production is carried on or not, hence they should not form part of the cost of production. There is no justification for apportioning such costs to the volume of work-in-progress or finished goods at end of the period. Such costs should be recovered from the margin (contribution) derived after deducting the variable costs from the value of sales. By doing so, the time cost of performing a particular a activity can be ascertained and used as a basis for sound managerial decision and cost control.

Difficulty in Classification of Variable Overhead Costs

Overhead cost may be broadly sub-divided into fixed and variable. Examples of fixed costs are, rent, insurance premimum, manager's salary, office salary etc. and that of variable are electricity costs, factory supplies, power etc. Overheads are taken into account for the determination of costs. It may not be easy to find out the amount of variable overhead costs. Many costs may be semi-variable, *i.e.* part of it may be fixed and part variable. For example, telephone charges will include telephone rent (fixed) and call charges (variable) and it may be difficult to find out variable portion out of the semi-variable overhead costs: Similarly, electric power, depreciation, repairs etc. are examples of semi-variable expenses. We shall discuss briefly how the problem can be solved.

A semi-variable cost is a cost which varies in total amount with changes in the volume of output, but the change is not proportionate to the change in output.

There are several methods for the separation of variable cost out of semi-variable cost, but one of them which is simple is explained below.

Two levels of production are chosen and on the basis of past experience, respective total semi-variable costs are found out. The difference in the volume of output and that in the cost shall suggest the answer. It is found that when the total production in a month was 100 units, the invariable cost amounted to Rs.400 and in another month, when the total output increased to 120 units, the semi-variable cost amounted to Rs.440.

Units produced	*Semi-variable costs*
	Rs.
100	400
120	440

An analysis of the above position shows that with an increase in production by 20 units, the semi-variable cost increased by Rs.40 *i.e.*, average increase is Rs. 2 per unit. Now we can ascertain that when 100 units were produced, total variable overhead cost would have amounted to Rs. 200 (Rs. 400 - Rs. 200) was fixed overhead cost out of the semi-variable cost of Rs. 400. The variable cost of Rs. 200 is the marginal cost to be used in marginal costing.

Features

From what has been discussed above we come to the conclusion that the following are the special features of marginal costing.

(i) Profit is calculated in a special manner. Marginal costs are deducted from the value of sales arid the difference is termed as "contribution", which is meant to cover the fixed casts and profits, if any. If the contribution exceed the fixed casts, there will be net profit and if it is less than the fixed costs, there is loss.

(ii) The unit cost of a product means the average variable cast of manufacturing the product which varies directly with production. Fixed casts are not allocated to the products and are charged against the revenue of the period. Generally variable selling and dispibutive costs are not considered here.

(iii) The valuation of work-in-progress and finished goods is done at the marginal casts. The reason being that fixed costs are period casts, that is, they relate to a particular period of time, hence if any portion of such costs is apportioned, to the work-in-progress or finished goods, that portion of fixed cast will be carried over to the next year and will remain recouped during the period in which these expenses have been incurred.

The contribution can be Gross or Net. If only the manufacturing variable expensės have been deducted from the sales revenue, the difference is termed as Gross Contribution. If variable administration costs are deducted from the Gross Margin, the balance will be the Net Margin.

There are two terms which confuse the students generally. These are marginal cost and marginal costing. Marginal cost, is the change in the aggregate costs with the increase or decrease of one unit of production. If 1,000 units are produced and the marginal cost is Rs.3 per unit then the total cost will be Rs. 3,000. If the production is increased to 1001 units of production then the total cost will be Rs.3,003. The change in the aggregate cost is Rs. 3 and is marginal cost. In this context a unit may be a single, a batch of articles, an order, a stage of production capacity or a department. It relates to the change in output in the particular circumstances under consideration.

Marginal costing is the ascertainment of marginal costs by differentiating between fixed costs and variable costs and to see the effect of profit of changes in volume or type of output. Thus marginal costing includes two things *i.e., (i)* the ascertainment of marginal cost and *(ii)* the cost volume-profit relationship.

ASCERTAINMENT OF MARGINAL COST

We have already seen how total cost is presented in the cost sheet with various divisions of costs. The presentation is made under the method of absorption or total cost method. Under this method the total cost as absorbed in the units of production. But presentation under marginal cost is different from the absorption costing. Under marginal costing the cost is ascertained as under:

	Rs.	
Sales.	XXXXXXX	
Less: Marginal cost:		
Direct Material	XXXXX	
Direct Wages	XXXXXX	
Direct Expenses	XXXXXX	
Variable Overhead	XXXXXX	XXXXXXX
	------------	-------------
Contribution	XXXXXX	
Less: Fixed Costs	XXXXXXX	

Profit (or Loss)	XXXXXXX	

Thus, we find that out of sales, marginal cost is deducted in order to calculate the gross margin or contribution.

Economists' and Accountants' views on Marginal Cost

Economists define. Marginal Cost as "the amount at any given volume of output by which aggregate costs are changed if the volume of output is increased or decreased by one unit". Suppose the aggregate cost of production of 1,000 units of a product is Rs. 10,000 and that of 1,001 units is Rs. 10,008, then the marginal cost of producing one additional unit is Rs. 8 (Rs. 10,008-10,000). Thus the additional cost of producing one additional unit is the Marginal cost according to the economists. According to economists variable costs are supposed to increase or decrease at a charging rate. At low level of activity, the variable cost per unit is supposed to decline with every additional unit of production as a result of increased efficiency of workers or better utilisation of production facilities. The law of increasing return or diminishing cost operates at a low level of activity, on the other hand, at a very high level of activity, variable cost per unit is supposed to rise with every additional unit of production on account of bottlenecks, over-crowding or excessive use of facilities. The law of diminishing returns, or increasing cost comes into operation. Against this, according to accountants it is assumed that with changing volume of activity variable cost per unit remain constant with changing volume of production or sales. Hence Marginal Cost in accounting refers to the difference in the total variable cost which results from the addition or reduction of a certain number of units, not of a single unit. It is the aggregate of variable costs, that is, Prime Cost plus variable overhead. For example, if Rs. 20,000 of Direct Ma'erials, Rs. 10,000 of Direct Wages and Rs. 10,000 of variable overheads are incurred in producing 10,000 units of a product, the marginal cost will be:

Rs. 20,000 + 10,000 + 10,000/1000 = Rs. 4 per unit

MARGINAL COSTING AND DIFFERNTLAL COSTING

Marginal Costing is sometimes confused with Differential Costing. The term 'Differential Costing' means a technique used in the preparation of *ad hoc* information in which only cost and income differences between alternative courses of action are taken into consideration. Thus, in case of differential costing a comparison is made between the cost differential and income differential between two or more situations and decision regarding adopting a particular course of action is taken if it is on the whole profitable. This is illustrated with the following example.

Example.

Pioneer manufacturing Company, makers of a specialized line of toys, receives an order for 2,000 units of toy battle tanks, from a large mail order house at a price of Rs.3 per unit.

The company sells this type of toy to its other customers at Rs. 5 each but it has surplus capacity and can take the special order without adversely affecting its regular operations for the coming month.

The income statement of the company for the preceding month is as follows:

Net Sales - 10,000 units @ Rs. 5	50,000
Costs:	*Rs.*
Direct Material: Rs. 1.50 per unit	15,000
Direct Labour: Rs. 1 per unit	10,000
Factory Overhead	10,000
Selling and Administration Expenses	10,000
Total Costs	Rs. 45,000
Net Profit	Rs. 5,000

Direct material and direct labour costs to be incurred on the special order are estimated to be of the same amount per unit as for the regular business. Special tools costing Rs. 500 would be required to meet the specifications of the mail-order house.

You are required to prepare a differential cost analysis for deciding about the acceptance of the order.

You are required to prepare a differential cost analysis for deciding about the acceptance of the order.

Solution.

DIFFERENTIAL COST STATEMENT

Existing situation	*Proposed situation*	*Net Increase*	*Decrease*
	10,000 units	12,000 units	2,000 units
Sales (i) Rs.	50,000	56,000	6,000
Cost:			
Direct Materials	15,000	8,000	3,000
Direct Labour	10,000	12,000	2,000
Factory Overhead	10,000	10,000	
Selling & Adm. Expenses	10,000	10,000	
Special tools	—	500	500
Total Cost	45,000	50,500	5,500
Profit (i)-(ii) = (iii)	5,000	5,000	500

In the above case differential costs are Rs. 5,500 while differential sales are Rs. 6,000. Thus, acceptance of order from a large mail order house gives an extra profit of Rs. 500. The order may be accepted provided it does not adversely affect the present sales at Rs. 5 per unit.

Thus, in case of Differential Costing, the change in total costs (both fixed and variable) is taken into account. The term 'Differential Cost' means the net increase or decrease in total cost resulting from a variation in production. The differential cost is termed as 'Incremental Cost' when the cost increases and 'Decremental Cost' when the cost decreases. Thus, Differential Costing, Incremental Costing and Decremental Costing are alternative terms and they are different from Marginal Costing and Direct Costing.

The difference between Marginal Costing and Differential Costing can be summarised as follows:

1. In case of Marginal Costing, the entire fixed cost are excluded while in the case of Differential Costing such

fixed costs which are relevant for decision-making are considered.

2. Differential Costs are worked out separately as analysis statements while marginal costs may be embodied in the accounting system itself.
3. In Marginal Costing, the contribution and the profit-volume ratio are the main yardsticks for the purposes of performance evaluation and decision-making. While in case of Differential Costing; the differential costs are compared with incremental or decremental revenue as the case may be.
4. Differential Costing can be used both in case of Absorption Costing and Marginal Costing.

The manner of application of Differential Costing is somewhat different from that of Marginal Costing. Under Differential Costing, differential costs of various alternatives are compared with the differential revenues and the decisions are taken on the basis of maximum net gain. While evaluating the viability of different projects, making a choice out of several alternative proposals. Differential Costing helps in a better way than Marginal Costing. If under Marginal Costing, while deciding about the profitability of products or making cost-benefit analysis, fixed costs are also considered at some stage, it takes the shape of Differential Costing. Hence, practically the purpose of applying the two techniques is the same and here also we have not made any difference in the application of these techniques to the problems which management has to face in its routine or otherwise decision-making process.

ABSORPTION COSTING OR FULL COSTING

Absorption Costing technique is also termed as Traditional or Full Cost Method. According to this method, the cost of a product is determined after considering both fixed and variable costs. The variable costs, such as those of direct materials, direct labour, etc. are directly charged to the products while the fixed costs are apportioned on a suitable basis over different products manufactured during a period. Thus, in case of Absorption Costing all costs are identified with the manufacture products. This will be clear with the help of the :following example.

Example.

A company is manufacturing 3 products A, Band C. The costs of their manufacture are as follows:

	A	*B*	*C*
Direct Material per unit	Rs. 3	Rs. 4	Rs. 5
Direct Labour	2	3	4
Selling Price	10	15	20
Output	1,000 units	1,000 units	1,000 units

The total overheads are Rs. 6,000 out of which Rs. 3,000, are fixed and rest are variable. It is decided to apportion these costs over different products in the ratio of output. You are required to prepare a statement showing cost of each product and profit according to Absorption Costing.

Solution.

The cost of each product would be ascertained according to Absorption. Costing as follows:

STATEMENT SHOWING COST AND PROFIT
(According to Absorption Costing Technique)

	A		*B*		*C*	
	Per Unit *Rs.*	*Total* *Rs.*	*Per Unit* *Rs.*	*Total* *Rs.*	*Per Unit* *Rs.*	*Total* *Rs.*
Direct Materials	3	3,000	4	4,000	5	5,000
Direct Labour	2	2,000	3	3,000	4	4,000
Overheads:						
Fixed	1	1,000	1	1,000	1	1,000
Variable	1	1,000	1	1,000	1	1,000
Total Cost	7	7,000	9	9,000	11	11,000
Profit	3	3,000	6	6,000	9	9,000
Selling Price	10	10,000	15	15,000	20	20,000
Total Profit	Rs, 3,000 + Rs. 6,000 + Rs. 9,000 = Rs. 18,000					

Under Absorption Costing each unit of product has to bear its total share of cost. It may be true that some products may not be able to bear their full share of cost but may be able to contribute to the overall profitability of the firm. For example, a product can be sold at a price which is sufficient to recover more than its variable cost required to produce it, but may not be sufficient to recover its full share of fixed cost. On the other hand, there may be products which contribute much more than their share of variable and fixed costs. Under absorption costing, the management is interested in knowing whether or not a product can produce an adequate return on investment after absorbing its share of the overall cost whether fixed or variable or direct or indirect. This is because in the long run, all costs must be more than recovered to assure a satisfactory return to the investors on their investment.

However, charging of fixed costs creates problems. These costs are apportioned to different products on some suitable basis, *e.g.*, as a percentage of direct material, a percentage of direct labour or a rate per article, etc. But, there is always some doubt about the suitability of the method adopted for apportionment of these fixed costs. It cannot be said with definiteness that the fixed costs so charged are really the costs which should have been charged to each of the different products. It, therefore, brings more inexactness in costing. Moreover, fixed costs have to be incurred whether there is production or no production. It means cost of a product not only depends upon the costs which are directly incurred but also on the volume of output. For example, if the cost of direct material and direct labour for a unit is Rs. 3 and 4 respectively and the fixed costs are Rs. 2,000 and the volume of output is 1,000 units, the total cost of production will be as follows:

Costs of Direct Materials	Rs. 3,000
Cost of Direct Labour	4,000
Fixed Overheads	2,000
Total Costs	9,000

The cost per unit comes to Rs. 9. In case, the output is 800 units only, the cost of production will be as follows:

Direct Material	Rs. 2,400
Direct Labour	3,200
Fixed Overheads	2,000
Total Cost	7,600

The cost per unit comes to Rs, 9,50 per unit.

From the above example, it is clear that the cost of the product has gone up by 50 paise per unit not because of any increase in price of direct materials or increase in the rates for direct labour, but because of lower volume of production. This seems to be a bit illogical. Some people, therefore argue that the fixed costs should not be considered while computing the cost of the product. But this should be charged against the total fund arising out of excess of selling price over variable cost. Marginal Costing, as explained below, is a technique of costing which deals with this concept.

Absorption and Marginal Costing

Both the types of cost accounting determine the cost of product, job or service either individually or collectively for the enterprise. Both the systems lend themselves to adoption of historical or estimated basis of absorption of costs.

The most differentiating features are as follows:

(a) In Marginal Costing the variable expenses are absorbed in the product cost or cost of goods sold whereas Fixed costs in their entirety are charged against the revenues of that period. Against this, in Absorption Costing not only variable but also fixed costs are charged to the cost of production to the cost of goods sold. Hence fixed cost is not entirely charged against the revenue of the period. Thus, under Absorption Costing, a portion of fixed cost will remain submerged in the value of closing inventories. The carry-over in opening inventories will bias computation.

(b) The main cause of difference between the profits in the two systems is the variation between the fixed costs absorbed in the opening and closing inventories. The net operating income under Marginal Costing is to be reconciled with that in Absorption Costing by adjusting of the difference in fixed overheads merged in the valuation of opening and closing inventories.

(c) In Absorption Costing the concept of period cost assumes a lesser significance as a portion of it is absorbed in the inventory cost and not viewed as an expense till sales are affected. Thus the profitability for a period may not be true till the quantum of fixed charges merged in the opening and closing balance of inventories is allowed to play its part in full in the computation of profitability.

(d) The profitability as realised in both the systems will differ. In Marginal Costing, the entire fixed costs are treated as period cost and thus are charged off against the revenues of that period without any relation to sales and production quantities. If the sales turnover in quantities is more than the production output in quantities, the profits will stand inflated and *vice-versa*.

(e) The Marginal Costing, either on a historical basis or estimated, rates of recovery of overheads are developed only for variables while in Absorption Costing two rates are developed, one for the fixed cost and the other for variables or alternatively a comprehensive rate to recover the entire cost. Both these systems permit computation of overheads for any volume of activity.

(f) The main elements of cost like Direct Material, Direct Labour and Direct Expenses, if any, will be accounted for in both the systems alike. The difference is only in overheads.

(g) In Marginal Costing the entire fixed expenses actually incurred are charged off, overhead variance due to variation in volume does not affect the computation while in Absorption Costing it does as over-absorption or under absorption.

However, Marginal Costing is easy to operate and facilitates a better and quicker understanding of the position of profitability with reference to anticipation and enables management to frame a future course of action.

The following example will show how presentation of accounts differs from each other.

Example.

ALLIED Co. LTD.

The following data relate to selling price and cost of a product:

Fixed Costs.

Manufacturing	Rs. 40,000
Selling & Administrative	Rs. 10,000

Variable Cost per unit.

Manufacturing	Rs. 4 per unit
Selling and administrative	Rs. 2 per unit
Selling price per unit	Rs. 15 per unit

The company produced 10,000 units of the product during the year and there was no opening inventory.

Solution.

	Absorption Costing	*Marginal Costing*
Units sold	10,000	10,000
	Rs.	*Rs.*
Sales Revenue (10,000 units @ Rs. 15 per unit)	1,50,000	1,50,000
Cost of goods sold:		
Variable manufacturing cost	40,000	40,000
Fixed Manufacturing cost	40,000	
Total manufacturing cost	80,000	40,000
Gross Profit	70,000	—
Contribution margin (Gross)	—	1,10,000
Less: Selling and administrative expenses:		

Variable selling & administrative expenses (10,000 × Rs. 2)	20,000	20,000
Fixed selling & administrative expenses	10,000	—
Tortal Selling & Administrative expenses	30,000	20,000
Net Profit	40,000	—
Contribution Margin (net)	—	90,000
Less Fixed costs:		
Manufacturing		40,000
Selling & admipistrative		10,000
Total period costs		50,000
Net Profit		40,000

The above data shows that there was neither any stock of finished goods at the beginning of the year nor at the end because the firm manufactured 10,000 units and sold all of them. As no portion of fixed costs was transferred to this year (because there was no opening stock) and no fixed costs have been transferred from this year to the next year, the amount of profits under the two do not differ. The difference arise under the two because of the price at which the opening and closing stocks have been charged.

It should be noted that while, under absorption costing, the cost of manufacturing the product has been calculated by taking both variable and fixed manufacturing costs which amount to Rs. 8 per unit (variable cost Rs. 4 per unit plus fixed cost Rs. 4 per unit), whereas in Marginal Costing, the same amounted to Rs. 4 per unit *i.e.*, the variable manufacturing cost.

MARGINAL COSTING AND STANDARD COSTING

Standard costs are the scientifically poredetermined costs of manufacturing a single unit or a number of units or product or of rendering a service during a specified future period. According to the terminology standard cost is a pre-determined cost calculated in relation to a prescribed set of working conditions correlating technical specifications and scientific measurements of materials and labour to the prices and wage rates expected to apply during the period to which the standard cost is intended to relate with an addition of an appropriate share of budgeted overhead. Its main purposes are to provide bases for control through variance accounting for the valuation of stocks and work-in-progress and in exceptional cases for fixing selling prices. The standard costs are planned costs of a product under current or anticipated conditions. The term standard cost consists of two parts, *viz.* standard and cost. Standards involve the expression of standards so established in values. Standard costing is the system of costing which seeks to control the cost of each unit or batch through determination beforehand of what should be the cost and then its comparison with actual cost. Thus the system of standard costing is based on standard cost.

The essential nature of standard costs is that in represents costs that should have been incurred rather than cost that were incurred. On the other hand marginal costs are direct costs or variable costs which vary according to the volume of production. Though an estimate of future marginal costs can be made but if the cost figures have been obtained for the expired period they will be historic costs. As a matter of fact, standard costing and marginal costing both are variable tools of cost control and marginal planning.

If a firm practises standard costing on proper lines *i.e.*, standards are themselves determined in a way which will not impose too great a burden on the workers or other employees of the firm, it may infuse in the minds of the staff a desire to achieve the standards and thus show greater efficiency. The objective of standard costing is avoidance of all losses and wastages as far possible.

Marginal costing also known as direct costing or variable costing is a comparatively new area in the field of accounting. It is very useful in decision making. It refers to the method of costing which is concerned with changes of any product. It deals primarily with changes in future cost. Projected cost provide very helpful guidelines for managerial decisions on pricing, sales, budgeting, production planning and marketing. According to the Institute sales. Cost and Works Accounts, London, "marginal costing is an ascertainment by differentiating between fixed costs and variable costs, of marginal cost and the effect on profit of changes in volume or type of output". Marginal Costing is a process of determining and analysing the marginal costs. Marginal cost it the amount of any given volume of output by which aggregate costs an changed if the volume of output is increased or decreased by one unit.

The concept of marginal costing is based on the important distinction between product costs and period costs, the former being related to the volume of output and the latter to the period of time rather than the volume production. Marginal costing regards as product costs only those manufacturing costs which have a tendency to vary directly with the volume of output. This is the complete contrast to the conventional system of costing under which all manufacturing costs—fixed as well as variable are treated as product costs variability with volume is the criterion for the classification of cost into product and period categories.

Thus marginal costing necessitates analysis of costs into fixed and variable. Even the semi-variable costs have to be closely and critically analysed in order to resolve themselves into their fixed and variable components depending upon whether they tend to remain fixed or vary with the compute.

Differential Costs and Incremental Costs

The terms have been defined by John G. Blocker and W. Keith Weltmore as:

> "The increase or decrease in total costs that result from producing and distributing additional or fewer units of a productor from a change in method of production of distribution such as the use of improved machinery, addition of a product or territory, or selection of a additional channel".

Incremental cost measures the addition to unit cost which results from an addition to output. The incremental cost is generally expressed as a cost perunit while differential cost is expressed in aggregate.

USEFULNESS OF MARGINAL COSTING OR VARIABLE COSTING OR DIRECT COSTING

(1) Profit Planning. With the rising cost and shrinkage in profit margin attention is now directed more and more by management towards a better and fuller understanding of the relationship between profit and the major factors affecting it like sales volume, production, selling price, sales mix, production and selling costs etc. This is simply because all these factors are variable in nature. Unless these relationships are known, there can be no assurance that the plans and subsequent actions to control activity will lead to the anticipated profits. Marginal or variable costing as method of evaluating the result of operation is designed to specify the need for a simple presentation of operating results which clearly show the cost volume-profit relationship. It attempts to improve the procedure for collecting and presenting information regarding these relationships. This type of information is not necessary for the determination of net income or for the measurement of production cost, but it is important to have such information for purposes of budgeting and profit planning, in selecting product lines and in deciding upon the relative importance to be given to each line of activity, in appraising the performance of sales personnel, in establishing price policy, and as a basis for decisions involving choice amongst alternatives.

(2) Decision-making. The technique of marginal costing is a valuable aid to management for decision-making under changing conditions. Business policies which form the basis of budgeting and which must be followed to secure desired results are formulated with the help of marginal cost analysis. Thus, one of the important duties of the cost accountant is to advise management on business policies arising out of marginal costing. Some of the important areas of decision-making where marginal cost analysis becomes unseful are mentioned below:

(i) ***Determination of Selling Price and Volume of Output.*** If the total revenue can be projected on the basis of anticipated prices and volumes of production, the increase in revenue at different levels of Production and at different prices can be compared with the marginal costs at those

levels of activity. Then the selling price which will maximise profits can be determined fasily by comparing the marginal costs and incremental revenue. Production should be increased as long as the increment in revenue is more than the marginal cost of producing the additional output. It will not be profitable any more to increase production when marginal revenue is equal to the marginal cost.

(ii) ***Make or Buy Decision.*** Manufacturers have sometimes to decide whether components or parts should be bought from the market or produced in the factory. The marginal cost of producing the parts compared with the market price gives an accurate basis for taking the decision to make or buy.

(iii) ***Determining Optimum Product or Sales-mix.*** Business firms producing and selling two or more products often face the problems of determining the ratio in which the different items should be produced and sold so as to maximise profits or minimise costs. As the fixed overheads are constant whatever be the mix, the most profitable mix is that which would give the highest amount of gross margin (excess of selling price over the variable costs). Application of the marginal costing technique is very appropriate in this connection. The decision will naturally depend on the effect of alternative combinations on the use of labour, materials, machine time, selling techniques, storage space, etc.

(iv) ***Replacement of Machinery.*** Whether it would be more profitable to replace existing machinery by new and improved ones is question which management in every concern has to face from time to time. The differential cost of keeping the old machine in use and using new machinery is the proper basis for making decisions of this nature.

(v) ***Acceptance of Special Order.*** If a special order is proposed and the price offered is less than the average total cost, a comparison of the additional revenue and marginal cost is necessary to decide whether the order is worthwhile to accept. Assuming that the order executed at the offered price will not affect the selling price in the market, it will be profitable to accept the offer so long as the additional revenue exceeds the marginal cost of supplying the order.

(vi) ***Submitting Tenders and Quotations.*** When a tender is submitted, the additional production involved will mean an increase in total cost. To make a competitive bid, the minimum price has to be quoted. The marginal cost indicates the floor below which the quotation will be unprofitable. This implies that any price above the marginal cost may be quoted so as to increase the total profit, provided the quoted price does not lower the normal price for the rest of the market.

(vii) ***Alternative Use of Plant Facility.*** If the manufacture of a particular product or component is possible by different methods techniques it needs to be decided whether one machine should be used instead of another, or how many operators should be used with a machine, or whether the processing should be carried out by manual or machine work. Marginal costing may be used in comparing the effect of alternative techniques on profit. The variable cost affected by alternative technique will lead to varying gross margins and this can be on the basis of deciding upon the best alternative.

(3) Cost Control. The importance of cost controller accomplishing the objective of profit maximisation is widely recognised in business houses. But neither all costs are controllable by any individual nor are all costs controllable by management at all times. Therefore, it is appropriate and logical that a clear distinction should be made between controllable costs. However, it is also necessary for effective cost control that the responsibility of control must lie with those who make the cost incurring decisions. This is possible to ensure through the marginal cost technique where variable and fixed costs are normally separated.

As Marginal Costing recognises the behaviour of costs in relation to volume and/or time, only variable costs are charged to product processes or functions per unit basis while the fixed expenses incurred to keep capacity and sell in readiness for use, are not charged to products and can be controlled by functional responsibility centres. Hence, the foreman is no longer accountable for depreciation and rent over which he has no control. Fixed costs are referred to the controlling authority involved. Thus, marginal costing ensures reporting only such costs to individual managers which are relevant and appropriate.

Further, under Marginal Costing it is possible to accumulate costs by cost centres, the smallest area of responsibility like, for instance, a department. Thus reports to foremen include only those costs which are subject to his control. Reports to higher managers include costs items in either detailed or summary form, because more costs are controllable as the scope of management responsibility enlarges. For instance, the production superintendent is responsible for all costs of the production department and own office costs. The production manager is responsible for costs of the production and service departments. The reports sent to management thus summarise the controllable costs at each stage.

Fixed costs are collected and reported in the income statement as separate deductions from marginal income *i.e.*, contribution margin instead of being merged with the cost of goods sold and inventory. This helps management to clearly understand the expense behaviour and not to loose sight of individual items of fixed expenses.

In short, the most important requirement of cost control, that costs within the functional area of responsibility be identified and controlled by people who make the cost incurring decisions; is fulfilled in marginal costing it follows a logical principle that costs which are not controlled by the responsibility individual should be omitted or separated from the costs which the individual is expected to control. This is technically referred to as "Responsibility Accounting".

Marginal Costing facilitates management by exception by focussing attention of the management towards results which are moving out of line and prompt them to initiate timely action for correction. Moreover, it helps higher level management personnel in evaluating the performance of men responsible to them. The impact of fixed expenses over specific functions and in the firm as a whole is conveyed to management in a more meaningful form under marginal costing. This helps management to ensure better utilisation of existing facilities and personnel.

To sum up, as a tool of management, the marginal costing technique highlights relationships between profits and the major factors affecting profits. The significance of marginal costing is particularly established, in multi-product companies and situations in which there is under-utilised capacity, and in connection with cost reporting to managers at different levels in the organisation. Variable costs and fixed costs require different approaches for purposes of control. From this point of view, marginal costing followes a logical principle that costs which are not controllable by operating managers should be separated from costs which are expected to be controlled by them.

Limitations of Direct Costing/Marginal Costing Variable Costing

Under certain conditions, some of the advantages listed in the previous section can be considered disadvantages of for example, the management of a company were prone to make all decisions both short and long-term, on the is of contribution, it might be a disadvantage to have the monthly accounting statements reflect contribution. In addition to these disadvantages that may apply in particular cases there are five disadvantages to direct costing.

(1) Inventories are Undervalued. The first disadvantage of direct costing is that inventories are undervalued. There is no question that inventories will have a lower value under a direct costing system than under a full absorption system and, in this respect, could be considered undervalued. Whether this disadvantage applies to any situation will depend on what effect this lower inventory value has. (The same disadvantage applies to the LIFO method of inventory valuation.) To the extent that in, direct costing inventories are smaller than in full absorption costing, internal statements will show a lower profit (in the year of the change over).

(2) Internal Financial Statements Differ from Published Reports. The Second disadvantage is that the internal financial statements will differ from the published reports. This results because most direct costing methods are not considered acceptable by the public accounting profession for external financial statements. Consequently, when a company uses direct costing, it is necessary to increase the value of the inventory to reflect full accounted costs. This adjustment may cause confusion because the internal profit figure will be different from that included in the annual report.

The seriousness of this disadvantage depends on the ability of management to understand the situation. If management understands and agrees that a direct costing system is more useful there should be little problem. If, however, management is not able (or willing) to understand why internal and external statements are different, this factor could be an important consideration in deciding whether to adopt a direct costing system.

The calculation to adjust the inventories to full cost is usually not an involved problem with respect to either the public accountant or the Internal Revenue Service. Acceptable methods are available that can be applied to the entire inventory value so that it is not necessary to recalculate the cost of each item. The clerical cost of making this calculation is relatively small.

(3) Monthly Profits Tend to Fluctuate more Widely. The third disadvantage of direct costing is that monthly profits will tend to fluctuate widely where the demand is seasonal. Under a full absorption system, if production is relatively constant, the effects of seasonal than changes in sales will be considerably mitigated. With direct costing, however the same amount of fixed costs will be reflected in the income statement each month regardless of the sales volume; therefore, profits will be higher in above-average months and lower in below-average months.

The seriousness of this disadvantage will depend upon several things, first, upon whether seasonal demand exists; if it does exist, upon whether production is more constant than sales (if it is not, the monthly profit fluctuations will not be mitigated), third, upon whether management, understands the limitations of the monthly profit estimates. As in the other situations, this is considering the adoption of a direct costing system.

(4) Direct Costing Requires a Change in the Present System. The fourth disadvantage of direct costing is that for most companies it entails a departure from accounting methods that have been in effect for some period of time. Any change causes a certain amount of trouble and confusion. A change to a direct costing system, therefore should not be made unless there are positive advantages for doing so. A company should not change its internal accounting system simply because "it appears to be the thing to do". Direct costing (or any other costing) is not a panacea for management ills. A direct costing system may aid management to make better decisions but it will not compensate for inadequate management.

(5) It is Difficult to Calculate Variable Costs. The fifth disadvantage, offered by proponents of full costing, is the inability of some companies to calculate variable costs, or even to agree on a definition. Management must make decisions based on differential costs and, consequently, these costs must be estimated. No matter how inexact the estimate, it is generally better than no estimate at all. The objection refers to having these variable costs reflected on the books of account. Since the variability of costs will differ under different circumstance, the usefulness of a single calculation of the variability of overhead costs is questioned. The answer to this question must also be decided in the context of a specific situation. If management must take many decision where variable cost may be very widely, a separate study will be required for each decision. Under these circumstances, little would be gained in having a single, arbitrarily deemed variable cost reflected on the books of account. If however, the variability of overhead costs does not differ much for different types of decisions, the fourth objection to direct costing is not valid.

❑